Violence, Imagination, and
Resistance

VIOLENCE, IMAGINATION, AND RESISTANCE

Socio-legal Interrogations of Power

Edited by Mariful Alam, Patrick Dwyer, and Katrin Roots

Copyright © 2023 Mariful Alam, Patrick Dwyer, and Katrin Roots
Published by AU Press, Athabasca University
1 University Dr, Athabasca, AB T9S 3A3
https://doi.org/10.15215/aupress/9781778290022.01

Cover image: Rawpixel 2477763
Cover design by Derek Thornton/Notch Design
Printed and bound in Canada

Library and Archives Canada Cataloguing in Publication

Title: Violence, imagination, and resistance : socio-legal interrogations of power /
     edited by Mariful Alam, Patrick Dwyer, and Katrin Roots.
Names: Alam, Mariful, editor. | Dwyer, Patrick, editor. |
     Roots, Katrin, editor.
Description: Includes bibliographical references.
Identifiers: Canadiana (print) 2022044305X | Canadiana (ebook) 2022044322X |
     ISBN 9781778290022 (softcover) | ISBN 9781771993678 (EPUB) |
     ISBN 9781771993661 (PDF)
Subjects: LCSH: Sociological jurisprudence—Canada. | LCSH: Power (Social
     sciences)—Canada. | LCSH: Settler colonialism—Canada. | LCSH: Race
     discrimination—Canada.
Classification: LCC KE3098 .V56 2023 | DDC 340/.1150971—dc23

We acknowledge the financial support of the Government of Canada through the
Canada Book Fund (CBF) for our publishing activities and the assistance provided
by the Government of Alberta through the Alberta Media Fund.

Canada   Alberta
                  Government

Contents

Part III Resistance and Social Transformation

Foreword

This book is the result of overlapping collective, collaborative, and interdisciplinary journeys. It is primarily the work of three young scholars who set out to write about doing socio-legal research on violence and resistance in Canada. In presenting this work, the editors and authors also enjoin us to question the very terms that hold the project together: socio-legal research, violence, and Canada.

Socio-legal research has become increasingly visible as a distinct field of study defined by core questions, critical sensibilities, and theoretical commitments shared across a range of institutional and disciplinary affiliations. Earlier generations of socio-legal scholars might have been the only researchers in their home department or faculty—whether law, sociology, political science, or communications—to pursue interdisciplinary law and society scholarship. This relative isolation throughout the years heightened the importance of scholarly associations, conferences, and journals dedicated to socio-legal scholarship in order to think and write across disciplinary divides. Later generations of socio-legal scholars built collaborative research centres as well as specialized departments and programs for undergraduate and graduate studies. The editors, as well as many of the contributors to this book, have studied and taught at some of these specialized socio-legal research hubs, such as York University's graduate program in socio-legal studies and Carleton University's graduate program in legal studies. These relatively recent institutional foundations provide new platforms for asking about and narrating the history of socio-legal studies: how do we talk about the histories and theories on which we build our work? The focus is no longer on communicating across disciplinary divides but on critically examining the theoretical foundations inherited from earlier generations.

When socio-legal studies emerged at a set of loosely connected institutions in the United Kingdom, the United States, and various settler colonies, the shared theoretical affinities frequently clustered around small groups of mostly white and mostly male theorists. Their work has proven insufficient for understanding the operations of law, power, and politics in settler colonies, let alone beyond them. In their introduction, the coeditors emphasize their intellectual debts to settler-colonial and Indigenous studies, to critical race theory, and to Black studies. These debts are also symptoms of historical omissions and refusals by previous generations of socio-legal researchers. Contemporary law and society scholarship needs to reflect on the limitations of its institutional roots as it embraces a broader set of intellectual foundations. Several chapters in this book provide excellent avenues for addressing these gaps, silences, and exclusions.

Professional organizations, conferences, and journals are frequently organized along the lines of nation-states. Yet what, for example, does the "Canadian" in Canadian law and society research refer to? Does "Canada" denote the citizenship and/or place of employment of the researchers or the geographic focus of their work? In this volume, the authors do not consider "Canadian" to refer to an uncomplicated subject position or a self-evident focus of their research. Rather, they use "Canada" as a starting point, a complicated relationship, and a responsibility.

The chapters by Stacy Douglas and by Carmela Murdocca, Shaira Vadasaria, and Timothy Bryan thematize the interplay between myths and violence in the foundation and constitution of Canada as a settler colony shaped by dispossession, genocide, and intersecting logics of racialization. Read together, these chapters powerfully illustrate that law cannot be reduced to either violence or language. The force of Western law is derived from its ability to appeal to "jurisfictions" backed by the threat of physical violence, but the metaphors and narratives on which legal language is based exert their own force: they shape our imagination of what is possible and thinkable as law, of how we imagine persons, relationships, and humanity. Here, the role of socio-legal research is not only to show how violent and arbitrary these foundations of Western law are but also to create space for us to imagine different futures built on different relationships, laws, and responsibilities.

Other contributions to this volume decentre Canada by taking an explicitly transnational approach: the introduction frames racialized police violence as a North American problem without denying the Canadian specificities, the chapter on #MeToo by Emily Lockhart, Katrin Roots, and Heather Tasker takes a transnational perspective rooted in an understanding of how racial and gendered hierarchies are expressed in Canadian law, and Heather Tasker's analysis of photographic projects in humanitarian spaces is rooted in an analysis of complex global hierarchies in which the images produced by refugee children are read, circulated, and repositioned. In these works, "Canada" is not the unquestioned frame, but it becomes framed, contextualized, and questioned through multiple methodologies.

In centring violence and resistance, the volume draws on a range of traditions of theorizing the boundaries of violence, the use of power, and the place of resistance. In arguing that (Western) law is inescapably tied to violence, the afterword by Mariful Alam and Irina Ceric challenges readers to think about forms of justice and community beyond the law as well as forms of law beyond the worn models of Western legality. At the heart of law's violence, we sometimes find silence: the quiet bureaucratic machinery that produces legal classifications of "terrorism," as the chapter by Yavar Hameed and Jeffrey Monaghan shows, or the insistence on state secrecy in the face of access to information requests by researchers and activists, as described by Alex Luscombe and Kevin Walby.

Read together, the contributions in this volume provide a valuable snapshot of methodological directions, theoretical foundations, and practical orientations in contemporary socio-legal studies in Canada. They highlight the work of researchers who are reshaping the field through careful, imaginative, and collaborative work.

Christiane Wilke

Acknowledgements

We want to thank the many friends, colleagues, and mentors who contributed to this work on its long road to publication, including Carmela Murdocca, Stacy Douglas, Ummni Khan, Amanda Glasbeek, and Matt McManus. Thank you to the faculty members of York University's department of socio-legal studies for their enthusiasm and support for the project.

A special thank you to James Williams and Beverly Orser. James provided us with mentorship and encouragement as we initially began the project. And Beverly played an important role in forming the original ideas for this book.

Thank you to the staff at Athabasca University Press and our editor, Pamela Holway, for her guidance and direction, as well as Megan Hall, Karyn Wisselink, and Derek Thornton, our cover designer. Thank you also to Scribe Inc. for copy-editing.

We are grateful to the anonymous reviewers of this manuscript who took the time to engage with our work and for their invaluable feedback and suggestions that undoubtedly helped strengthen this book.

Lastly, we are very grateful to the authors of the chapters in this collection for their patience and commitment throughout this long process and for their brilliant chapters that capture important conversations about the law's role in reproducing various forms of violence.

Violence, Imagination, and
Resistance

Introduction
Socio-legal Perspectives on Law's Violence

Mariful Alam, Patrick Dwyer, and Katrin Roots

YOUR HONOR: In addressing this court I speak as the representative of one class to the representative of another. I will begin with the words uttered five hundred years ago on a similar occasion, by the Venetian Doge Faheri, who addressing the court, said: "My defense is your accusation; the causes of my alleged crime your history!"

—August Spies

In the summer of 2020, news coverage of the recent outbreak of COVID-19 was temporarily displaced by stories about the death of George Floyd at the hands of four Minneapolis police officers, in what has become an almost-iconic portrait of police brutality. On 25 May 2020, Floyd, a Black man, was arrested on suspicion of passing a counterfeit twenty-dollar bill. The police knew him to be intoxicated, yet he was neither behaving violently nor reported to be armed. In the course of the arrest, Floyd, already handcuffed, resisted attempts to move him into a police vehicle. Finally, two officers forced him into the car and then proceeded to drag him across the back seat and onto the street, where he was violently pushed to the ground. There he lay while Derek Chauvin, a white police officer, pressed his knee into Floyd's neck as Floyd repeated, again and again, "I can't breathe." Chauvin kept his knee in place long after Floyd was unconscious, releasing it only after medical help arrived and he was ordered to stop. By the time the ambulance reached the hospital, Floyd was dead (*New York Times* 2022). Chauvin kept his knee on Floyd's neck for a total of nine minutes and twenty-nine seconds (Levenson 2021).

Floyd's death sparked a massive outpouring of anger and waves of protests on the part of Black communities and their supporters not only in the United States, but in Canada and around the world. Floyd's death was noteworthy for the intense public scrutiny that surrounded the case and the charges brought against the four officers. Derek Chauvin was ultimately convicted on two counts of murder and one count of manslaughter and sentenced to twenty-two and a half years in prison—considerably longer than is standard under Minnesota law (Chappell 2021). The other three officers involved in the incident were charged with violating Floyd's civil rights and have since received sentences ranging from two and a half years to three and a half years. It bears remembering that while the killing of a Black man by police is not new, rarely are police convicted and jailed. In this case, it was a combination of the public visibility of Floyd's murder—which was caught on video by several witnesses—the slow and deliberate actions of Chauvin (in contrast to the split-second decision-making often blamed for police killings), and on-the-ground activism by Black Lives Matter (BLM) and other organizations that led to a public outcry and ultimately prosecution.

Although Canadians also joined in protests against the act of racialized police violence that occurred in the United States, they are perhaps too quick to forget that similar instances of police violence against BIPOC communities routinely take place in Canada (see Cole 2020; Maynard 2017; Razack 2015), even as Canadian law enforcement officials regularly strive to compare themselves favourably to their American counterparts (see Glasbeek, Roots, and Alam 2019; Glasbeek, Roots, and Alam 2020, 335–36). Consider, for instance, the deaths of

- Ejaz Choudry, a sixty-two-year-old Punjabi man living in the Toronto suburb of Mississauga who was shot and killed by police on 20 June 2020 after his family called for help because Choudry, a person living with schizophrenia, was having a mental health crisis (Nasser 2021);
- Jason Collins, a thirty-six-year-old Indigenous man who was shot and killed by Winnipeg police on 9 April 2020 during a domestic violence call in which Collins aimed (what turned out to be) a BB gun at them (CBC News 2021);

- Eishia Hudson, a sixteen-year-old Indigenous woman who was shot and killed by Winnipeg police on 8 April 2020 shortly after they stopped the vehicle in which she and several others were attempting to flee after robbing a liquor store (Cram and Frew 2021);
- Andrew Loku, a forty-five-year-old Black man living with PTSD who was shot and killed by a Toronto police officer on 5 July 2015 as he "advanced on him [the officer] with a hammer" (Gillis 2017); and
- Sammy Yatim, an eighteen-year-old immigrant from Syria who was shot a total of eight times and killed by a Toronto police officer on 27 July 2013 after the police were summoned because Yatim was behaving erratically and waving a switchblade around on a streetcar (CBC News 2015; O'Brien 2022).

These are only a few instances of police violence carried out with the permission of and in the name of law in Canada.

The incidents above highlight obvious examples of the state's use of direct force—what can be defined as naked violence—a more overt and visible form of violence that involves physical force or coercion, such as imprisonment, war, genocide, and police brutality (Poulantzas 1978). Yet the death of racialized people at the hands of the police is merely one aspect of a larger structure of settler colonialism and white supremacy enabled and maintained through law. Here, it is fruitful to consider Rob Nixon's concept of *slow violence*—a form of violence that, as he explains, occurs

> gradually and out of sight, a violence of delayed destruction that is dispersed across time and space, an attritional violence that is typically not viewed as violence at all. Violence is customarily conceived as an event or action that is immediate in time, explosive and spectacular in space, and as erupting into instant sensational visibility. We need, I believe, to engage a different kind of violence, a violence that is neither spectacular nor instantaneous, but rather incremental and accretive, its calamitous repercussions playing out across a range of temporal scales. (2011, 2)

Nixon builds on the work of Johan Galtung (1969), who distinguished what he termed *structural* (or *indirect*) violence from *personal* (or *direct*) violence. Galtung argued that violence needs to be defined as more than simply actions carried out by a specific person that cause immediate physical or psychological harm; it must also include violence that has no direct agent but is instead "built into the structure and shows up as unequal power and consequently as unequal life chances" (171). For Galtung, structural violence is often invisible and more insidious than personal violence because it is embedded within our social and political structures, which can perpetuate suffering and harm over long periods of time. Accounting for structural violence "helps with identifying links to present structures that the 'sensational visibility' of violent acts often conceals" (Holterman 2014, 60). We note that structural violence is associated with social injustice while contributing to violence against individuals and groups. Forms of structural violence may legitimize naked or personal violence, as we saw with the police killings noted above. Both slow and structural violence are indirect and are maintained through repressive structures (Nixon 2011, 11). However, while structural violence is static and constantly present, slow violence occurs over time, and the violence is gradually "decoupled from its original causes by the workings of time" (ibid.). For instance, consider the effects of residential schools—the last of which closed in 1996—on Indigenous people in Canada. The structural violence in this context can be seen in the operation of residential schools and the laws and policies that supported it, while the concept of slow violence captures the long-term and intergenerational effects that residential schools have had on Indigenous populations over time. Decoupled from its original source, the effects of this slow violence can and have been erroneously attributed to a variety of sources rooted in individuals, Indigenous cultures, and societies.

Although Nixon writes about violence in the context of environmental degradation, his conceptualization of slow violence has a much wider application. Geoff Ward, for example, draws on the concept of slow violence to examine the role of the state in perpetuating settler colonialism and white supremacy. As he explains, "slow violence" is victimization that is "attritional, dispersed, and hidden" (2015, 299), therefore making it more difficult to trace it to specific structures, organizations, policies, or laws. Indeed, as Ward contends, it is more common to see "subtler personal or structural violence contributing to dis-accumulation, collective under-development and general disadvantage" (302), therefore making it imperative to examine this form of violence. This is further clarified by Kelly Struthers Montford and Tessa Wotherspoon, who contend that "slow violence is a *specific form* of violence that is insidious, not easily identifiable as racism or violence, and is not reducible to the intent of an individual acting against another. Instead, it is structural, routine, and elongated in its harm and effects" (2021, 81).

As we detail below, the role of law in creating and supporting conditions for naked and structural violence has been widely discussed in socio-legal scholarship. Yet, law's role in enabling and perpetuating slow violence—a concept we believe should also be considered alongside naked and structural force—is seldom discussed. The contributors in this volume focus on violence in all its forms—slow, structural, and naked—as it pertains to law. While the objective here is not to debate or move forward the scholarly discussion on theoretical differences between these forms of violence, we believe they are important to take into consideration when analyzing the power of law. In order to understand how violence enters into socio-legal conceptualizations of law, it is pertinent to first take a step back to briefly consider the diverse scholarly approaches to what law is and how scholars in the developing field of socio-legal studies understand the relationship between law and violence. Centering the law in these discussions allows us to dissect the ways in which authoritative bodies of text, which are often taken as neutral, objective, and intended to promote the well-being of everyone in society, are contributing to state-sanctioned and often invisible violence directed particularly toward certain groups. Socio-legal scholars have already begun this process and are contributing to the advancement of the field of socio-legal studies. As such, we now turn the discussion to the development and expansion of this field in Canada and consider the various ways in which socio-legal scholars conceptualize and theorize "the law."

Socio-legal Studies: A Brief History

The core identity of socio-legal studies emerges from its juxtaposition with traditional legal scholarship. As Kitty Calavita writes, traditional legal scholarship is rooted in law schools that often present the law as a "set of principles and rules that relate to each other according to a particular logic or dynamic" (2010, 4). Following the Second World War, scholars began recognizing that legal power could no longer be reduced to "black letter law" and that a richer, more nuanced and interdisciplinary approach was needed (Arthurs 1983). This shift was reflected in the development of undergraduate law and society programs, Marxist-inspired critical legal studies, and feminist movements (Brophy and Blokhuis 2017). A question these movements sought to investigate was not simply whether a particular law was just or appropriately applied but what impact law has on society and social relations. In the context of the

1970s economic crisis and the ongoing civil rights movement (ibid.), socio-legal scholarship emerged from a range of interdisciplinary fields engaged in exploring the impact of legal dynamics both inside and outside of the courtroom, including women's studies, critical race studies, sociology, criminology, Marxist political economy, anthropology, history, political science, and psychology, to name a few. Many of these fields critically addressed law's role in upholding and reproducing structural inequalities.

The notion of "law" and "society" as distinct spaces and fields of practice was challenged in the 1980s and 1990s by critical scholars who viewed the legal and the social as mutually constitutive (Feenan 2013, 7; see also Ewick and Sarat 2015). For instance, Patricia Ewick and Susan Silbey reject the conceptual distinction between law and society, suggesting we must look at "the presence of law in society" (1998, 35). Another critique of treating the social and the legal as distinct is offered by Peter Fitzpatrick, who argues that both the "legal" and the "social" have proved to be inadequate in providing a focus for the field of socio-legal studies (1995; see also Cotterrell 2009; Silbey 2013). According to Fitzpatrick, despite attempts by scholars to frame law as having, what he calls, a "determinate existence," the law only exists in relation to something else—whether that be society, economy, class, or another social component.

One key insight central to the work of many scholars is that the field of socio-legal studies cannot be defined by, nor confined to, specific parameters. It thus lacks an identifiable canon, or a "fixed, timeless and bounded set of works" (Guillory 1993; Seron, Coutin, and Meeusen 2013, 289). The interdisciplinary nature of socio-legal studies makes it difficult to establish a canon, since, as Carroll Seron, Susan Bibler Coutin, and Pauline White Meeusen point out, "to be interdisciplinary is to be inclusive" (293). In their view, interdisciplinarity is the only approach that can adequately examine the complex issues presented by law, legal decisions, and the legal terrain overall (290). Ultimately then, the central contribution of socio-legal studies lies not only in the absence of a coherent canon (Arthurs and Bunting 2014; Ewick and Sarat 2015) but also in the impossibility of creating one.

The challenge of defining the field was highlighted during a panel on publishing and peer review observed by one of the editors at the 2019 Law and Society annual conference, where panelists (including publishers, editors, and members of editorial boards) were presented with the question "What constitutes a law and society paper?" A long silence ensued, following which one of the panelists suggested that "there is no clear answer," and another admitted that this is one of the hardest questions they face in their work. Our experience of working on this manuscript and writing this introduction has been similar. Each time we surveyed colleagues on their thoughts about the field, we were given different ideas as to what the introduction should cover, what might be missing, and where the conversation needed to go. We thus encountered what Fitzpatrick described as a "strategy of confession and avoidance: the field is there but its 'definition' is attended with unspecific and unrelieved 'problems', 'difficulty' and a general absence of clarity in its 'lines of demarcation'" (1995, 105). This volume reflects the empirical and theoretical richness, diversity, and even "messiness" of this discipline as the authors engage with a broad range of topics, issues, theoretical framings, and methodological approaches.

Situating "the Law" in Socio-legal Studies

While the boundaries of the field remain undefined, socio-legal scholars collectively focus on the relationship between law and power. One important debate within the field is whether law is repressive or merely one of many governing tactics. Our objective is not to revive the debates about law's power to repress and/or govern but simply to provide an overview and context for our discussion of law's role in supporting violence in all its forms.

The "law as repression" approach recognizes law's role in enabling and perpetuating systems of domination through social structures, including capitalism, racism, patriarchy, and settler colonialism. While we recognize the diverse perspectives captured by the "law as repression" umbrella, here we focus specifically on key arguments agreed upon by those whose work aligns with this perspective. Marxist accounts of law, particularly the instrumentalist approach, often emphasize law's role in dominating, repressing, and coercing the lower classes while ensuring the values and interests of the ruling class are internalized and obeyed (see Cain and Hunt 1979; Chambliss and Seidman 1971; Hay 1975). The approach suggests that the legitimacy of law is maintained through legal devices such as the rule of law and the promise of liberty and equality for all. As Stephen Brickley and Elizabeth Comack (1987, 98) argue, the liberal state and its judicial apparatus are not independent entities but coercive instruments used by economic elites to protect private property rights and accumulate capital. As they point out, a rigid instrumentalist approach sees the language of equality and neutrality that underpins the rule of law as nothing more than a myth and illusion that masks the hegemonic power of the ruling classes. The instrumentalist approach reminds us that the fundamental fear of the ruling classes of having their right to private property undermined or challenged through popular struggle led to the emergence of policing and security apparatuses as techniques for enforcing a capitalist social order by disciplining and wielding control over workers and vagrants who resisted (Neocleous 2008, 26–31).

Like Marxists, critical race theorists also see law as repressive but as an avenue for enabling and reproducing racist practices (Crenshaw 1995, 2003; Delgado and Stefancic 2017; Haney López 1996). In effect, critical race theorists hold that law constitutes racism. As Constance Backhouse (1999) explains, law has historically been used to force the assimilation of Indigenous peoples to European culture, inhibit the entry of certain immigrant populations into Canada, oppress racialized groups, and construct racial discrimination and racial hierarchies. To protect the economic relations, culture, and values of the white dominant class, legislation was often drafted to carry out the desired effect. Although historically we saw the enactment of explicitly exclusionary and racist legislation, this has shifted over time to take on more subtle forms of legal domination through universalized rights, colour-blind laws, and neutral practices (Freeman 1995; Haney López 1996; Williams 1992). The policing and security apparatuses used to enforce these laws therefore not only are limited to maintaining capitalism, as noted above, but also extend to settler colonialism. In Canada, the North-West Mounted Police (NWMP)—one of two police forces that later merged to become the Royal Canadian Mounted Police (RCMP)—was established both to maintain the authority of white settler colonialism and to suppress Indigenous rebellions (see Comack 2013; Whitaker, Kealey, and Parnaby 2013; Wright and Binnie 2009). The NWMP was established in 1873—around the same time as the Canadian state was also establishing and formalizing new colonial legal policies, such as the Gradual Enfranchisement Act of 1869 and later the Indian Act in 1876. The RCMP continues this legacy of colonial violence in the name of protecting the nation, as exemplified by their removal of the Wet'suwet'en blockade in February 2020, demonstrating that the Canadian state's repression of dissent and claims of Indigenous sovereignty continue in an effort to defend settler capitalism (Dafnos 2013; see also Ceric 2020). When analyzing law's role in enabling violence, we must also consider how law produces forms of violent racial governance, parsing out how slow, structural, and naked violence work together to target populations. Racism and settler colonialism are important forces that not only are enabled by law and constitute law's power but also extend significantly beyond law.

Lastly, we must consider law's role in constituting patriarchal relations. For instance, 'examine the Marxist-inspired feminist Catherine MacKinnon, who takes a structuralist perspective on law's role in regulating gender relations. MacKinnon replaces class division with patriarchy as a form of oppression and argues that women's unequal social position is a result of their sexuality, which is distorted and manipulated by the dominant sex for their benefit. MacKinnon (1982) explains that the law is merely an arm of the state, which maintains masculine standards disguised as objective and neutral. She takes the position that the law cannot be used to bring about change, since in aiming for equality under the law, we are really striving for masculine standards. While Catherine MacKinnon's work has been criticized for being too essentialist, feminists have nonetheless built upon her ideas to show how patriarchy continues to operate through legal structures (see Chan, Chunn, and Menzies 2005; Chunn and Lacombe 2000; Craig 2018; Smart 1989, 1995; Ursel, Tutty, and leMaistre 2008). Indeed, Kimberlé Crenshaw (1991), Patricia Hill Collins (2015), and other intersectional feminists acknowledge that structural inequality is mutually constituted by multiple forms of oppression, including race, gender, class, age, ethnicity, and ability. Feminists using an intersectional perspective recognize the importance of historical context, culture, time, place, and space for understanding structural inequality and, in our case, structural violence.

Although "law as repression" scholars focus on law as a form of domination, it would be simplistic to end on the conclusion that law can only be reduced to repression and physical violence. Drawing on structural approaches to Marxism, we recognize that the state and its institutions are relatively autonomous (Gramsci 1971; Althusser 1971). And while the state and its legal system certainly have repressive functions that enable the ruling classes to accumulate capital, they do not operate on repression alone; they also, as Nicos Poulantzas (1978) suggests, rely on legitimization and consent. For example, the state must sometimes go outside of the interests of capital by winning "the loyalty of the economically and socially oppressed classes" (Brickley and Comack 1987, 100) to ensure the smooth functioning of capitalism and avoid crises of legitimacy (Gramsci 1971). Consider, for instance, legislation that protects labour rights, the right to strike, and workplace safety regulations won by the labour movement. In this instance, overruling the short-term interests of some capitalists and providing the working class with a set of real rights and liberties ensured that the fundamental structure of capitalist social relations was not disrupted (see Palmer 2003; Tucker 1988, 2019). Similarly, critical race theorists such as Patricia Williams (1992) acknowledge the importance of legal rights in challenging racial violence and inequality for Black people in America, even if only as formal (rather than substantive) rights.

More than the rule of law being a myth or an illusion, the structuralist approach helps us understand how these positive developments have compelled individuals to accept as real its ideological principles of neutrality and equality. Poulantzas summarizes this perspective and writes that the universal, formal, and abstract character of law presupposes "agents who have been 'freed' from the personal-territorial bonds of precapitalist, and even serf, societies"; therefore, people assume they are "free and equal before the law" when, in actuality, exploitation and violent coercion underpin our entire political structure (1978, 80–81). Poulantzas also acknowledges how this mythology plays a fundamental role in mediating the relationship between slow, structural, and naked violence through law: "In every State, law is an integral part of the repressive order and of the organization of violence. By issuing rules and passing laws, the State establishes an initial field of injunctions, prohibitions and censorship, and thus institutes the practical terrain and object of violence. Furthermore, law organizes the conditions for physical repression, designating its modalities and structuring the devices by means of which it is exercised" (77). As Poulantzas observes, "State-monopolized physical violence permanently underlies the techniques of power and mechanisms of consent; it is inscribed in the web of disciplinary and ideological devices; and even when not directly exercised, it shapes the materiality of the social body upon which domination is brought to bear" (81). As we see in this volume, the mythology of law protects the colonial system while denying Indigenous rights to sovereignty and autonomy, thereby legitimizing the use of state violence against these groups.

While contemporary structuralist scholars concur that capitalist social relations are reinforced through legal norms, those who critique structuralism argue that we must understand law in a more nuanced manner, leading them to examine the possibility of law as an avenue for social change. One of these scholars is E. P. Thompson (1975), who takes the position that although the rules of society may support ruling class power, they also at times curb this power and its intrusions. For Thompson, the law cannot be separated from the social, as it is "deeply imbricated within the very basis of productive relations, which would have been inoperable without this law" (261). Another such scholar is Alan Hunt (1993), who argues that the law is neither autonomous nor dependent but is constitutive through unstable and changing links between institutions. He explains that the law is part of a system of modes of regulation, but it maintains its proximity to the state, even while involved in the process of governance and social regulation (Hunt 1993, 207). For Hunt, then, law constitutes "a field within which social relations are generated, reproduced, disputed and struggled over" (293). Importantly, Hunt takes the position that law should be prioritized as a site for social justice and social transformation—a position that is challenged in the afterword to this volume by Alam and Ceric, who claim that "*it will never be possible* to separate the force of law from violence, whether that violence is metaphysical, social, or political." Yet rather than debate the merits of law as a site of struggle, Alam and Ceric call on socio-legal scholars to imagine and conceptualize radical alternatives to law to generate a dialogue on new transformative possibilities.

Although structural perspectives widen our understanding of law's power, law and governance scholars are critical of these structuralist debates, noting the limited scope of these accounts in two ways. First, they contend that the reliance of structuralist approaches on a rather unified view of state power does not offer clarity on how less formal, nonstate technologies of power play a role in social and political relations. And second, they critique the structuralist perspective's guiding focus on repressive relations of power and thus failure to offer ways to investigate the productive potential of legal power. It is our view that law as governance perspectives offers socio-legal scholars a conceptual toolkit to investigate how violence is not only exercised through law but also incorporated and normalized into other aspects of the body politic. Adopting a governmentality perspective *alongside* law as repression scholarship offers scholars a more fruitful avenue for analyzing how violence operates.

The "law as governance" approach is inspired by Michel Foucault's analysis of power, particularly his work on governmentality. Many scholars, inspired by Foucault, expanded their focus to analyze not only how the law represses, dominates, and controls but also how it produces subjectivities, norms, and identities in mutually constitutive ways (Ewick and Silbey 1998; Hunt 1993; Rose, O'Malley, and Valverde 2006; Rose and Valverde 1998; Valverde 2003; Williams and Lippert 2006). These Foucauldian-inspired works emphasize the importance of exploring legal power beyond the state. Foucault's work directs us to consider power more broadly rather than as something that's simply enshrined in the state. He famously called on scholars to "cut off the king's head"—that is, to study power relations by widening the concept of power beyond a sovereign, king, or ruling class (Foucault 1980, 121). Instead, Foucault suggests we should consider how power operates as a decentralized force through multiple sites and institutions. Foucault's analysis emphasizes that power is fragmented, dispersed, and omnipresent ([1978] 1990, 93). As Kevin Walby points out, an investigation of law's power under a Foucauldian analytic would include a "range of multifarious and irreducible governmental sites," including but not limited to the law (2007, 555). Consequently, a central feature in Foucault's analytical inquiry was a move away from investigating power as possessed and inherently negative or repressive and instead exploring its productive dimensions. By inverting the relations of power, Foucault (1980) believed scholars could more concretely grasp the variety of mutually constitutive social practices, knowledges, and technologies that bring into play our understanding of reality and subjectivity.

Although Foucault never produced a coherent theory of law, his analysis of power has influenced the law as governance approach. Rather than viewing law as solely grounded in violence and sovereignty, Foucault recognized law as "something that could be used to enforce certain norms and behaviour" (Newman 2004, 43). Law as governance scholars have noted that law and modern forms of power are both interdependent and opposing (Beck 1996; Golder and Fitzpatrick 2009). Instead of referencing the law as a singularity, Nikolas Rose and Mariana Valverde, for instance, believe it's best to use the term *legal complex* to describe the "assemblage of legal practices, legal institutions, statutes, codes, authorities, discourses, texts, norms, and forms of judgment" (1998, 542). Legal complexes are one of many diverse forms of power for governing, as they are often combined with other forms of knowledge, including psychiatric or medical knowledge. We see this observation as particularly fruitful, as it allows us to expand our analysis of how violence is enabled through and in conjunction with these "nonviolent" extrajudicial knowledges.

While many suggest Foucault's work does not consider the role of legal violence or state repression and offers very little in imagining the possibilities of social transformation and resistance (see Hunt and Wickham 1994; Poulantzas 1978; Mbembe 2003), we believe these analyses overlook many insights provided by Foucault. In contrast to the argument made by Nicos Poulantzas, who writes that Foucault underestimates "the role of law in the exercise of power within modern societies" by failing to understand "the function of the repressive apparatuses (army, police, judicial stem, etc.) as means of exercising physical violence that are located at the heart of the modern state" (1978, 77), we believe Foucault acknowledged the role of violence as a key element of modern politics (see also Oksala 2010). In numerous interviews and lectures delivered shortly before his death, Foucault argued that violence is deeply embedded within our social structures, pointing out that "humanity settles each one of its violences *within a system of rules*, and thus goes from domination to domination" (1980, 91; emphasis added). Here, we agree with Saul Newman's commentary that Foucault's analysis of power demonstrates violence has, in fact, "creeped into the very structures, laws, hierarchies, and institutions that have been established to suppress it" (2004, 578). Through this lens of the pervasiveness of violence to constitute ruling power relations, we can begin to see that violence is not merely exercised by the state as a spectacle through naked force. Violence is also exerted slowly through social structures and institutions. In other words, the law and legal complexes are both productive *and* violent (see Newman 2004; Poulantzas 1978). While we agree that examinations of law's power must expand beyond black-letter law and include its variations in the form of policies, norms, and discourses, we suggest that law, in its many forms and expressions, continues to be a unique source of power. In contrast to scholars who believe Foucault expelled law or simply viewed law as the sovereign right to engage in violence (see Hunt and Wickham 1994), we take the perspective advanced by scholars such as Carol Smart (1989, 1995) who highlight that the mythology of law as neutral and objective for evaluating information and determining truth is part of its unique power.

Consider Smart's (1989) critique of law claiming to have the method for finding "the truth." In this discovery process, Smart reminds us that the law disqualifies other knowledges and experiences, thus determining what becomes established as "the truth." This is enabled by law's ability to set itself apart from the social order and in doing so create the perception that it is able to reflect on the world in a neutral and objective way (Smart 1989, 11). The law also relies on other knowledges, such as psychiatric and medical knowledges, to inform both legal and extralegal forms of governance and extend its power beyond legal truth-making (16–17). Law's "claim to truth," Smart writes, is not manifested in its practice but "in the ideal of law" (11). Not only does law evaluate truth; it also creates legal fictions that maintain and reinforce settler colonialism, the production of criminal others, and the preservation of gender and racial inequality amongst other forms of inequality.

The Relationship between Slow, Structural and Naked Legal Violence

Our goal in this book is not to revisit the debate on the metaphysical essence of law but instead to provide a snapshot of how some Canadian socio-legal scholars address the ways in which legal power draws on, maintains, and perpetuates various forms of violence, whether through subtle and mundane governing practices or through overt coercion and force. We believe that law's power should be examined in new and creative ways that go beyond narrow conceptual debates between law as repression and law as governance. Instead, we draw on both approaches to make sense of the complex and varied ways in which law not only continues to organize overt coercion but also helps sustain the structural and slow violence of white supremacy, patriarchy, and settler colonialism.

One of the most obvious examples of the relationship between naked, structural, and slow violence is Canada's contemporary and historical treatment of Indigenous people. Given our focus on Indigenous struggles in the sections that follow, it is important that we position ourselves in this discussion. All three of the editors of this book are settlers in Canada. In discussing Indigenous issues, it is not our intention to suggest that we possess personal insight about Indigenous experiences and culture. We are writing about these concerns as allies, supporters, and accomplices with recognition and concern for the ongoing impact of settler colonialism.

Despite its earnest show of support for the ninety-four calls to action issued by the Truth and Reconciliation Commission (2015), the Canadian government has taken little by way of concrete action in response to racism, poverty, inadequate health care, lack of education, overincarceration, police violence, and the denial of other basic human rights to Indigenous peoples. For instance, Indigenous communities have spent decades attempting to focus attention on the issue of missing and murdered Indigenous women and girls. Statistics Canada reported that, over the period from 2001 to 2015, Indigenous women and girls were six times more likely to be killed than their non-Indigenous counterparts (Hotton Mahony, Jacob, and Hobson 2017, 22) and that, as of 2014, they faced a rate of serious violence twice as high as that of Indigenous men and triple that of non-Indigenous women (Boyce 2016, 3). An analysis conducted in 2016 by Maryanne Pearce and Tracey Peter revealed that the situation was even worse than it had previously appeared: Indigenous women and girls were twelve times more likely to be murdered than non-Indigenous women and girls and sixteen times more likely than white women (cited in National Inquiry into Missing and Murdered Indigenous Women and Girls 2019, 1a:55). The most recent statistics from 2020 suggest a slight decline in the homicide rate for Indigenous women. Based on this information, Indigenous women are five times more likely to be killed compared with non-Indigenous women, though the authors caution this could be affected by statistics collection practices, as all statistics since 2019 now refer to the gender identity of the victim instead of their biological sex (Perreault 2022, 27).

International attention was drawn to this issue more than a decade earlier, with the release of the Amnesty International report *Stolen Sisters: A Human Rights Response to Discrimination and Violence Against Indigenous Women in Canada* (2004). In 2013, Human Rights Watch released a report calling for the Canadian government to launch a national commission of inquiry and, with guidance from Indigenous leaders, to develop a national action plan to address the issue of missing and murdered Indigenous women and girls (2013, 15). Then in 2015, the United Nations' Committee on the Elimination of Discrimination Against Women found that Indigenous women and girls in Canada face "grave and systemic" rights violations that urgently need to be addressed by the Canadian state (2015, 3). The Conservative government in power at the time, led by Prime Minister Stephen Harper, did not consider it important to address this issue, noting that the murders should be understood as crimes rather than as a "sociological phenomenon" (quoted in Ditchburn 2014). It was in 2015, after the Liberal government came into power, that a national inquiry into the issue was finally announced. The results of the national inquiry were released in a report published in June 2019 and found that the Canadian state committed genocide against Indigenous peoples through systemic forms of racism and disregard (National Inquiry into Missing and Murdered Indigenous Women and Girls 2019; see also Palmater 2016; Jolly 2019; McDiarmid 2019).

The report of the inquiry also found that the genocide was empowered by colonial structures evidenced most notably by the Indian Act, the principal instrument through which federal jurisdiction was exercised over Indigenous peoples enacted in 1876. The Indian Act adopted a highly paternalistic view of Indigenous people, treating them as "wards of the state" unable to manage their own lives. It also gave discretion to Canadian governing authorities to determine who qualified as an "Indian," which land belonged to Indigenous peoples, and to what extent Indigenous people had the right to engage in their traditional social, cultural, and economic practices (Morgensen 2011, 62; see also Diabo 2017; Miller 2004). Canadian governing practices have long been informed by what Wolfe (2006) conceptualizes as "a logic of elimination," which has the objective of gradually destroying Indigeneity through techniques of regulation and assimilation and replacing it with a new settler nation and identity characterized by liberalism and private property regimes (see also Crosby and Monaghan 2012, 425). Indeed, an important tactic that facilitated the settler-colonial project was the deployment of what Jean Comaroff and John Comaroff (2006) call *lawfare*, whereby authorities drew on coercive legal instruments to "realize [the] project of [Indigenous] elimination" and "securitize settler-colonial spaces" (Crosby and Monaghan 2012, 425). These lawfare strategies are continuing to be employed today through legal tactics. One such example is corporations applying for court injunctions to forcefully remove Indigenous protesters and blockades defending unceded land and territory (Ceric 2020; Pasternak 2017; Simpson and Le Billon 2021).

The Indian Act also authorized the operation of residential schools, which were central to the colonial project of assimilation. Residential schools aimed to transform Indigenous children and youth into "proper English-speaking Canadians loyal to the Crown" (Talaga 2017, 9; see also Regan 2010; Woolford and Gacek 2016). Revisions to the Indian Act in 1920 made it mandatory for parents to send their children to these boarding schools, which were often far from the child's home. If parents refused, the RCMP was tasked with rounding up the children and delivering them to the school—by force, if necessary. Parents were also threatened with sanctions, including being jailed and having their rations cut until they surrendered their children (Hopper 2021; see also Talaga 2017; Metatawabin with Shimo 2015). Indigenous children experienced significant abuse and neglect, as well as sexual, physical, and psychological abuse; starvation; torture; and other acts of violence in residential schools (Bourgeois 2015; MacDonald and Hudson 2012; Metatawabin with Shimo 2015; Talaga 2017). And while residential schools are no longer in operation, these practices have not stayed in the past but persist through the impacts of intergenerational trauma and the continued placement of Indigenous children into the child welfare system at rates greater than at the height of residential schools, a system that has been called the second generation of residential schools (Bourgeois 2015).

In the late spring and early summer of 2021, the remains of well over a thousand Indigenous children were discovered in unmarked graves near several former residential schools in British Columbia and Saskatchewan.[1] Many more grave sites are believed to exist in Canada (Austen 2021; Blackstock and Palmater 2021) and are stark reminders of the relationship between slow, structural, and naked violence. While concentrating on naked violence narrows the focus to the moments of abuse and murder, attention to structural and slow violence broadens the inquiry to the laws and policies that enabled the operation of residential schools and their long-term impacts, including the intergenerational trauma generated by these forms of violence within Indigenous communities. These events contain both momentary (immediate) and continuous forms of violence. To try to separate these forms of violence as either naked, slow, or structural is akin to seeing from one eye rather than using our entire field of vision. The harms of residential schools on Indigenous populations bring together the naked violence of the past with the sustained and intergenerational trauma of these experiences on Indigenous communities.

It is fit to remember that violence perpetrated against Indigenous populations, in part by and through residential schools, relied on the mythology of law as a neutral and objective method for evaluating information and determining truth (Naffine 1990). These "objective" legal approaches were key for the settler-colonial project. "Neutral" legal concepts such as *terra nullius* allowed for the "erasing" of space already inhabited by Indigenous people, both conceptually and physically, therefore being instrumental for building and settling in the new world. Through a process of slow, structural, and naked violence, the law has played, and *continues* to play, a vital role in the production and erasure of Indigenous social, political, and cultural practices and identities (Williams 1990; Anghie 1996; Blomley 2003; Miller 2004; Comaroff and Comaroff 2006).

The relationship between slow, structural, and naked violence can also be examined in the context of the criminal legal system, in which the path from the spectacle of police arrests through to the relative nonspectacle of incarceration marks the transition from coercive and structural force to slow violence that has long-term consequences for racialized and Indigenous communities. Consider, for example, the impact of the 1986 Anti-Drug Abuse Act in the United States—one assault in what Richard Nixon famously dubbed the "War on Drugs." Among other things, the act mandated harsher penalties for the possession and sale of drugs and increased the number of drug-related offenses that carried a mandatory minimum prison sentence. In particular, the amount of crack cocaine required to trigger a mandatory sentence was set far lower than the amount of powder cocaine, a provision widely recognized for its racist agenda: the large majority of crack users were Black, whereas powder cocaine was primarily a drug used by affluent whites. Inner-city Black neighbourhoods were accordingly targeted as havens for drug users and pushers, and Black people were arrested and imprisoned at vastly disproportionate rates (Alexander 2012, 59–80; see also Davis 2017, xi–xvii). The situation was exacerbated by the "tough on crime" policies of the 1990s, notably the 1994 Violent Crime Control and Law Enforcement Act, which sent the number of inmates in the United States soaring, again with a significant overrepresentation of both Blacks and Hispanics. Although incarceration rates have been steadily declining since the late 2000s, an obvious racial imbalance persists. As of the end of 2018, Blacks still made up about 33 percent of the prison population, in comparison to their 12 percent share of the US population as a whole, and were incarcerated at a rate roughly five times that of white people (Gramlich 2020).

In Canada, the criminalization of drug possession and sale has also disproportionately targeted Black and Indigenous people (Maynard 2017), contributing to the overrepresentation of these groups in Canadian prisons. In January 2020, Canada's Office of the Correctional Investigator reported that, although Indigenous people account for only 5 percent of the population of Canada overall, the proportion of Indigenous inmates out of the total federal prison population had now exceeded 30 percent, their number having increased by 43.4 percent (or 1,265) since April 2010. Similarly, in 2013, the Office of the Correctional Investigator noted in their annual report that the number of Black inmates in Canada's federal prisons had grown by nearly 90 percent between 2003 and 2013, with the result that Blacks then made up 9.5 percent of the federal prison population despite representing only 2.9 percent of the Canadian population (2013, 3, 9). While a series of recommendations were made in 2013 by the correctional investigator and in 2017 by a UN human rights working group to change the governance structure of Correctional Service Canada (CSC) and provide more national training, CSC has mostly ignored these recommendations (Office of the Correctional Investigator of Canada 2022, 39–43; UN Human Rights Council Working Group of Experts on People of African Descent 2017).

These statistics reaffirm our contention that inserting the concept of slow violence into the analysis helps us better understand the power of law and the experiences of racialized groups who are subjected to racist and colonial violence—not only naked and structural violence but also slow violence at the hands of law. The intention and outcome of the law may not be immediately evident nor present itself in obvious ways, at least not in all its forms. What becomes clear is that while the threat of physical coercion always lurks beneath the law, it also operates and creates conditions for discrete forms of violence that disproportionately target BIPOC, sexual minorities, and economically disadvantaged communities. While Poulantzas reminds us that physical coercion underpins our entire political and legal structure, we must also consider that violence is inscribed within a "web of disciplinary and ideological devices" (1978, 77). This violence remains the determining element of all relationships of power, even when it is not exercised in a direct and open manner (81). Building on Poulantzas, we take the position that slow, structural, and naked violence are all mutually constitutive and should be examined together if we are to understand their full impact.

Overview of the Chapters

The chapters in this volume contribute to and advance the discussions outlined above, demonstrating the subtle, practical, and persistent ways law's violence continues to be maintained and perpetuated in Canadian society.

The chapters in part 1 focus on law's relationship to settler colonialism and racism in Canada, providing theoretical and methodological approaches for deconstructing these structures. In chapter 1, Carmela Murdocca, Shaira Vadasaria, and Timothy Bryan focus their analysis on race and colonialism, contending that Canadian socio-legal scholars must move beyond the institutional framing of race and racism and suggesting that they are constitutive of law. By adopting a methodological approach that addresses the continuities of race and colonialism, as well as their relationalities, the authors argue socio-legal scholars can better attend to the continuities of racial legal governance and the spatial and temporal dimensions across disparate sites of violence.

The second chapter, by Stacy Douglas, further highlights how settler colonialism is constitutive of Canadian law, noting the imaginative and mythological foundations of this law through a postcolonial case analysis. The chapter considers how a focus on imagination can problematize the legacy of colonialism and white supremacy present throughout the Canadian legal landscape. Douglas explores the application for judicial review brought by the Mikisew Cree against the Canadian government for its failure to carry out the Crown's duty to consult with Indigenous communities before introducing legislation that would make changes to environmental protections. Douglas seeks to provide what Peter Fitzpatrick termed an *internal decolonization* of the settler-colonial legal infrastructure by subverting the myths of law's rationality. This chapter highlights how law's imaginative properties reproduce settler colonialism, generating legal fictions that maintain settler-colonial violence against Indigenous groups.

The essays in part 2 continue our discussion of law's violence and reproduction of inequalities, focusing specifically on law's power in producing racism and gender violence and depoliticizing racial violence. The authors highlight the ways that the violence of the law against certain segments of society is invisibilized through legal creations of categories of a "crime" and a "criminal," which are deeply racist, sexist, xenophobic, and misogynistic and target most marginalized populations. The chapters underline questions about who becomes the focus of the law's attention (and discourse) as a perpetrator or a victim, an exercise that brings to light deep social inequalities.

In chapter 3, Yavar Hameed and Jeffrey Monaghan continue the conversation on law's imaginative properties. The authors demonstrate the ways in which racist ideologies used in policing practices and communications animate the production of Islamic terrorists and how the law extends and reinforces the equation of Muslim bodies with threats to national security. More specifically, Hameed and Monaghan investigate the ways in which the crime-making dynamics inherent in the "war on terror" are embedded with racialized constructions of "menacing Islam" in counter-terrorist practices. The authors draw on Richard Ericson's work to outline how various practices in the Canadian criminal legal system combine to determine what cases are transformed into acts of terrorism and how suspects, once identified, are accordingly positioned as terrorists. This chapter contributes to one of the anthology's themes: law relies on the production of fictions, including fictional enemies, to maintain both overt and discrete violence against marginalized groups, as the state arrests and incarcerates where possible while engaging in long-term surveillance of the Muslim population.

Contributing to discussions on race, gender, and law's power, in chapter 4, Emily Lockhart, Katrin Roots, and Heather Tasker trace the development of key feminist concerns in relation to gendered violence, coming to settle in our contemporary moment dominated by discussions of #MeToo and increased public awareness of the prevalence of sexual harassment and assault. The authors suggest that the broad publicity and, therefore, hypervisibility of activism and the resulting attention paid by the criminal legal system to those who formerly escaped its power should not be mistaken for a universalized transformation in enactments of justice through legal developments. Instead, they argue that the spectacularism attached to the hypervisible cases drawing attention in the #MeToo movement, such as those of Harvey Weinstein and R. Kelly, serve to stand in for sexual harm broadly. The attention these events receive is powerful in mobilizing limited legal responses, but in drawing the eye to spectacular and individual cases, the everyday experiences and executions of violence, including violence committed by and through law primarily against marginalized and racialized people, remains routinized, invisibilized, and when seen, barely read as violence at all.

In chapter 5, Heather Tasker offers a critical analysis of the United Nations High Commissioner for Refugees' "Do You See What I See?" (DYSWIS) photography project. Tasker demonstrates how legal power, through its absence and presence, contributes to violence that depoliticizes and silences racialized groups living in refugee camps. Through an analysis of the DYSWIS project, the chapter explores how humanitarian logic is materialized through the medium of photography and the ways that this impacts Western consumption of images produced by refugee youth. The chapter focuses on how projects such as DYSWIS influence international norm-making in ways that entrench humanitarian principles such as impartiality and neutrality. She argues that DYSWIS serves to exclude, or silence, politicized and context-specific conversations about conflict, displacement, and law.

The contributions in this book not only explore law's power but suggest transformational possibilities for those seeking to challenge law's violence and power. The chapters in the final section outline paths for resistance and social transformation. In chapter 6, Alex Luscombe and Kevin Walby provide a conceptual framework for understanding the practice of feral lawyering, where socio-legal scholars use freedom of information laws to broker access to hidden documents. They note not only law's power to exclude and protect information but also how socio-legal scholars can demand, negotiate, and challenge the state and state power, as well as disrupt the state's ability to hide information. The chapter points to feral lawyering as a practical strategy for challenging legal violence, revealing the inner workings of its bureaucracy.

In chapter 7, Nergis Canefe argues that socio-legal scholars must address the rigidities and silence of our field, including providing more attention to law's power beyond its productive and creative potential and instead including law's violence and law's ability to both produce and justify violence against individuals from many subjectivities and identities. Canefe suggests that rather than simply engaging in academic discussions, the objective of early socio-legal scholarship was to develop ways critical legal scholarship could benefit populations that are oppressed, marginalized, and discriminated against in society. For Canefe, although socio-legal scholars reveal uncertainties about law, they pay little attention to violence in everyday life. To account for the rigidities and silences of the field, Canefe notes that we must explore the relationship between hegemony, legal consciousness, and ideology. According to the author, it is not enough to see legal consciousness as a theoretical concept or research topic, but it must instead be seen as inherently tied to legal hegemony and ideology.

Mariful Alam and Irina Ceric conclude the volume with an afterword on social transformation and future possibilities, suggesting that the force of law cannot be separated from violence. While socio-legal scholars often focus on the role of law in creating or subverting social change, Alam and Ceric argue that we must consider a vision of a society without a state or law. The chapter outlines lessons learned from social movements and prefigurative politics when creating visions of justice beyond law and the state. Spoke councils, sanctuary cities, and anti-carceral feminist movements all provide examples of how we can reimagine democracy and justice, providing interventions to address injustice without state violence.

Note

1 These discoveries brought home the violent realities of colonization, provoking outrage and expressions of remorse. The Ontario Human Rights Commission (2021), for example, called upon all Canadians to recognize the brutal legacy of colonialism manifest in intergenerational trauma and in the continued

dispossession and marginalization of Indigenous peoples. Beyond that, the Native Women's Association of Canada (2021; see also Lao 2021) demanded detailed investigations and called for criminal charges to be brought against the religious and government officials and others still living who were found to be directly implicated in these deaths. Following the lead of Idle No More (n.d.), many also campaigned for the cancellation of Canada Day, in part to highlight the fact that Canada has not done nearly enough to rectify the damage done to Indigenous communities and to put a stop to this violence in the present day. As Mi'kmaw activist Robert Leamon stated at a rally in St. John's on Canada Day, rather than celebrate, those in attendance "choose to instead gather to recognize all of the lives who have been lost due to racism, colonialism and ongoing genocide and oppression by Canada" (quoted in Moore 2021).

References

Alexander, Michelle. 2012. *The New Jim Crow: Mass Incarceration in the Age of Colorblindness*. New York: New Press.

Althusser, Louis. 1971. *Lenin and Philosophy and Other Essays*. Translated by Ben Brewster. New York: Monthly Review Press.

Amnesty International. 2004. *Stolen Sisters: A Human Rights Response to Discrimination and Violence Against Indigenous Women in Canada*. London: Amnesty International.

Anghie, Antony. 1996. "Francisco De Vitoria and the Colonial Origins of International Law." *Social & Legal Studies* 5 (4): 321–36.

Arthurs, Harry. 1983. *Law and Learning / Le droit et le savoir: Report to the Social Sciences and Humanities Research Council of Canada by the Consultative Group on Research and Education in Law*. Ottawa: Information Division, Social Sciences and Humanities Research Council of Canada.

Arthurs, Harry, and Annie Bunting. 2014. "Socio-legal Scholarship in Canada: A Review of the Field." *Journal of Law and Society* 41 (4): 487–99.

Austen, Ian. 2021. "The Indigenous Archaeologist Tracking Down the Missing Residential Children." *New York Times*, 30 July 2021. https://www.nytimes.com/2021/07/30/world/canada/indigenous-archaeologist-graves-school-children.html.

Backhouse, Constance. 1999. *Colour-Coded: A Legal History of Racism in Canada, 1900–1950*. Toronto: University of Toronto Press.

Beck, Anthony. 1996. "Foucault and Law: The Collapse of Law's Empire." *Oxford Journal of Legal Studies* 16 (3): 489–502.

Blackstock, Cindy, and Pamela Palmater. 2021. "The Discovery of Unmarked Children's Graves in Canada Has Indigenous People Asking: How Many More?"

Guardian, 9 June 2021. https://www.theguardian.com/commentisfree/2021/jun/
09/discovery-mass-graves-canada-indigenous-people-first-nations-residential
-schools.

Blomley, Nicholas. 2003. "Law, Property, and the Geography of Violence: The
Frontier, the Survey, and the Grid." *Annals of the Association of American
Geographers* 93 (1): 121–41.

Bourgeois, Robyn. 2015. "Colonial Exploitation: The Canadian State and the
Trafficking of Indigenous Women and Girls in Canada." *UCLA Law Review* 62
(6): 1426–63.

Boyce, Jillian. 2016. "Victimization of Aboriginal People in Canada, 2014." Juristat:
Statistics Canada, Catalogue no. 85–002-X, 28 June 2016, https://www150.statcan
.gc.ca/n1/en/pub/85-002-x/2016001/article/14631-eng.pdf?st=licIR_Q-.

Brickley, Stephen, and Elizabeth Comack. 1987. "The Role of Law in Social
Transformation: Is a Jurisprudence of Insurgency Possible?" *Canadian Journal of
Law & Society* 2 (2): 97–120.

Brophy, Susan Dianne, and J. C. Blokhuis. 2017. "Defining Legal Studies in Canada."
Journal of Commonwealth Law and Legal Education 12 (1): 7–18.

Cain, Maureen, and Alan Hunt. 1979. *Marx and Engels on Law*. New York:
Academic Press.

Calavita, Kitty. 2010. *Invitation to Law and Society: An Introduction to the Study of
Real Law*. 2nd ed. Chicago: University of Chicago Press.

CBC News. 2015. "Video Reveals Details of What Happened the Night Sammy
Yatim Was Shot." 21 October 2015. https://www.cbc.ca/news/canada/toronto/
sammy-yatim-trial-1.3281596.

———. 2021. "No Charges for Winnipeg Officers Who Killed Man in One of 3
Shootings Last April: Police Watchdog." 5 May 2021. https://www.cbc.ca/news/
canada/manitoba/iiu-winnipeg-police-jason-collins-police-shooting-1.6015046.

Ceric, Irina. 2020. "Beyond Contempt: Injunctions, Land Defense, and the
·Criminalization of Indigenous Resistance." *South Atlantic Quarterly* 119 (2): 353–69.

Chambliss, William J., and Robert B. Seidman. 1971. *Law, Order, and Power*.
Reading, MA: Addison-Wesley.

Chan, Wendy, Dorothy E. Chunn, and Robert Menzies, eds. 2005. *Women, Madness
and the Law: A Feminist Reader*. London: GlassHouse.

Chappell, Bill. 2021. "Derek Chauvin Is Sentenced to 22½ Years for George Floyd's
Murder." NPR, 25 June 2021. https://www.npr.org/sections/trial-over-killing-of
-george-floyd/2021/06/25/1009524284/derek-chauvin-sentencing-george-floyd
-murder.

Chunn, Dorothy E., and Dany Lacombe, eds. 2000. *Law as a Gendering Practice*.
Toronto: Oxford University Press.

Cole, Desmond. 2020. *The Skin We're In: A Year of Black Resistance and Power*. Toronto: Doubleday Canada.

Collins, Patricia Hill. 2015. "Intersectionality's Definitional Dilemmas." *Annual Review of Sociology* 41:1–20.

Comack, Elizabeth. 2013. *Racialized Policing*. Halifax: Fernwood.

Comaroff, Jean, and John Comaroff. 2006. "Law and Disorder in the Postcolony: An Introduction." In *Law and Disorder in the Postcolony*, edited by Jean Comaroff and John Comaroff, 1–56. Chicago: University of Chicago Press.

Committee on the Elimination of Discrimination Against Women. 2015. *Report of the Inquiry Concerning Canada of the Committee on the Elimination of Discrimination Against Women Under Article 8 of the Optional Protocol to the Convention on the Elimination of All Forms of Discrimination Against Women.* New York: United Nations. https://digitallibrary.un.org/record/836103?ln=en.

Cotterrell, Roger. 2009. "Spectres of Transnationalism: Changing Terrains of Sociology of Law." *Journal of Law and Society* 36 (4): 481–500.

Craig, Elaine. 2018. *Putting Trials on Trial: Sexual Assault and the Failure of the Legal Profession*. Montréal and Kingston: McGill-Queen's University Press.

Cram, Stephanie, and Nicholas Frew. 2021. "Hundreds Gather in Memory of Eishia Hudson, 16, Who Was Fatally Shot by Winnipeg Police a Year Ago." CBC News, 8 April 2021. https://www.cbc.ca/news/canada/manitoba/eishia-hudson-vigil -winnipeg-police-1.5980336.

Crenshaw, Kimberlé. 1991. "Mapping the Margins: Intersectionality, Identity, Politics and Violence Against Women of Colour." *Stanford Law Review* 43 (6): 1241–99.

———. 1995. "Race, Reform, and Retrenchment: Transformation and Legitimation in Anti-discrimination Law." In *Critical Race Theory: The Key Writings That Formed the Movement*, edited by Kimberlé Crenshaw, Neil Gotanda, Gary Peller, and Kendall Thomas. New York: New Press.

———. 2003. "Demarginalizing the Intersection of Race and Sex: A Black Feminist Critique and Antidiscrimination Doctrine, Feminist Theory, and Antiracist Politics" In *Critical Race Feminism: A Reader*, 2nd ed., edited by Adrien Katherine Wing. New York: NYU Press.

Crosby, Andrew, and Jeffrey Monaghan. 2012. "Settler Governmentality in Canada and the Algonquins of Barrier Lake." *Security Dialogue* 43 (5): 421–38.

Dafnos, Tia. 2013. "Pacification and Indigenous Struggles in Canada." *Socialist Studies / Études socialistes* 9 (2): 57–77.

Davis, Angela J. 2017. "Introduction." In *Policing the Black Man*, edited by Angela J. Davis, xi–xxiv. New York: Pantheon.

Delgado, Richard, and Jean Stefancic. 2017. *Critical Race Theory: An Introduction*. New York: NYU Press.

Diabo, Russell. 2017. "The Indian Act: The Foundation of Colonialism in Canada." In *Whose Land Is It Anyway? A Manual for Decolonization*, edited by Peter McFarlane and Nicole Schabus, 22–26. Vancouver: Federation of Post-Secondary Educators of BC. https://fpse.ca/sites/default/files/news_files/Decolonization%20Handbook.pdf.

Ditchburn, Jennifer. 2014. "Reports Contradict Stephen Harper's View on Aboriginal Women Victims." CBC News, 3 September 2014. https://www.cbc.ca/news/indigenous/reports-contradict-stephen-harper-s-view-on-aboriginal-women-victims-1.2754542.

Ewick, Patricia, and Austin Sarat. 2015. "On the Emerging Maturity of Law and Society: An Introduction." In *The Handbook of Law and Society*, edited by Austin Sarat and Patricia Ewick, xiii–xxii. Chichester, UK: Wiley-Blackwell.

Ewick, Patricia, and Susan S. Silbey. 1998. *The Common Place of Law: Stories from Everyday Life*. Chicago: University of Chicago Press.

Feenan, Dermot, ed. 2013. *Exploring the "Socio" of Socio-legal Studies*. New York: Palgrave Macmillan.

Fitzpatrick, Peter. 1995. "Being Social in Socio-legal Studies." *Journal of Law and Society* 22 (2): 105–12.

Foucault, Michel. (1978) 1990. *The History of Sexuality*. Vol. 1, *An Introduction*. Translated by Robert Hurley. New York: Vintage.

———. 1980. *Power/Knowledge: Selected Interviews and Other Writings, 1972–1977*. Edited by Colin Gordon. Translated by Colin Gordon, Leo Marshall, John Mepham, and Kate Soper. New York: Pantheon.

Freeman, Alan David. 1995. "Legitimizing Racial Discrimination Through Antidiscrimination Law: A Critical Review of Supreme Court Doctrine." In *Critical Race Theory: The Key Writings That Formed the Movement*, edited by Kimberlé Crenshaw, Neil Gotanda, Gary Peller, and Kendall Thomas, 29–45. New York: New Press.

Galtung, Johan. 1969. "Violence, Peace, and Peace Research." *Journal of Peace Research* 6 (3): 167–91.

Gillis, Wendy. 2017. "Andrew Loku Coroner's Inquest Revealed Crucial New Details." *Toronto Star*, 23 June 2017. https://www.thestar.com/news/crime/2017/06/23/andrew-loku-coroners-inquest-revealed-crucial-new-details.html.

Glasbeek, Amanda, Katrin Roots, and Mariful Alam. 2019. "Postcolonialism, Time, and Body-Worn Cameras." *Surveillance and Society* 17 (5): 743–46.

———. 2020. "Seeing and Not-Seeing: Race and Body-Worn Cameras in Canada." *Surveillance and Society* 18 (3): 328–42.

Golder, Ben, and Peter Fitzpatrick. 2009. *Foucault's Law*. New York: Routledge.

Gramlich, John. 2020. "Black Imprisonment Rate in the U.S. Has Fallen by a Third Since 2006." Pew Research Center, 6 May 2020. https://www.pewresearch.org/fact

-tank/2020/05/06/share-of-black-white-hispanic-americans-in-prison-2018-vs
-2006/.

Gramsci, Antonio. 1971. *Selections from the Prison Notebooks.* London: Lawrence and Wishart.

Guillory, John. 1993. *Cultural Capital: The Problem of Literary Canon Formation.* Chicago: University of Chicago Press.

Haney López, Ian. 1996. *White by Law: The Legal Construction of Race.* New York: NYU Press.

Hay, Douglas. 1975. "Property, Authority, and the Criminal Law." In *Albion's Fatal Tree: Crime and Society in Eighteenth Century England*, edited by Douglas Hay, Peter Linebaugh, John G. Rule, E. P Thompson, and Cal Winslow, 18–62. London: Allen Lane.

Holterman, Devin. 2014. "Slow Violence, Extraction and Human Rights Defence in Tanzania: Notes from the Field." *Resources Policy* 40:59–65.

Hopper, Tristan. 2021. "'This School Is a Jail House': Documents Reveal the Horrors of Indian Residential Schools." *National Post*, 3 June 2021. https://nationalpost .com/news/canada/this-school-is-a-jail-house-documents-reveal-the-horrors-of -indian-residential-schools.

Hotton Mahony, Tina, Joanna Jacob, and Heather Hobson. 2017. "Women and the Criminal Justice System." In *Women in Canada: A Gender-Based Statistical Report, 7th ed.* Statistics Canada, Catalogue no. 89–503-X, 21 June 2017. https://www150 .statcan.gc.ca/n1/en/pub/89-503-x/2015001/article/14785-eng.pdf?st=kRbTsx8l.

Human Rights Watch. 2013. "Those Who Take Us Away: Abusive Policing and Failures in Protection of Indigenous Women and Girls in Northern British Columbia, Canada." 13 February 2023. https://www.hrw.org/report/2013/02/13/those-who-take -us-away/abusive-policing-and-failures-protection-indigenous-women.

Hunt, Alan. 1993. *Explorations in Law and Society: Toward a Constitutive Theory of Law.* New York: Routledge.

Hunt, Alan, and Gary Wickham. 1994. *Foucault and Law: Towards a Sociology of Law as Governance.* London: Pluto.

Idle No More. n.d. "#CancelCanadaDay." Accessed 10 December 2022. https://idlenomore.ca/cancelcanadaday/.

Jolly, Joanna. 2019. *Red River Girl: The Life and Death of Tina Fontaine.* Toronto: Viking.

Lao, David. 2021. "People Complicit in Canada's Residential School Deaths Should Be Charged, Group Says." Global News, 24 June 2021. https://globalnews.ca/news/7978394/canada-residential-school-criminal-charges/.

Levenson, Eric. 2021. "Former Officer Knelt on George Floyd for 9 Minutes and 29 Seconds—Not the Infamous 8:46." CNN, 30 March 2021. https://www.cnn.com/2021/03/29/us/george-floyd-timing-929-846/index.html.

MacDonald, David B., and Graham Hudson. 2012. "The Genocide Question and Indian Residential Schools in Canada." *Canadian Journal of Political Science* 45 (2): 427–49.

MacKinnon, Catherine A. 1982. "Feminism, Marxism, Method, and the State: An Agenda for Theory." *Signs* 7 (3): 515–44.

Maynard, Robyn. 2017. *Policing Black Lives: State Violence in Canada from Slavery to the Present.* Halifax: Fernwood.

Mbembe, Achille. 2003. "Necropolitics." Translated by Libby Meintjes. *Public Culture* 15 (1): 11–40.

McDiarmid, Jessica. 2019. *Highway of Tears: A True Story of Racism, Indifference, and the Pursuit of Justice for Missing and Murdered Indigenous Women and Girls.* Toronto: Doubleday Canada.

Metatawabin, Edmund, with Alexandra Shimo. 2015. *Up Ghost River: A Chief's Journey Through the Turbulent Waters of Native History.* Toronto: Vintage Canada.

Miller, J. R. 2004. *Lethal Legacy: Current Native Controversies in Canada.* Toronto: McClelland and Stewart.

Moore, Mike. 2021. "Cancel Canada Day Rally in St. John's Draws Support, Solidarity for Indigenous Community." CBC News, 1 July 2021. https://www.cbc .ca/news/canada/newfoundland-labrador/cancel-canada-day-nl-1.6087553.

Morgensen, Scott. 2011. "The Biopolitics of Settler Colonialism: Right Here, Right Now." *Settler Colonial Studies* 1 (1): 52–76.

Naffine, Ngaire. 1990. *The Law and the Sexes: Explorations in Feminist Jurisprudence.* Sydney: Allen and Unwin.

Nasser, Shanifa. 2021. "No Charges in Death of Ejaz Choudry, 62-Year-Old Shot and Killed by Police While in Crisis." CBC News, 6 April 2021. https://www.cbc.ca/ news/canada/toronto/ejaz-choudry-no-charges-siu-peel-police-1.5976266.

National Inquiry into Missing and Murdered Indigenous Women and Girls. 2019. *Reclaiming Power and Place: The Final Report of the National Inquiry into Missing and Murdered Indigenous Women and Girls.* 2 vols. https://www.mmiwg-ffada.ca/ final-report/.

Native Women's Association of Canada. 2021. "NWAC Demands Criminal Charges Against Governments, Churches, and Others Responsible for Deaths of Thousands of Children at Indian Residential Schools." News release, 24 June 2021. https://nwac.ca/media/2021/06/nwac-demands-criminal-charges-against -governments-churches-others-responsible-for-deaths-of-thousands-of-children -at-indian-residential-schools.

Neocleous, Mark. 2008. *Critique of Security.* Montreal: McGill-Queen's University Press.

Newman, Saul. 2004. "Terror, Sovereignty and Law: On the Politics of Violence." *German Law Journal* 5:569–84.

New York Times. 2022. "How George Floyd Died, and What Happened Next." 29 July 2022. https://www.nytimes.com/article/george-floyd.html.

Nixon, Rob. 2011. *Slow Violence and the Environmentalism of the Poor*. Cambridge, MA: Harvard University Press.

O'Brien, Abby. 2022. Inquest into Fatal Shooting of Sammy Yatim by Toronto Police Set for November. CTV News, 24 October 2022. https://toronto.ctvnews .ca/inquest-into-fatal-shooting-of-sammy-yatim-by-toronto-police-set-for -november-1.6122654.

Office of the Correctional Investigator. 2013. "Annual Report of the Office of the Correctional Investigator, 2012–2013." 28 June 2013. https://www.oci-bec.gc.ca/ cnt/rpt/pdf/annrpt/annrpt20122013-eng.pdf.

———. 2020. "Indigenous People in Federal Custody Surpasses 30%—Correctional Investigator Issues Statement and Challenge." News release, 21 January 2020. https://www.oci-bec.gc.ca/cnt/comm/press/press20200121-eng.aspx.

———. 2022. "Annual Report of the Office of the Correctional Investigator, 2021–2022." 30 June 2022. https://www.oci-bec.gc.ca/cnt/rpt/pdf/annrpt/annrpt20212022-eng.pdf.

Oksala, Johanna. 2010. "Violence and the Biopolitics of Modernity." *Foucault Studies* 10:23–43.

Ontario Human Rights Commission. 2021. "Statement on Unmarked Graves Found at Former Saskatchewan Residential School Site: Growing Numbers Must Lead to Growing Action." Accessed 8 December 2022. http://www.ohrc.on.ca/en/news _centre/statement-unmarked-graves-found-former-saskatchewan-residential -school-site-growing-numbers-must.

Owusu-Bempah, Akwasi, and Scott Wortley. 2014. "Race, Crime, and Criminal Justice in Canada." In *The Oxford Handbook of Ethnicity, Crime, and Immigration*, edited by Sandra M. Bucerius and Michael Tonry, 281–320. Oxford: Oxford University Press.

Palmater, Pamela. 2016. "Shining Light on the Dark Places: Addressing Police Racism and Sexualized Violence Against Indigenous Women and Girls in the National Inquiry." *Canadian Journal of Women and the Law* 28 (2): 253–84.

Palmer, Bryan D. 2003. "What's Law Got to Do with It? Historical Considerations on Class Struggle, Boundaries of Constraint, and Capitalist Authority." *Osgoode Hall Law Journal* 41:465–90.

Pasternak, Shiri. 2017. "Blockade: A Meeting Place of Law." In *Whose Land Is It Anyway? A Manual for Decolonization*, edited by Peter McFarlane and Nicole Schabus, 32–35. Vancouver: Federation of Post-Secondary Educators of BC. https://fpse.ca/sites/default/files/news_files/Decolonization%20Handbook.pdf.

Perreault, Samuel. 2022. "Victimization of First Nations People, Métis and Inuit in Canada," Juristat: Statistics Canada, Catalogue no. 85-002-X, 19 July 2022. https://www150.statcan.gc.ca/n1/pub/85-002-x/2022001/article/00012-eng.htm

Poulantzas, Nicos. 1978. *State, Power, Socialism*. London: Verso.

Razack, Sherene H. 2015. *Dying from Improvement: Inquests and Inquiries into Indigenous Deaths in Custody*. Toronto: University of Toronto Press.

Regan, Paulette. 2010. *Unsettling the Settler Within: Indian Residential Schools, Truth Telling and Reconciliation in Canada*. Vancouver: University of British Columbia Press.

Rose, Nikolas, Pat O'Malley, and Mariana Valverde. 2006. "Governmentality." *Annual Review of Law and Social Science* 2:83–104.

Rose, Nikolas, and Mariana Valverde. 1998. "Governed by Law?" *Social & Legal Studies* 7 (4): 541–51.

Seron, Carroll, Susan Bibler Coutin, and Pauline White Meeusen. 2013. "Is There a Canon of Law and Society?" *Annual Review of Law and Social Science* 9:287–306.

Silbey, Susan S. 2013. "What Makes a Social Science of Law? Doubling the Social in Socio-legal Studies." In *Exploring the "Socio" of Socio-legal Studies*, edited by Dermot Feenan, 20–36. New York. Palgrave Macmillan.

Simpson, Michael, and Philippe Le Billon. 2021. "Reconciling Violence: Policing the Politics of Recognition." *Geoforum* 119:111–21.

Smart, Carol. 1989. *Feminism and the Power of Law*. London: Routledge.

———. 1995. *Law, Crime and Sexuality: Essays in Feminism*. London: Sage.

Struthers Montford, Kelly, and Tessa Wotherspoon. 2021. "The Contagion of Slow Violence: The Slaughterhouse and COVID-19." *Animal Studies Journal* 10 (1): 80–113.

Talaga, Tanya. 2017. *Seven Fallen Feathers: Racism, Death, and Hard Truths in a Northern City*. Toronto: House of Anansi.

Thompson, E. P. 1975. *Whigs and Hunters: The Origin of the Black Act*. New York: Pantheon.

TRC (Truth and Reconciliation Commission) of Canada. 2015. "Calls to Action." In *The Final Report of the Truth and Reconciliation Commission of Canada*. Winnipeg: TRC of Canada.

Tucker, Eric. 1988. "Making the Workplace 'Safe' in Capitalism: The Enforcement of Factory Legislation in Nineteenth-Century Ontario." *Labour / Le Travail* 21:45–85.

———. 2019. *Administering Danger in the Workplace*. Toronto: University of Toronto Press.

UN Human Rights Council Working Group of Experts on People of African Descent. 2017. "Report of the Working Group of Experts on People of African Descent on Its Mission to Canada." Geneva: United Nations. https://digitallibrary.un.org/record/1304262?ln=en#record-files-collapse-header.

Ursel, Jane, Leslie M. Tutty, and Janice leMaistre, eds. 2008. *What's Law Got to Do with It? The Law, Specialized Courts and Domestic Violence in Canada*. Toronto: Cormorant.

Valverde, Mariana. 2003. *Law's Dream of a Common Knowledge*. Princeton: Princeton University Press.

Walby, Kevin. 2007. "Contributions to a Post-sovereigntist Understanding of Law: Foucault, Law as Governance, and Legal Pluralism." *Social & Legal Studies* 16 (4): 551–71.

Ward, Geoff. 2015. "The Slow Violence of State Organized Race Crime." *Theoretical Criminology* 19 (3): 299–314. https://doi.org/10.1177/1362480614550119.

Whitaker, Reg, Gregory S. Kealey, and Andrew Parnaby. 2013. *Secret Service: Political Policing in Canada from the Fenians to Fortress America*. Toronto: University of Toronto Press.

Williams, James, and Randy Lippert. 2006. "Governing on the Margins: Exploring the Contributions of Governmentality Studies to Critical Criminology in Canada." *Canadian Journal of Criminology and Criminal Justice* 48 (5): 703–20.

Williams, Patricia J. 1992. *The Alchemy of Race and Rights*. Cambridge, MA: Harvard University Press.

Williams, Robert A., Jr. 1990. *The American Indian in Western Legal Thought: The Discourses of Conquest*. New York: Oxford University Press.

Wolfe, Patrick. 2006. "Settler Colonialism and the Elimination of the Native." *Journal of Genocide Research* 8 (4): 387–409.

Woolford, Andrew, and James Gacek. 2016. "Genocidal Carcerality and Indian Residential Schools in Canada." *Punishment and Society* 18 (4): 400–419.

Wright, Barry, and Susan Binnie, eds. 2009. *Canadian State Trials*. Vol. 3, *Political Trials and Security Measures, 1840–1914*. Toronto: University of Toronto Press.

Part I
Lawfare and Settler Colonialism

1 Race and Colonialism in Socio-legal Studies in Canada

Carmela Murdocca, Shaira Vadasaria, and
Timothy Bryan

What is the story of race and settler colonialism in the legal landscape of present-day Canada? How do we tell these legal histories of settler-state racial violence in the context of the ongoing realities of Indigenous dispossession, anti-Black racism, and the experiences of civil death by migrants and displaced people? What does it mean to commit to this inquiry at a time when human rights discourse and projects of reparative justice corroborate with the legacies of white supremacy and racial colonial violence inherent in juridico-political mechanisms of liberal rights regimes? In this chapter, we maintain that socio-legal scholars in Canada need to do much more to address the historical, structural, and affective significance of race, racism, and settler colonialism in our socio-legal analyses and imaginations (Gomez 2012).[1]

Although the growing field of socio-legal studies has advanced particular considerations of law and nation building in Canada (see the chapters by Douglas and Hameed and Monaghan in this collection, for example), it is our position that the constitutive basis of race and colonialism in the afterlives of slavery and the ongoing effects of racism and colonialism in Canada require additional attention in the field of socio-legal studies. Defining the broad area of socio-legal studies is not without its challenges. The field emerged in the 1960s in Canada with an interdisciplinary intent of moving within and beyond an institutional and formal understanding of law to an inter-disciplinary view of law that addresses the social, political, economic, and cultural meanings of law.[2] Race and racism are still understood in quite an institutional framing in socio-legal studies (i.e., the systemic, differential, and experiential effects of racism in the legal system) despite decades of research and writing that connect an institutional legal framework to the cultural meanings of law, race, and colonialism advanced in critical race, Indigenous, post-colonial, and anti-colonial scholarship. Socio-legal scholarship that views race and the complex legacies of colonialism and racialization as variables to be measured in legal systems and as processes that often collapse race and identity in ways that do not attend to the structural, foundational, and epistemological ways that race and colonialism are imbricated in socio-legal processes. This observation has been made in a number of social science disciplines, including socio-legal studies. As Laura Gomez argues, "Law and society scholars have somewhat carelessly incorporated race into their research by treating it as a readily measurable, dichotomous (black/white) variable that affects law at various points" rather than in a more complex way (2012, 230). Indeed, this is not to suggest that research that considers race as a measurable variable is not politically potent, strategic, and important.[3] The task is to connect the consequences and experiential realities of the ongoing histories of colonialism and racialization (which may be revealed through quantifying encounters with police or overincarceration rates, for example) to "thick description," to borrow Clifford Geertz's phrase, which compels a "sorting out (of) the structures of signification" (1973, 9) and assists in revealing the meanings, observations, and conceptual, contextual, temporal, affective, aesthetic, and interpretive structures of socio-legal phenomena.[4]

Considering race and colonialism in socio-legal studies in Canada invites an inquiry into some of the significant contributions that have been made to the field. As we explore in this chapter, particular scholars have done much to expand our understanding of race, colonialism, and law in Canada and provide theoretical and methodological tools for examining the epistemological and ontological foundations of race, colonialism, and law. At a time when Indigenous and Black activists call for renewed attention to the racial and gendered violence manifest in the colonial and racial foundations of ongoing white settler colonialism and the anti-Black legacies of white supremacy in racial capitalism, socio-legal scholarship is in a unique interdisciplinary position to shed light on *how* and *in what particular ways* race and colonialism are manifest and sanctioned in and through socio-legal phenomena. How can socio-legal studies respond to police violence directed at Black, Indigenous, and other racialized people? How should socio-legal studies account for the structural violence experienced by Indigenous people and communities of colour? How can socio-legal studies address links between race, religion, and hate crimes? How can socio-legal studies address concerns about sovereignty, dispossession, and the logic of national security that criminalizes refugees? What role can socio-legal approaches play in addressing historical memory and the forms of injustice organized under Canadian settler-colonial legal orders?

In raising these questions, we also contend that these legacies have been addressed by scholars of race and settler colonialism who show that race is part of the defining constitution of state and nation.[5] In this collection, for example, we see how forms of racialization are alive in debates concerning Indigenous rights (Douglas), terrorism (Hameed and Monaghan), and gendered racial violence (Lockhart, Roots, and Tasker). Race is manifest through a range of modalities, schemes, articulations, and affective registers that effectively constitute and define norms, procedures, practices, logics, vocabularies, and discourses that configure state, nation, personhood, subjectivity, and resistance.[6] In the United States, these legacies have been described by Colin Dayan as "legal terror," which she elaborates as the ritualized making and remaking of legal conditions of civil death ("naturally alive but legally dead") through legal processes that define and redefine personhood (2005, 193). In this list of rituals, she includes citizens turned refugees through Hurricane Katrina in the United States, ghost detainees, and nooses found in trees and in university offices—to which, in the Canadian context, we add the murder of hundreds of Indigenous children buried in unmarked gravesites, the continued theft of Indigenous lands, the ongoing forms of anti-Black police violence, the profiling and racial hate crime violence directed at Muslim communities, structural and systemic racism, the racialization of poverty, the criminalization of race, the overincarceration of Indigenous and Black people, anti-immigrant policies and practices, the impunity for violence directed at Indigenous women and girls, the criminalization of refugees, and the use of solitary confinement in prison among the many processes of racism alive in our communities today. We suggest that these racial legal terrors shed light on historical and current material and symbolic rituals of violence and dispossession directed at Black, Indigenous, and other racialized people. Tracing racial forms of dispossession in settler colonialism and racial capitalism requires an analysis of the legacies of racial colonial terror and the capacity to repurpose racial governance. As Brenna Bhandar and Davina Bhandar suggest, dispossession "reflect(s) the uneven impact of several hundred years of capitalist accumulation, centralised through the agency of the possessive individual and its corollary, the subject (always-already) ontologically and politically dispossessed of the capacity to appropriate and own, to be self-determining" (2016, n.p.). Racial legal terrors and the enduring "cultures of dispossession" encompass discursive, affective, material, and symbolic practices that form the basis of "pedagogical instruction in a symbolic order that might be obscured by modern state forms and discourses" as well as projects of decolonization, resistance, and rupture (Rao 2011, 626). How might socio-legal researchers and educators respond to the convergence of these contemporary legal, political, economic, social, and cultural experiences and contestations?

When attempting a review of the field in the Canadian context, certain questions arise: What kind of work on race and colonialism is recognized as socio-legal? Is there a recognized canon of socio-legal studies on race and colonialism? Where and how are race and colonialism represented in socio-legal research? Is Indigenous studies recognized as socio-legal scholarship? How is Black studies included in the canon of socio-legal studies? What has the study of race and colonialism added to the field of socio-legal studies? What methodological approaches have been useful in advancing this field of study? These are theoretical and methodological questions and charged political questions. We do not offer a comprehensive response to these questions; however, we identify the work of several scholars inspired by critical race, post-colonial, Indigenous, Black, and cultural studies and anti-colonial approaches whose work is arguably empirically grounded in socio-legal studies. In this chapter, we highlight specific theoretical and methodological contributions in these works that treat race and colonialism not as a subfield of socio-legal scholarship but as the terrain animating socio-legal studies in Canada. The scholarship chosen does not provide an exhaustive historical or genealogical account of research in race and the law emerging from a Canadian context; rather, the aim and intent are to identify how select scholars empirically trace the relationships between law and racial power highlighting *race* as a key constituent of power that shapes legal discourse and practices and racial colonial white settler nation building. Through canvassing selected contributions that have engaged in this work, we notice two methodological trends that have connected the relationship between race, colonialism, and law in instructive ways: (1) *continuity*, a genealogical method that attends to the historical continuities of race and colonialism in socio-legal processes in Canada; and (2) *relationality*, an analytic that pays attention to the ways racial ideas and practices travel through and across temporalities and spatialities. We understand these two methodological interventions as interconnected insofar as they allow scholars to engage contemporary forms of racial violence through a historical and globally situated lens while paying close attention to the specificities of localized forms of legal terror. In this chapter, these analytics function as descriptions of how to conceptually link subjects, objects, and practices through law and reveal how we are all differently positioned in relation to ongoing settler colonialism and racial capitalism. We propose that a historical and structural account of race and colonialism in socio-legal scholarship requires an analysis of *continuity* and *relationality* to better account for the ways that *race and colonialism* constitute law and legal processes.

In order to explore some of the ways that race and colonialism are taken up in socio-legal scholarship, this chapter is divided into two sections. The first section explores what we are describing as the continuities (indeed, genealogies) of race and colonialism. This section attends to the genealogical, historical, and continuous forms of white settler colonialism and racial capitalism that structure socio-legal processes in Canada. In this section, the work of key scholars is identified for the theoretical and methodological contributions to addressing the continuous legacies of colonialism and racism as expressed and experienced in and through law. The second section explores the relational ways that race and colonialism circulate spatially and temporally and bind national subjects through processes of racialization. As discussed, a theoretical and methodological framework of relationality offers a corrective to comparative approaches to race and colonialism that at times mute the particularity of distinct locales through analogy or by treating racial and colonial formations as discrete phenomena. In each section, we identify *how* and in *what* particular ways an approach offers a focus on *continuity* and *relationality* as overlapping and conceptually descriptive accounts of how racial colonial processes assist in advancing an analysis of law and socio-legal studies scholarship in Canada. The scholars identified canvass the diverse issues of the criminalization and regulation of Indigenous identity and cultural practices, including violence against Indigenous women, the treatment of Black defendants in Ontario courts, the racialization of incarceration and criminalization, the racial and spatialized violence directed at Japanese Canadians during the 1940s, and the links between race, colonialism, and humanitarianism. In this chapter, our aim is to offer modest theoretical and methodological proposals to socio-legal scholars and researchers in view of a collective goal to make race and colonialism matter in our socio-legal research agendas and pedagogical approaches.

Continuities of Race and Colonialism

Socio-legal scholarship on race and colonialism can be described as offering approaches that address the continuities of racial and colonial formations in law. Such approaches can be characterized as genealogical accounts of the racial and colonial formations in settler colonialism. The word *genealogy* as it is employed in critical social theory owes much to Michel Foucault's use of the term in his effort to write "histories of the present" (1977, 39). Departing from positivist methods of inquiry, Foucault describes his approach to genealogy as one that attempts to "desubjugate historical knowledge, to set them free, or in other words to enable them to oppose and struggle against the coercion of a unitary, formal and scientific theoretical discourse" (10). Part of Foucault's approach to genealogy is to excavate subaltern knowledges (i.e., "historical contents that have been buried or masked in functional coherences of formal systemizations" [7]). As Foucault explains further, "If you like, we can give the name genealogy to this coupling together of scholarly erudition and local memories which allows us to constitute historical knowledge of struggles and to make use of that knowledge in contemporary tactics" (8). It is through this approach to the study of how things come to be that we are provided a method for accounting for a *history of the present.*

As David Garland describes, genealogy can be viewed as "a method of writing critical history: a way of using historical materials to bring about a 'revaluing of values' in the present day" (2014, 372). Rather than searching for a single point of "origins," Foucault (and Nietzsche) were more interested in tracing genealogy as "the erratic and discontinuous process whereby the past became the present: an aleatory path of descent and emergence that suggests the contingency of the present and the openness of the future" (Garland 2014, 373). Garland continues,

> Genealogical analysis traces how contemporary practices and institutions emerged out of specific struggles, conflicts, alliances, and exercises of power, many of which are nowadays forgotten. It thereby

enables the genealogist to suggest—not by means of normative argument but instead by presenting a series of troublesome associations and lineages—that institutions and practices we value and take for granted today are actually more problematic or more "dangerous" than they otherwise appear. (372)

In reviewing socio-legal scholarship on race and colonialism, it is apparent that a genealogical approach assists in identifying continuity alive in and through the historical and ongoing processes of racial governance in ongoing settler colonialism and white supremacy. Examining continuity allows us to trace (1) the violent, annihilative, and carceral consequences of white supremacy, racial capitalism, and settler colonialism; (2) the remaking of racial formations for new and renewed legal, political, and economic conditions; and (3) the ways in which racial governance can be viewed as a liberal mark of "progress." The work of Renisa Mawani, Pamela Palmater, Barrington Walker, Val Napoleon, and Sherene Razack individually and collectively illustrates the continuity of race and colonialism in socio-legal studies.

Identifying the continuity of race and colonialism as genealogical also suggests a temporal approach to considering racial colonial phenomena. The genealogical continuity of race and colonialism is temporal to the extent that historical phenomena can be viewed in relation to the present, and similarly present phenomena can be examined for traces of the past. In this regard, genealogical continuity can be said to also open up possibilities for the future. Considering law as genealogy requires attention to historicity and the temporal dimensions of law, race, and colonialism. As Renisa Mawani suggests, considering law *as* genealogy requires a focus on the temporal dimensions of law: "Law as temporality moves beyond history and historicity and invites an exploration into law's deployment of time as a means of capturing and obscuring, albeit not always successfully, the density of lived time" (2014, 93). In her research, Mawani demonstrates the genealogical and temporal orientation of law through an analysis of the way in which "free" British Indians in the early twentieth century established and advocated claims as settlers in South Africa in relation and opposition to "other racially inscribed and enumerated populations including Indian indentures, Asiatic migrants, and most notably, native Africans" (68). Emphasizing the temporal and continuous racial formations in South Africa and across the British Empire, Mawani argues that these "juridical-racial taxonomies were also *temporal divisions* that fomented legal subjectivities ascribed with unequal degrees of worth and value, disparate rights to land, and with distinct claims to imperial polity" (68). These temporalities of racial colonial rule reveal the continuous and shifting racial formations—the connections between state formation and subjectivity—that respond to particular political and economic conditions in settler-colonial contexts. The significance of genealogical understandings of law, race, and settler colonialism—as temporality attenuated to ongoing histories of the present—has been taken on by a number of Indigenous and non-Indigenous scholars in a multitude of ways.

Pamela Palmater's study of genocidal policies and practices aimed at the disappearance of Indigenous peoples on Turtle Island (North America) is a robust example of this work. Rather than reading legislative policies aimed at Indigenous extinction as remnants of a distant past, Palmater centres the continuity in scalping bounties targeting Indigenous peoples in Nova Scotia (2014, 32).[7] For example, alongside an examination of forced sterilization, Palmater examines the long-standing and intergenerational terror of residential schools to the legal regulation of Indigenous identity and band membership through the Indian Act. While these methods of colonial control vary in technique and scale, they are linked through the use of law and, in particular, the intent behind legislative efforts to erase Indigenous peoples in North America. For example, through her analysis of the Indian Act, we come to appreciate how a policy first introduced in 1876 with the intent to "amalgamate all pre-and post-confederation legislation with regards to Indians and bring their control under the full jurisdiction of the federal government" (Palmater 2014, 34) continues to define (via registration) who counts as Indigenous, which Indian bands are recognized, and how reserve land can be used. As argued by Palmater, this comprehensive act stretches into almost every aspect of Indigenous life and has had the effect of legally eliminating (by means of registration and regulation) "who is and is not an Indian" (34).

"Ghost people" (i.e., those referred to as "non-status Indians") are among those barred from legal recognition in a number of ways, including rights to land. Relying on case law to explain further (in particular, *Sharon McIvor and Jacob Grismer v. Canada* 2010), between 1876 and 1985, "the criteria for federal recognition as 'Indian' was largely based on a one-parent descent rule—so long as descent was from a male person of Indian blood" (Palmater 2014, 35).[8] The effect of 12(1)(b) of the Indian Act—which many scholars have addressed as a patriarchal, heterosexist, and racist statute[9]—was that Indigenous women who married non-Indigenous men lost their status, and by extension, their offspring also lost legal recognition. Tracing the juridical category of Indian status, Brenna Bhandar elaborates on how the very act of defining who counts as "Indian" (as calculated through blood) was a project inextricably linked to broader structures of racial capitalism and the capacity to determine who had rights to enjoy and hold land (Bhandar and Bhandar 2016, 3). Contributing to this discussion on the legislative regulation and juridical erasure of the category "Indian," Bhandar explains how racist, sexist, and patrilineal provisions outlined in the Indian Act provided the necessary legal grounds to further land dispossession. As Bhandar notes, "In the definition of 'Indian' we see the erasure from the juridical category of Indian of First Nations women as independent subjects; they are categorised either as the child or the wife of a man" (2016, 3). This example of demographic management was one of the many ways that Canada's settler government maximized control of land while minimizing both the existence of and their obligations to Indigenous peoples. Palmater's examination of the legislative changes in the Indian Act reflects the myriad ways that the Canadian government has made Indigenous peoples the target of what she names as "legislative extinction" (2014, 28). Through a genealogical examination of colonial legal orders, Palmater provides a historical and analytical lens to address the continuities between seemingly disparate and differently scaled sites of settler-colonial violence.

Another noteworthy contribution to genealogical approaches to the study of Indigenous claims to land and identity in Canada is Val Napoleon's article "Delgamuukw: A Legal Straightjacket for Oral Histories?" (2005). Examining the treatment of Gitxsan *adaawk* or oral history as legal evidence of Gitxsan land ownership, Napoleon shows how the denial of Indigenous knowledge systems and notions of Indigenous "inferiority" continue to be central to the securing of a settler state. By way of delineation, Napoleon recounts the *Delgamuukw* case and the decades-long legal battle launched by the Gitxsan and Wet'suwet'en hereditary chiefs before the British Columbia Supreme Court, the province's Court of Appeal, and finally the Supreme Court of Canada between the mid-1980s and the mid-1990s. The case turned on the admissibility of the *adaawk* (oral history), which formed the basis of the Gitxsan and Wet'suwet'en claim to their land. Among the Gitxsan people, the *wilp* (or "House") is the primary unit of social organization, and the *adaawk* functions as the "formal institution" that maintains the identity of each *wilp* (Napoleon 2005, 126). *Adaawk* were presented and shared between *wilps* and represented a formal narrative distinct from folklore and contained implications for the privileges, territories, and political relations of the Gitxsan people. The Gitxsan and Wet'suwet'en argued that the *adaawk* is "a living institution" and a valid and trustworthy historical record (153).

Napoleon argues that the *adaawk* was forced into a "straightjacket of standard form evidence" that made it fundamentally unacceptable and incommensurable with Western legal rules, ultimately resulting in Justice McEachern's refusal to consider it as official evidence at trial (2005, 125). As Napoleon explains,

> What becomes clear from the transcript is that the Court was not able to hear or accept the *adaawk* as presented—a legal and political institution rather than a simple cultural artefact or chronological history record. The forms of expression, symbolism, and inter-connections between the worlds of spirits, humans, and animals proved to be beyond the grasp of the Court. Consequently, McEachern C.J. characterized much of the *adaawk* as mythology, not history, and in the end accorded it no weight as evidence. (154)

Despite the place of the *adaawk* in Gitxsan life as a formal record of Gitxsan territorial claims, oral history was viewed as heresy, myth, or culture. The Gixksan *adaawk* needed to be in a fixed, unchanging, and singular form in order to be accepted as evidence. The trial transcripts reveal that at every point in the legal process, the court advanced a "distorted legal truth" about Indigenous oral histories, one in which the *adaawk* could never be considered a "legal and political institution" rather than simply a "cultural artifact or [a] chronological history record" (154).

Napoleon's article shows the continued work of settler colonialism through the invalidation of Indigenous knowledge. In this case, we see how the formal legal tests that determine the reliability of evidence function as colonial governance insofar as it delegitimizes Indigenous knowledge systems in Western fields of knowledge. The exclusion of the Gitxsan *adaawk* and the outcome of the *Delgamuukw* case sanction colonial strategies of governance to secure territory by dismissing Indigenous claims to and sovereignty over land and resources. Another way we can understand genealogical approaches to the study of race in Canadian courtrooms is by attending to the ways that colonial identity comes to be renewed and represented against racialized logics of Black criminality.

Barrington Walker's *Race on Trial: Black Defendants in Ontario's Criminal Courts* examines the treatment of Black defendants in Ontario's courts from 1858 to 1958. He provides a unique account of the ways in which death penalty cases are an important site for crafting a benevolent white settler identity. Walker examines how judges exercised "discretionary justice" in cases involving Black defendants (2010, 45) and shows how Black communities—caught between formal legal equality on the one hand and social, political, and legal discrimination on the other—were precariously positioned and, similar to Indigenous offenders, routinely subject to harsher punishments than their white counterparts. In so doing, he demonstrates how racial stereotypes and imagery became tools for defense lawyers and government officials to secure convictions and to selectively advocate against harsher sentences.[10]

In a number of death penalty cases in Ontario during the late nineteenth and the early twentieth centuries, notions of Black docility or unintelligence were used strategically by lawyers to support claims that defendants should be subject to more lenient punishments. Through Walker's research, we see how debates about criminal sentencing were tied to Canadian nation building and the ways in which efforts to preserve a particular notion of Canadian identity are maintained through law. Rather than countering or displacing racism, discrimination, and white supremacy, rare instances of judicial leniency toward Black offenders reveal links between Canadian benevolence and the role of law in nation building. The significance of Walker's work is that it highlights the paradoxical nature of racial justice and law in Canada and the colonial logics that come to reproduce moral ideas of benevolence in representational systems of law.

Sherene Razack's groundbreaking essay *Gendered Racial Violence and Spatialized Justice: The Murder of Pamela George* provides a significant genealogical intervention that shows the entanglements between white supremacy, misogyny, and settler-colonial violence.[11] In Razack's sobering account of the murder of Pamela George, she traces the legal narratives that animate a story about George, a Saulteaux woman who participated in sex work in the economically depressed area of the Stroll in Regina, Saskatchewan. The legal narratives that shaped representations of her in the courtroom work to disavow histories of dislocation, settler violence, economic disadvantage, and spatial containment. Razack shows how legal narratives produced about George and the white men that murdered her are robust signposts of settler colonialism, both at the level of encounter and in subsequent legal representation. By "unmapping" the racial histories of the men and George, their victim, Razack foregrounds the historical and contemporary participation of white settlers in the dispossession of Indigenous lands and in physical and sexual violence toward Indigenous peoples and shows precisely how the law works to normalize, naturalize, and legitimate these conditions. Razack illustrates a continuity of colonial strategies of spatial containment. Noting how the Indigenous confinement on reserves facilitated the "near absolute geographical separation of the colonizer and the colonized" (Razack 2002, 131), she further shows how sexual violence toward Indigenous women, economic marginalization, and spatial containment were integral to strategies of colonial domination that prefigured the encounter between George and her murderers. The spatial containment of Indigenous people on reserves, such as the Sakimay reserve where George was born, and the geographical separation of reserves from economically vibrant urban centres created "in-migration" in which Indigenous people would travel from reserves into predominantly white cities for employment. These movements, as Razack shows, are often characterized by violent encounters and sexualized violence toward Indigenous women. This violence becomes a form of boundary-making that secures the status of the colonizer, confirms the status of the colonized, and marks marginal spaces such as the Stroll, in which violence is normalized and naturalized, from the respectable white spaces of the suburbs and university campuses. At trial, colonialism, racial/spatial violence, and gendered racial violence were disqualified as factors contributing to George's death. Instead, George's status as a sex worker, the Stroll's existence as a space of perceived danger and degeneracy, and drunken male violence were believed to be the causes of the crime (Razack 2002).

Here we see how particular colonial histories materialize in contemporary sexualized violence toward George and other Indigenous women in spaces deemed degenerate, which naturalize such violence, and state indifference (via the exoneration of white male violence) to murdered Indigenous women. According to Razack, "uncovering" the ways in which "justice" was delivered to George's murderers "helps us to see how race shapes the law by informing notions of what is just and who is entitled to justice. It enables us to see how whiteness is protected and reproduced through such ideas as a contact between autonomous individuals standing outside of history" (156). Razack's methodological intervention is instructive for another reason: it helps us see what happens to racial and colonial violence at the levels of trial, national inquiry, and commission. She shows how racism and ongoing colonialism are "made to disappear" in legal proceedings or are reconfigured in order to exonerate those who maintain this work. Structural violence is recast as isolated incidents or the unfortunate outcome of a benevolent state with good intentions.

An analytic of *continuity* serves as an important corrective to frameworks that analyze colonial and racial processes as legacies of a distant past rather than as ongoing, permanent, and renewed relations. As the scholarship reviewed here demonstrates, identifying empirical studies that reveal the continuities of race and colonialism shows how racism is made durable in law; how law becomes a tool of violence, annihilation, and dispossession; and how racial governance is constitutive to the settler-colonial state.

Relationality and Race and Colonialism

Socio-legal scholars of race and colonialism have used the method of "relationality" to examine ongoing structures of colonialism. Relationality or what Walter Mignolo identifies as "relational ontology" is distinct from "comparativist" approaches to the study of orderings of race and racial difference. Explaining this idea further, Keith Feldman describes relationality as a methodological intervention that helps to "account descriptively and analytically for connections, linkages, and articulations across the institutionalization of difference in disciplines and the nation-state cartographies they reference" (2016, 110). Although differently positioned, scholars invested in this methodological orientation to the study of law reveal how colonial and racial relations are maintained in seemingly different sites of racial violence. For instance, an analytic of relationality provides a clearer sense for thinking through the ways that seemingly disparate sites of racial violence and abandonment—such as a suicide crisis in the Northern Ontario Indigenous community of Attawapiskat and Canadian discourse surrounding the arrival of Syrian refugees—are connected (Murdocca 2020).

Second, relationality signals to the ways that broader structures and logics of race and white supremacy travel within and across racial formations and colonial frontiers. In this way, a relational framework allows us to link these systems of control and domination in order to explain how the specificities of these formations are at times constitutively interactive and entangled. These passages of race often travel across colonial temporalities and spatialities in horizontal and multidirectional ways.

While this analytical approach might seem similar to a lens of comparative analysis, David Theo Goldberg has insisted that relationality widens our analysis in ways that a strictly comparativist account prohibits. As Goldberg notes, comparisons pivot from an outward reference that assumes and maintains a discrete separation from the object of analysis in question, including the idea of local and national boundaries (2009). Drawing on the work of Bernard Cohn (1996) and Ann Laura Stoler (2002, 2006), Goldberg (2009) invokes relationality to explain what he refers to as the *globalization of the racial*. For example, Goldberg explains that racial ideas and racial thinking were exercised through experimentation in the colonies as "laboratories for metropolitan class rule," which later became "rehearsals in the intimacies and moral class life" (1275), and by extension and design, the ordering structures of race relations within the metropole. While racist institutional arrangements and control were "made local to apply to lived conditions of the everyday" in the colonies, Goldberg's approach to relationality centres the heterogeneous ways that the project of race circulates between time and space. In so doing, he insists that an analytical framework of "relationality" offers a way of seeing how "state formations or histories, logics of oppression and exploitation are linked" and that these linkages "stress the (re-) production of relational ties and their mutually effecting and reinforcing impacts" (1275–76). Thus what we can borrow from Goldberg through his invocation of relationality is a method for seeing how race travels in multidirectional ways and finds resonance in locally specific but historically tied imperial projects.

Third, relationality opens up analytical possibilities to examine the contingency of racial formations and processes (i.e., how racial groups are, at different points in history, pitted against one another to maintain the work of settler-colonial governance) through various juridical orderings. Distinct from frameworks that centre a comparativist approach to the study of race, relationality allows us to think about how we are differently implicated and located in settler-formations like Canada and complicit—albeit in different ways—in maintaining white supremacy. Rather than studying racialization as a discrete or individualized sets of practices, this analytic opens up particular ways to read the relational structures that animate and renew projects of race and racism through law and in settler-colonial nation building.[12] To further illustrate how this analytic has been adopted by scholars of race and colonialism in a Canadian legal context, we briefly canvass some key contributions to the field of socio-legal studies, including the work of Mona Oikawa (2010), Renisa Mawani and David Sealy (2011), and Carmela Murdocca (2020).

In "Cartographies of Violence: Women, Memory, and the Subject(s) of the 'Internment,'" Mona Oikawa (2010) adopts a relational lens to examine the carceral policies and spatialities of internment used to incarcerate Japanese Canadians in the making of white settler-colonial nationhood. As Oikawa historicizes, the racial violence inflicted upon twenty-two thousand Japanese Canadians during the 1940s took place in a number of ways, such as imprisonment, dispossession, detention, low-waged labour, and displacement (73). Examining the long-term effects on Japanese Canadians subjected to the War Measures Act, internment camps, work camps, and prisoner of war camps in the British Columbia interior, the sugar beet farms, and more insidious sites of carceral violence such as "self-support" sites (73), Oikawa addresses what these forms of carceral violence enabled in the reproduction of racial social orders and the making of Canada as a white nation (74). Drawing from Japanese Canadian women's testimonies—as sites of spatial analysis—across different generations (those that were expelled and their daughters), she uncovers the heterogeneous experiences of violence made possible through spatial arrangements of violence. Moreover, she demonstrates how these testimonial accounts of spatialized violence structure ongoing relationships to memory and subjectivity in Canada.

Oikawa's analysis draws from a relational lens in several ways. First, she shows how these spatialities of incarceration and displacement were constructed across both material and discursive lines that worked to define national subjects as being against one another and anchored in a temporality of colonial modernity (Oikawa 2010, 82). The modernizing discourses imbued in the confinement of Japanese Canadians (i.e., that the separation of Japanese Canadians from their ties to community would accomplish the civilizing goal of assimilation) was secured through a racialized logic of primitiveness. It was not just that Japanese Canadians and, in particular, Japanese Canadian masculinity was racialized through orientalist and emasculating discourses but that these discourses also worked to form representations of white subjecthood: "Racializing, gendering and classing processes were spatialized through these carceral sites. Japanese-Canadian masculinities were produced in relation to white masculinities. Japanese-Canadian women were constructed in relation to white women. Japanese-Canadian men and women were constructed in relation to each other" (80).

This interlocking analysis points to the ways that systems of domination— "male domination, white supremacy, economic domination, heteronormativity, and ableism"—structured the very conditions upon which whiteness and Japanese Canadian bodies came to be relationally constituted and represented juridically (Oikawa 2010, 80). More importantly, this relational analysis insists that these shifting signifiers of domination were constituted across a dispersed and heterogeneous set of spatial arrangements. As Oikawa concludes, "The ability of these women to locate their losses spatially and relationally instructs us to think further about our implications in the enforced scattering of Japanese Canadians and in the 'scattered hegemonies' of nation-building and citizen constitution" (98). Another way we might think about an analytic of relationality and its contribution to the study of race and law is by attending to how it challenges causal understandings of race and criminality.

In Renisa Mawani and David Sealy's critique of dominant criminological approaches to the race-crime link, they argue that such studies often reduce racial profiling and the administration of justice to racial bias, prejudice, and stereotyping that results in the "arrest, prosecution and incarceration of racial minorities" (2011, 162). The problem with the "race-crime" link is that it often assumes a deterministic relationship between race and crime; crimes related to issues such as "drugs" or "gang violence" are marked as racial (and are sometimes theorized in relation to racist nation-building policies), and because drug-related crimes are marked as racial (i.e., street level drugs), this inevitably leads to the criminalization of people of colour (e.g., racial profiling, stop and frisk policies, mass incarceration). At best, these criminological approaches make broader connections between, for instance, the overincarceration of Indigenous people, people of African ancestry, and South Asians in Canada (through a political economy of capitalism and slavery), thereby showing how the overincarceration of racialized peoples is a phenomenon rooted in more than simply racial prejudice. However, the problem with these approaches, as Mawani and Sealy point out, is that they assume that racial profiling can be resolved by "better criminological knowledges of discretionary processes" and "antiracist criminal justice policy initiatives," thereby ignoring the underlying sensibilities around race and criminality as produced through *colonial knowledge* (162). Pointing to the ways that criminological approaches actually "ignore the ways in which black criminality is assumed from the start" (164), they argue that we need to be more attentive to the ways that racialized processes of criminal justice practice are already imbued in *racialized knowledge* formed through assumptions about Black criminality (ibid.).[13]

One of the reasons that might account for why the "race-crime link" ignores the salience of colonial (racial) knowledge is because it centres nineteenth century conceptions of race and racism (rooted in scientific racism and biopolitics). In so doing, this historical framing disavows the forms of racialization produced out of carceral institutions such as racialized slave labour. In an attempt to reinterpret and relocate the "race-crime link" in a broader historical context of carcerality in socio-legal studies, we might turn to imaginings and practices of race and racialization that emerged through colonial governance in the fifteenth century onward and the rise of necropolitical experimentation institutionalized through plantation slavery (Mbembe 2003, 21). By examining the ways that ideas about Black criminality emerge through historical processes that license social and material death under colonial modernity, we are challenged to think about how the "race-crime link" emerges in relation to ideas about race and incarceration prior to the emergence of the penal system, therefore inviting a differently positioned epistemic reading of the relationship between race and crime.

In Carmela Murdocca's article "'Let's Help Our Own': Humanitarian Compassion as Racial Governance in Settler Colonialism" (2020), she invokes a method of relationality to account for two seemingly unrelated discourses of racial violence: the arrival of recently settled Syrian refugees into Canada and the suicide crisis in the Indigenous community of Attawapiskat, Ontario. In bringing these two crises into a common analytic framework that centres humanitarianism under white settler colonialism, Murdocca's work shows how public and media discourse surrounding these two events signals the racial intricacies within "legal obligations that work to define human and racial difference" (20).

Examining Canadian media representations of the arrival of Syrian refugees and the ongoing conditions of violence within the Attawapiskat community, Murdocca's work asks, "What forms of racial violence evoke compassion and the language of humanitarianism?" and equally important, "Who gets to live and die in settler colonialism?" This sample of media accounts attending to Syrian refugees and the Attawapiskat community reveals the disparate reactions present in Canadian news media. Pivoting between antirefugee rhetoric and humanitarian pleas to support Indigenous struggles within Canada, we see a common but complex racial grammar that reveals a telling national story. While editorials and letters to the editor of one of Canada's leading newspapers raised the question of what it means for the Canadian state to give generously to Syrian refugees while ignoring the suicide crisis in the Attawapiskat community, this narrative circulates within a discourse of both antirefugee rhetoric and depoliticized humanitarian logic. A closer examination of this entanglement compels us to ask, as Murdocca does, "How is the racial project of the modern liberal state in Canada made possible by positioning different racial groups dialectically against one another in the formation of new regimes of racial governance" (2020, 1279)? Explaining further, she contends that "to track the conceptual mobility of compassionate humanitarianism in Canada is to address how liberal humanitarianism is made possible through ongoing racial and structural violence. Attending to how, *and in what particular ways*, histories and ongoing experiences of racial violence emerge coterminous with invocations of compassionate humanitarianism reveals how appeals to liberal conceptions of justice necessitate and require racial violence" (1283).

In helping us see the *globalization of the racial* (Goldberg 2009), Murdocca's work signals one of the ways that race circulates in a moral economy of human rights discourse. Rather than comparing the treatment of Indigenous communities in Canada to newly arrived Syrian refugees, her analysis instead asks us to think about the ontological parameters of difference that bring the "over there" and "over here" into relation.

Through canvassing some of the literature that has contributed to sociolegal scholarship emerging from Canada, we have attempted to illustrate how such literature has enriched our understanding of the mobilization of race and law under histories and ongoing structures of settler-colonial nation building. This body of scholarship and its methodological orientations are indebted to post-colonial, feminist, and post-structural scholarship that have inspired an epistemic landscape for tracing "histories of the present." In making us curious about the symbolic and material ways that racial subjects are formed, reconstituted, and contested, and the ongoing legal structures that maintain structures of white supremacy, we are challenged to recalibrate understandings of law that often emerge from liberal and neoliberal logics and sensibilities.

Conclusion

As researchers and educators, we are in a position to advance, support, and be the gatekeepers of particular kinds of knowledge production in socio-legal studies. Our role occasions and invites consideration of the historical and structural dimensions of race and colonialism in order to address and reflect on life, death, and possibilities for justice for Black, Indigenous, and other racialized people. This task also requires that we attend to the legal structures and systems of white supremacy that organize race relations and simultaneously challenge forms of accountability and reparative justice.

We are writing in a time when white supremacy and racial terror are alive—in both the spectacular and the quotidian senses. In fact, we continue to witness how incidents and expressions of racial violence—as sanctioned by legal governance—work to obscure the very boundaries between the spectacular and what takes place in the ordinary. Whether we turn to white nationalist torch-lit rallies in Canada or the United States or the ongoing everyday police harassment and violence against Black, Indigenous, and other racialized people in Canada, these expressions of racial violence are sanctioned and made possible through law. The contributions canvassed reveal how the genealogies of race and colonialism structure the epistemological and ontological foundations of law. These contributions permit and compel an analysis of the complex genealogies of race and colonialism and the ways in which differently positioned racial groups are subject to projects of racial governance under settler colonialism. We propose that a focus on both the continuity and relationality of race and colonialism reveal that race and colonialism should not be treated as a subfield of socio-legal studies; rather, attending to processes of race and colonialism indicates complex and intersecting relations between colonial racial violence, dispossession, sovereignty, criminality, migration, and subjectivity that illuminates the colonial and racial "force of law" (Derrida 1992).

Through exploring the *continuity of race and colonialism*, we maintain that socio-legal research on race and colonialism must be attentive to the continuities of racial legal governance—the continuous foundational logics, legitimating discourses, forms of regulation, techniques of control, criminalization, dispossession, containment, securitization, relocation, murder, violence, destruction, and theft. Key to attending to the continuities of race and colonialism is also examining how seemingly progressive reform may reproduce the very logics of colonial racial rule.[14] Through identifying the *relationality of race and colonialism,* we have explained how such an approach may be used to address how racial ideas and practices travel across time and through space in order to reveal how disparate sites of racial violence and control are linked and interconnected. Further, through viewing the legacies of race and colonialism as relational, we are able to address the constitutive ways that racialization circulates to bind subjects and practices together across different temporalities and spatialities.

Notes

1 This call is echoed by Laura E. Gomez in her presidential address to the American Law and Society Association. See Gomez (2012).
2 Harry Arthurs and Annie Bunting (2014) note that Canadian law and society research emerged "as in other jurisdictions . . . in the 1960s as a challenge to narrow vocational understanding of law" (488).
3 The recent call by activists from Black Lives Matter Toronto, for example, to keep statistics based on race and policing (supported by the work of socio-legal researchers) has assisted, in part, in fostering a public conversation about policing, racial profiling, and the importance of social movements in the context of white supremacy. This convergence also reveals the ongoing importance of linking socio-legal research on race to the work of social movements, law, and policy advocates.
4 Heather Love provides a useful genealogy of Geertz's notion of thick description (see Love 2013, 401–34).
5 Some of the works that are not discussed directly in this chapter but that serve as analytical inspirations for scholarly contributions to the study of race and colonial nation building include Fanon, Frantz. 1963. *Wretched of the Earth.* New York: Grove; McClintock, Anne, Aamir Mufti, and Ella Shohat. 1997. *Dangerous Liaisons: Gender, Nation, and Postcolonial Perspectives.* Minneapolis: University of Minnesota Press; Said, Edward. 1993. *Culture and Imperialism.* London: Vintage; Hartman, Saidiya 1997. *Scenes of Subjection: Terror, Slavery, and Self-Making in Nineteenth-Century America.* New York: Oxford University Press; Razack, Sherene 2007. "Stealing the Pain of Others: Reflections on Canadian Humanitarian Responses." *Review of Education, Pedagogy, and Cultural Studies* 29 (4):375–94; Razack, Sherene 2008. *Casting Out: The Eviction of Muslims from Law and Politics.* Toronto: University of Toronto Press; Razack, Sherene 2015. *Dying from Improvement: Inquests and Inquiries into Indigenous Deaths in Custody.* Toronto: University of Toronto Press; Yuval-Davis, Nira 1997. *Gender and Nation.* London: Sage; Backhouse, Constance 1999. *Colour-Coded: A Legal History of Racism in Canada, 1900–1950.* Toronto: University of Toronto Press; Lawrence, Bonita 2003. "Gender, Race, and the Regulation of Native Identity in Canada and the United States: An

Overview." *Hypatia* 18 (2): 3–31; Mackey, Eva 2002. *The House of Difference: Cultural Politics and National Identity in Canada*. Toronto: University of Toronto.

6 For example, see Comack (2013), Henry and Tator (2006), Razack (1998), and Tanovich (2006).

7 Palmater notes that Governor Cornwallis of Nova Scotia offered financial rewards as incentives to kill Mi'kmaw adults and children. The effect of this order reduced the Mi'kmaw population by up to 80 percent (2014, 32).

8 Explaining further, Palmater identifies the one exception to this rule (enacted in 1951) as the "double mother clause," which stipulated that "male Indians whose mother and paternal grandmother were only Indians by virtue of having married an Indian, could lose their status at age twenty-one" (2014, 35).

9 See Lawrence (2004) and Monture-Angus (1999).

10 An example that Walker notes is the case of Frank Smith. Although Smith was convicted of the murder of James Conyers in what was described as a "drunken brawl" and was originally sentenced to death, the jury immediately recommended mercy. Concerns that the sentence was inconsistent with the ideals of British justice and a belief that the sentence was not fit for a "'poor unfortunate' . . . 'child of nature'" helped advance the argument (Walker 2010, 49).

11 At the time of writing, the top two articles cited in the *Canadian Journal of Law & Society* are Razack, Sherene 2000. "Gendered Racial Violence and Spatialized Justice: The Murder of Pamela George"; and Razack, Sherene 1999. "Making Canada White: Law and the Policies of Bodies of Colour in the 1990s."

12 Using the example of comparative analyses between apartheid regimes, in particular that of South Africa and Israel, Goldberg's analysis shows the limits of its reach in orienting our understanding of how racial processes map onto others in ways that are mutually reinforcing (2009, 1279). For example, although comparativist accounts between Israel and South Africa are made to uncover how Israel's treatment of Palestinians was analogous to the treatment of South Africa's Black population—with the political aim of introducing economic sanctions and cultural boycotts on Israel—there are important differences that become obscured in the comparative model. As Goldberg notes, in not accounting for the differences between formalized *segregation* (as illustrative of South African apartheid) and absolute *separation* as organized under Israeli apartheid, we ignore the differences between governing structures, thereby undermining anti-apartheid critique and organizing.

13 It is also worth noting the ways that moral regulation on drugs informed the racialization of East Asian masculinity and ideas about white femininity. As Constance Backhouse examines in her study of white women's labour laws, which prohibited "Japanese, Chinese or other Oriental persons" from employing white women from 1912 and 1969 in Saskatchewan, ideas about white femininity and racialized masculinity were operationalized through a moral panic on opium during the early twentieth century. Asian men were routinely described as being cowardly and untrustworthy and having the capacity to

lure white women "into the underworld to suffer a fate worse than death" (Backhouse 1999, 139). The emergence of these labour laws coincided with immigration policies that sought to restrict Chinese immigration to Canada and racialized drug fears that circulated around Asian men. It was precisely these fears that illicit drugs would make white women susceptible to sexual slavery that helped galvanize white support for these laws and support for organizations such as the Regina's Women's Labour League. See Backhouse (1999).

14 See Murdocca (2013).

References

Arthurs, Harry, and Annie Bunting. 2014. "Socio-legal Scholarship in Canada: A Review of the Field." *Journal of Law and Society* 41 (4): 487–99.

Backhouse, Constance. 1999. *Colour-Coded: A Legal History of Racism in Canada, 1900–1950*. Toronto: University of Toronto Press.

Cohn, Bernard. 1996. *Colonialism and Its Forms of Knowledge: The British in India*. Princeton, NJ: Princeton University Press.

Bhandar, Brenna, and Davina Bhandar. 2016. "Cultures of Dispossession: Critical Reflections on Rights, Status and Identities." *Darkmatter Journal: In the Ruins of Imperial Culture* 14. https://eprints.soas.ac.uk/22447/1/Cultures %20of%20Dispossession_%20Rights,%20Status%20and%20Identities%20_%20 darkmatter%20Journal.pdf.

Comack, Elizabeth, Lawrence Deane, Larry Morrisette, and Jim Silver. 2013. *Indians Wear Red: Colonialism, Resistance, and Aboriginal Street Gangs*. Halifax: Fernwood.

Dayan, Colin. 2005. "Legal Terrors." *Representations* 92 (1): 42–80.

Derrida, Jacques. 1992. "Force of Law: The 'Mystical Foundation of Authority.'" In *Deconstruction and the Possibility of Justice*, edited by Benjamin N. Cardozo, 3–67. New York: Routledge.

Feldman, P. Keith. 2016. "On Relationality, on Blackness: A Listening Post." *Comparative Literature* 68 (2): 107–15.

Foucault, Michel. 1977. *Discipline and Punish: The Birth of the Prison*. Translated by Alan Sheridan. New York: Vintage.

Garland, David. 2014. "What Is a 'History of the Present'? On Foucault's Genealogies and Their Critical Preconditions." *Punishment and Society* 16 (4): 365–84.

Geertz, Clifford. 1973. "Thick Description: Towards an Interpretive Theory of Culture." In *The Interpretation of Cultures*, 310–23. New York: Basic.

Goldberg, David T. 2009. "Racial Comparisons, Relational Racisms: Some Thoughts on Method." *Ethnic and Racial Studies* 33 (7): 1271–82.

Gomez, Laura E. 2012. "Looking for Race in All the Wrong Places." *Law & Society Review* 46 (2): 221–45.

Henry, Frances, and Carol Tator. 2006. *Racial Profiling in Canada: Challenging the Myth of 'A Few Bad Apples.'* Toronto: University of Toronto Press.

Lawrence, Bonita. 2004. *"Real" Indians and Others: Mixed-Blood Urban Native Peoples and Indigenous Nationhood.* London: University of Nebraska Press.

Love, Heather. 2013. "Close Reading and Thick Description." *Public Culture* 25 (3): 401–34.

Mawani, Renisa. 2014. "Law as Temporality: Colonial Politics and Indian Settlers." *UC Irvine Law Review* 4 (65): 65–96.

Mawani, Renisa, and David Sealy. 2011. "On Postcolonialism and Criminology." In *Criminology: Critical Canadian Perspectives*, edited by Kristen Kramar, 159–72. Toronto: Pearson Canada.

Mbembe, Achille. 2003. "Necropolitics." *Public Culture* 15:11–40.

Monture-Angus, Patricia. 1999. *Journeying Forward: Dreaming First Nations' Independence* Halifax: Fernwood.

Murdocca, Carmela. 2013. *To Right Historical Wrongs: Race, Gender and Sentencing in Canada.* Vancouver: University of British Columbia Press.

———. 2020. "'Let's Help Our Own': Humanitarian Compassion as Racial Governance in Settler Colonialism." *Oñati Socio-legal Series* 10 (6): 1270–88.

Napoleon, Val. 2005. "Delgamuukw: A Legal Straightjacket for Oral Histories?" *Canadian Journal of Law & Society* 20 (2): 123–55.

Oikawa, Mona. 2010. "Cartographies of Violence: Women, Memory, and the Subject(s) of the 'Internment.'" In *Race, Space and the Law: Unmapping a White Settler Society*, edited by Sherene H. Razack, 71–98. Toronto: Between the Lines.

Palmater, Pamela. 2014. "Genocide, Indian Policy, and Legislated Elimination of Indians in Canada." *Aboriginal Policy Studies* 3 (3): 27–54.

Rao, Anupama. 2011. "Violence and Humanity: Or, Vulnerability as Political Subjectivity." *Social Research* 78 (2): 607–32.

Razack, Sherene. 2002. "Gendered Racial Violence and Spatialized Justice: The Murder of Pamela George." In *Race, Space and the Law: Unmapping a White Settler Society*, edited by Sherene H. Razack, 121–56. Toronto: Between the Lines.

Razack, Sherene. 1998. *Looking White People in the Eye: Gender, Race, and Culture in Courtrooms and Classrooms.* Toronto: University of Toronto Press.

Stoler, Ann. 2002. *Carnal Knowledge and Imperial Power: Race and the Intimate in Colonial Rule.* Berkeley: University of California Press.

———. 2006. *Haunted by Empire: Geographies of Empire in North American History.* Durham, NC: Duke University Press.

Tanovich, M. David. 2006. *The Colour of Justice: Policing Race in Canada.* Toronto: Irwin Law.

Walker, Barrington. 2010. *Race on Trial: Black Defendants in Ontario's Criminal Courts, 1858–1958.* Toronto: University of Toronto Press.

2 Jurisfiction and Other Settler-Colonial Legal Imaginaries

Stacy Douglas

In 2012, Conservative prime minister Stephen Harper introduced and passed bills C-38 and C-45, two omnibus bills that made significant changes to environmental protections in Canada. This is remembered as the catalyst for the Idle No More movement, which saw thousands of Indigenous people and their allies take to the streets to draw attention to the contemporary colonial landscape of Canadian law and politics. In response, the Mikisew Cree First Nation in northeastern Alberta brought an application for judicial review against the Crown, arguing that the federal government had a duty to consult before introducing the legislation. Since 2014, the Mikisew have been embroiled in a legal campaign that has been both victorious (in the 2014 Federal Court case) and defeated (in the 2016 Federal Court of Appeal as well as the 2018 Supreme Court cases). The following chapter charts the decisions of these three courts to reveal the fickle and fictive accounts of settler-colonial sovereignty that they contain.

The most recent ruling from the Supreme Court holds that the Mikisew were not entitled to the duty to consult because ministers, when developing policy, act as parliamentarians, not as the Crown; only the executive is subject to the duty to consult. Below, I explore this reasoning to show that the court's insistence on the precise location of the Crown is performative at best. An analysis of the majority decision as well as the disagreement regarding the duty to consult from Justices Abella and Martin demonstrates that there is much more uncertainty at issue than the court concedes. On legal grounds alone, the tension between Canada's traditions of parliamentary and constitutional sovereignty combined with a commitment to truth and reconciliation makes this case far from closed. Moreover, the presumed clarity with which the Supreme Court speaks of the absolute distinction between parliament and executive is part and parcel of a long-standing narrative of the imagined truth of colonial sovereignty. The story goes something like this: Positive law is rational and absolute. Therefore, a simple objective analysis of existing law will reveal the correct legal decision. Nowhere in this conceptualization is any iteration of the silences, assumptions, or aporias that make up the mythology of modern law. As such, this supposedly rational and well-reasoned occidental law is always imagined as the better to its oriental, customary, and savage other (Fitzpatrick 1992). In this way, supposedly objective Western legal reasoning is always contingent on an imagined spectre; it is this supposedly irrational, subjective law that gives Western law its literal *raison d'état*. Revealing this imbrication with its supposedly savage other illustrates Western law's failed project of absolute sovereignty; and yet, its autobiography, spelled out in case law established by *Mikisew* (2018), continues to paint itself as the sole harbinger of objective truth, rationality, and authority. My aim is to render legible the falsity of this assertion and the effort that is put into mobilizing it. In short, I want to showcase the myth of settler-colonial legal superiority.

Of course, such a revelation is not new to many. Those communities on the receiving end of such mythology know full well the extent of settler-colonial legal mysticism. And yet, there is a formidable public that remains captured by the enchantment of legal positivism, refusing to see—or perhaps simply not subject to—the logical leaps employed by the occidental law that orients the nation-state. And so this chapter, at least in part, speaks to a public that believes in the superiority of the presumed secular and rational settler-colonial legal infrastructure. My goal is to draw attention to the logic that holds this imaginative infrastructure in place, what Peter Fitzpatrick, drawing on Edward Said, has called a project of "internal decolonization" through an exoticization of the domestic (1992, 14). What can a focus on "imagination" do to upset the legacy of colonialism and white supremacy that grips the Canadian national landscape (and beyond)? This last sentence may sound odd to some. How can an imagination grip a landscape? But I think the phrasing gets at the problem directly. The way in which law is narrativized impacts the power of settler-colonial sovereignty. A nation's imagination of strong sovereignty fuels legal claims to land and ownership. Stories matter. Following in the footsteps of anti-colonial scholars from a range of colonial and settler-colonial contexts, I focus on mythical stories of law's authority as a small contribution to thinking through the project of material decolonization.

But this collection not only focuses on the imaginations of courts and legal practitioners; it also takes up socio-legal scholars' research questions, methods, and analyses. My other aim in this regard is to show that some older texts are too quickly forgotten and some jurisdictions are too lionized as unique in current academic, socio-legal trends; in short, it is important to see how colonial logics are confined not only to the Canadian or settler-colonial contexts. Big and broad thinking about colonial law may—and I argue does—inspire new and important insights in contemporary Canada. As such, my approach herein is to use some aging anti-colonial legal theory with new case law to draw attention to the ways in which many of the same problems can and do persist across decades and legal orders.[1] Moreover, contemporary case law analysis offers a fruitful place from which to destabilize the grasp that the myth of law's absolute rationality has on the settler-colonial imagination. What is the end game to such destabilization? Perhaps it is to suggest that non-Western law should not be dismissed as irrational or unconcerned with process; it is to make room for other law(s) both within the confines of the existing settler-colonial legal framework and also outside of it. Ultimately, I argue that the Mikisew's claim for prelegislative consultation can easily be granted and that it should be, even if such a victory does not represent the horizon of possibility for decolonization.

There is another paper to be written on the fact that the Federal Court's 2015 decision misspells Mikisew as *Misikew*. The argument of this fictive article may be that the misspelling is illustrative of the enormous contempt that the settler legal system has for Indigenous communities or the great disparity of language and worldviews between the two. Or perhaps it is an argument about the gravity of seemingly small mistakes, even when committed by a data processor. In either case, I think the error speaks to the importance of confronting settler socio-legal imaginaries and their seemingly (to settlers) subtle violence. Herein I include the misspelled name in all citations from the Federal Court decision to let that mistake resound.

Background

In 2014, the Federal Court found that the Mikisew's claim was valid; the changes to the Fisheries Act, the Species at Risk Act, the Navigable Waters

Protection Act, and the Canadian Environmental Assessment Act provided "a sufficient potential risk to the fishing and trapping rights [. . .] so as to trigger the duty to consult" (*Courtoreille* 2014, para. 93). Importantly, the Supreme Court of Canada (SCC) found in *Haida Nation v. British Columbia* that actual harm need not be done in order to trigger the duty to consult but that the "potential existence" of harm was sufficient (2004, para. 35), and in 2014, Justice Hughes of the Federal Court found this to be the case for the Mikisew. Justice Hughes concluded mildly that "notice should have been given to the Misikew [*sic*] in respect of those provisions that reasonably might have been expected to possibly impact upon their 'usual vocations' together with an opportunity to make submissions" (*Courtoreille* 2014, para. 103) and that the relief given to the Mikisew should be declaratory. Hughes noted that the court must respect the separation of powers and also that anything more than a declaration at this point (i.e., an injunction) would present too many logistical and legal problems in respecting jurisdiction between the courts and parliament but that "a declaration to the effect that the Crown ought to have given the Misikew [*sic*] notice when each of the Bills were introduced into Parliament together with a reasonable opportunity to make submissions may have an effect on the future respecting continuing obligations to the Misikew [*sic*] under Treaty No. 8" (para. 109).

Two years later in *Canada (Governor General in Council) v. Mikisew Çree First Nation* (2016), the Federal Court of Appeal (FCA) found that Justice Hughes improperly conducted a judicial review of legislative action contrary to the Federal Courts Act (1985) and that, by subjecting legislation to judicial review, he failed to respect the doctrine of separation of powers and the principle of parliamentary privilege. While the Mikisew argued that ministers, when proposing legislation, acted as members of the executive, the FCA found that ministers, when making legislation, acted as parliamentarians and so were not subject to judicial review. Further, Justice Yves Montigny, writing for the court, claimed that Justice Hughes was not respectful enough of the boundary between courts and parliament. For Montigny and the FCA, imposing a legal duty to consult during the legislative stage "would not only be impractical and cumbersome and potentially grind the legislative process to a halt, but it would fetter ministers [*sic*] and other members of Parliament in their law-making capacity" (*Canada* 2016, para. 60). Yet in the very next paragraph, Montigny also claimed that "it is good politics to engage stakeholders such as Aboriginal groups on legislative initiatives which may affect them or regarding which they have a keen interest, before introducing legislation into Parliament" (para. 61). For the Federal Court of Appeal then, consultation on legislation may be good politics, but it is not good law.

In *Mikisew Cree First Nation v. Canada (Governor General in Council)* (2018), the SCC sided with the FCA against Justice Hughes and declared that the courts do not have jurisdiction for judicial review because "while Cabinet ministers are members of the executive, they participate in this process . . . not in an executive capacity, but in a legislative capacity" (*Mikisew* 2018, para. 113). In essence, parliamentary privilege and the separation of powers prevents courts from interfering in the legislative process. To grant the Mikisew their appeal would be to "empower plaintiffs to override parliamentary privilege by challenging the process by which legislation was formulated, introduced or enacted" (para. 124). Clearly, one of the most salient themes to emerge from the SCC case is the issue of jurisdiction.

On Travelling Crowns, or Where Is the King?

The FCA and SCC rely on the Federal Courts Act (1985) to say that Justice Hughes erred in his determination that parliamentarians drafting legislation could be subject to the duty to consult.[2] The higher courts claim that, although the lawmakers in question are ministers (and as such are part of the cabinet, which is part of the executive or Crown, the body subject to the duty to consult), at the time of drafting, they function as parliamentarians, which makes their actions immune to judicial review.

Justice Hughes thoughtfully addressed these issues in the initial 2014 decision from the Federal Court. He claimed that, in accordance with the Federal Courts Act, no member of "the House of Commons, nor any committee or member of either house" would be subject to judicial review (Federal Courts Act 1985, sec. 2[2]); the Mikisew were not seeking judicial review of the content of the omnibus bills nor a decision made by a member of parliament, nor a minister to implement legislation (*Courtoreille* 2014, para. 22). Rather, "the Applicant is seeking to *engage the process* that Ministers of the Crown undertake before legislation has been drafted and presented to Parliament" (para. 22, emphasis mine). He goes on to do a careful reading of the legislative process as outlined in a guide published by the Canadian Privy Council Office in 2001 (submitted by the Mikisew First Nation), as well as oral arguments and cross-examination, to conclude that there is ample space to accommodate the duty to consult within the existing legislative process before a bill goes before parliament:

> At the very least, a duty to consult arises during the Policy Development and Cabinet Approval of Policy stages of the law-making process in this case, and at the very least, the duty to consult could attach to all steps up to the review and sign off of the sponsoring Minister. This means that the duty to consult would arise before Cabinet provides notice to Parliament, and thus before the introduction of the Omnibus Bills into Parliament. (*Courtoreille* 2014, para. 36)[3]

Justice Hughes also notes the inherent tension between Canada's commitment to a clear separation of powers on the one hand and a constitutional duty to consult in the name of the honor of the Crown, given force with section 35 of the Constitution Act (1982) on the other. At issue here is the slippery nature of the separation of powers when attempting to address Crown conduct that "has the potential to adversely affect an Aboriginal claim or right of which the Crown has actual or constructive knowledge" (*Courtoreille* 2014, para. 39). And indeed recent case law has allowed for judicial interventions in the name of the duty to consult, even during planning stages (*Courtoreille* 2014, paras. 41–43; *Haida Nation* 2004; *Mikisew Cree* 2005).[4] Moreover, Justice Hughes argues that simple suggestions that court interference in the law-making process is detrimental to governing fails to recognize the laborious, multistep process of law-making in the first place (*Courtoreille* 2014, para. 62). In short, for Justice Hughes, "the steps that Cabinet Ministers undertake during the law-making process prior to introducing a bill into Parliament do indeed constitute Crown conduct that can give rise to the duty to consult" (*Courtoreille* 2014, para. 84). But this suggestion was rejected by the FCA and the Supreme Court; they insist, against Justice Hughes, that there is a clear separation between parliament and executive. However, the image of such absolutely autonomous spheres requires some fantastical leaps of its own.

The Supreme Court relies on a formulation from Walter Bagehot's 1872 *The English Constitution* to conjure two metaphors to describe the relationship between the legislative and executive branches. In so doing, the court admits that "there is no doubt overlap between executive and legislative functions in Canada; Cabinet, for instance, is 'a combining committee—a *hyphen* which joins, a *buckle* which fastens, the legislative part of the state to the executive part of the state'" (*Mikisew* 2018, para. 33). But they then counter this by claiming that there *is* a clear distinction and that they do not believe "ministers act in an executive capacity when they develop legislation. The legislative development at issue was not conducted pursuant to any statutory authority; rather, it was an exercise of legislative powers derived from Part IV of the *Constitution Act, 1867*" (*Mikisew* 2018, para. 33). Although the court gives little detail on precisely what they mean here (and doesn't explain the seeming contradiction that the Constitution Act is indeed statutory), they emphasize that ministers are acting as members of the House of Commons in developing legislation, duties granted under Part IV of the Constitution Act (1867).

But let me explore these two metaphors to their full extent in order to ask just what kind of a relationship between branches we are to infer. In the first instance, if the cabinet is a hyphen, it looks something like this, "legislature-executive," where the cabinet is the unspoken presence connecting the two. Are we to assume, then, that if we add the third branch in the popularly imagined trinity of state power, "legislature-executive-judiciary," that the hyphen infers another silent partner between the executive and the courts? If so, who or what is it? Is there yet another combining committee between the courts and the legislature?

In the second metaphor, the cabinet is a buckle. Does Bagehot, and by extension the SCC, mean a buckle on a shoe where legislators are the shoe, the cabinet is the buckle, and the executive is the foot it all stays fastened to? Or perhaps legislators are the foot (doing all the walking), the executive is the shoe that protects the legislators, and the cabinet (the buckle) is what keeps the shoe from sliding off? Or maybe Bagehot means a belt buckle, whereby legislators are one end of the buckle, and the executive is the other side. In this metaphor, perhaps the cabinet is the publicly viewable frontispiece that ties them together, while parliament and the executive constantly run seamlessly together around the back? In either metaphor, the court undoes their hard and fast claim that there is a distinct separation between legislature and the executive by using the metaphor of the cabinet as a combining committee.

Moreover, in the very next paragraph, the court claims that "the development of legislation by ministers is part of the law-making process, and this process is generally protected from judicial oversight" (*Mikisew* 2018, para. 34). Despite the striking use of the word *generally*, which introduces a very direct admission that there are exceptions to this supposedly hard and fast separation, the justices also concoct an image of law-making as pure and sacrosanct, immune to any type of regulation or interference. While lawmakers know that, this process is rife with interjections, consultations, and even reviews by an unelected second chamber,[5] it has also more recently been subject to court intervention. For example, in *British Columbia Teachers' Federation v. British Columbia* (2016), the government was found to have failed to consult in good faith prior to the introduction of legislation.

The 2016 case between the British Columbia Teachers Federation and the province seems to introduce profound dilemmas about the separation of the branches asserted in *Mikisew*. In this remarkable case, the SCC relied wholly on the reasons given by the British Columbia Court of Appeal in 2015, choosing not to elaborate on the reasons for their decision whatsoever. Even more surprising was the fact that the majority of the SCC sided with the lone dissenting judge from the Court of Appeal, Justice Ian Donald. In the earlier case, Justice Donald, dissenting, argues that the province did not meaningfully consult with the teachers' union and, as such, the legislation in question (Bill 22) is not constitutionally valid. Justice Donald, and in turn the SCC majority that agree with him, makes bold claims that there is a constitutional "right to a meaningful process that is not continually under threat of being rendered pointless" (*British Columbia* 2015, para. 285) and that "a Charter breach cannot always be seen within the four corners of legislation, but must sometimes be found to occur prior to the passage of the legislation, when the government failed to consult a union in good faith or give it an opportunity to bargain collectively" (para. 288). Although he is speaking in the context of the Charter right to "freedom of association" (sec. 2d) as it pertains to unions, it is not difficult to see how this might be relevant to the context of meaningful consultation with Indigenous communities pursuant to section 35 of the Constitution Act (1982). I return to the issue of meaningful consultation and its constitutional requirement below, but let me note that Justice Donald goes further to complicate the relation between branches when it comes to prelegislative consultation. Again, speaking in the context of labour relations, he states that prelegislative consultation is done by the executive, not the legislature. Moreover, he cites Justice Major in *Wells v. Newfoundland*, [1999] 3 S.C.R. 199, as he asks for a reality-check when it comes to the myth of the absolute separation of powers in Canada:

> [Wells] said, "The Court should not be blind to the reality of Canadian governance that, except in certain rare cases, the executive frequently and de facto controls the legislature": Wells at para. 54.

The same acknowledgement of reality is required in this case. Thus, the unilateral imposition, alteration, or deletion of employment terms by the Legislature is, in most circumstances, the final step in an agenda of the executive branch; the same executive branch that both develops policy and has a constitutional obligation to consult or negotiate with collective representatives. (*British Columbia* 2015, para. 289)[6]

In this case, the Supreme Court refused to see the separation of powers as rigid and absolute, yet a clear distinction was drawn in *Mikisew*.

At issue in these cases is the discrepancy of when a minister becomes part of the executive—or, in other words, a dispute over where exactly the Crown lay. I suggest that a reading of the competing assertions of the Crown's true resting place among these three Mikisew cases illuminates a well-worn theme of colonial jurisprudence: the mythological foundations of modern law, to borrow from Peter Fitzpatrick's book title (1992). The take-away here is that the Crown is both everywhere and nowhere. The judges' careful reasoning suggests that there is a reasoned science, a legal rationality, that can pinpoint exactly where the Crown lies (or at what precise point a parliamentarian becomes a minister, and hence becomes subject to the duty to consult). But this is a ruse, although not an intentional one.[7]

In what follows, I provide examples of where observers can see an alternative narrative in *Mikisew*—not of a rational legal order navigated adeptly by experts of law but rather a messy, contradictory settler-colonial legal system enacted by competing agents that are often at odds with one another. The upshot of this analysis is to show that, while the *Mikisew* decision may foster a continued allegiance to the myth of legal positivism, it is part of a long and global history of case law that reveals the tenuous claim of colonial societies' legal power.

Parliamentary Versus Constitutional Sovereignty, or Choose Your Favourite Constitutional Principle

Even on strictly legal terms, *Mikisew* tells a confusing story of settler sovereignty. On the one hand, there is a strong claim among the SCC majority that judges cannot interfere in the legislative process (either to proscribe a duty to consult upon parliamentarians or to conduct a judicial review into the passing of the two omnibus bills in question) if parliamentary sovereignty is to be upheld. In this situation, parliamentary sovereignty reigns supreme, much like it does in UK law, subjugating all other legal considerations. On the other hand, there is also a narrative of constitutional supremacy adrift in this case, amplified by Abella and Martin. These insights draw attention to the principle of the "honour of the Crown," given weight via section 35 of Canada's Constitution. This unresolved tension between parliamentary and constitutional supremacy, a long-standing dilemma of Canadian constitutional law, gives insight into the conflicting claims of settler sovereignty.

Inherent in the concept of the honour of the Crown is the acknowledgement that there is an Indigenous claim to sovereignty that precedes Crown sovereignty (*Mikisew* 2018, para. 22). The principle is meant to promote negotiation outside of the courts (para. 22, citing *Taku River Tlingit* 2004, para. 24) and is considered to impose a "heavy obligation" on the Crown (para. 24, citing *Manitoba Metis* 2013, para. 68), even going so far as to be considered a "constitutional principle" (para. 24, citing *Beckman v. Little Salmon* 2010, para. 42). However, it carries no specific content: "It speaks to the way in which the Crown's specific obligations must be fulfilled. These obligations vary depending on the circumstances" (para. 60, citing *Manitoba Metis* 2013, para. 73).

But there is debate about how foundational a role the honour of the Crown should play. In their reasoning, Abella and Martin cite earlier case law to say that the honour of the Crown should be "the first consideration in determining whether the legislation or action in question can be justified" (*Mikisew* 2018, para. 64). This seems to suggest that case law stemming from *Sparrow* and *Haida* has already deemed constitutional supremacy to be paramount to parliamentary sovereignty. Abella and Martin further claim that the process of reconciliation demands a practice of "ongoing consultation," meaning that the "legislative sphere is not excluded from the honour of the Crown, which attaches to all exercises of sovereignty" (*Mikisew* 2018, para. 78). Amplifying the tension between parliamentary and constitutional sovereignty, they insist that case law has already decided that section 35 is to be understood as a limit on parliamentary sovereignty and that

> it seems to me quite ironic that parliamentary sovereignty would now be used as a shield to prevent the Mikisew's claim for consultation. With respect, such an approach reactivates the happily silenced spirit of *St. Catherine's Milling and Lumber Co. v. The Queen* (1888), 14 App.

Cas. 46 (P.C.), where Aboriginal rights were "dependent upon the good will of the Sovereign" (p. 54). (*Mikisew* 2018, paras. 85–86)

Abella and Martin go even further: "I do not accept an approach that replaces an enforceable legal right to consultation, with a vague and unenforceable right to 'honourable dealing.' The duty to consult is not a suggestion to consult, it is a duty, just as the honour of the Crown is not a mere 'incantation' or aspirational goal (*Haida Nation*, at para. 16)" (*Mikisew* 2018, para. 84). This resounding criticism of the majority reasoning should not go unheard. More than showing a difference of opinion, Abella and Martin are pointing to the fickle arguments of the courts—in *Sparrow*, constitutional supremacy was argued to reign supreme, and in *Mikisew*, it is subjugated to parliamentary supremacy.

Johan van der Walt writes about the somewhat arbitrariness of legal decisions in his book *Law and Sacrifice* (2005). He argues that, because decisions have to be made, the best we can do is draw attention to the losers. In opposition to Supreme Court decisions that do the work of narrating how the winners won, he argues that we also need stories of the losers so that we render legible the very real possibility that the losers could come back and win the legal argument on another day. While there is much to be gleaned from van der Walt's insights, this is not the case I am making here. More than rendering legible the losers, my project is to draw attention to the *construction of the narrative of the winners* to show how rife with contradictions the myth of legal rationality is; I want to disrupt a reading of it as well-reasoned and rational law. Taking cues from Said's insights in *Orientalism*, Fitzpatrick argues that "occidental being is impelled in a progression away from aberrant origins. It is formed in the comprehensive denial of the 'other'—in assertions of universal knowledge, imperious judgement and encompassing being" (1992, ix–x). This is what is happening in *Mikisew* (2018).

Narrating the supposedly solid ground of law for the SCC, Justice Karakatsanis claims that parliament reigns supreme—sort of:

> Parliamentary sovereignty mandates that the legislature can make or unmake any law it wishes, within the confines of its constitutional authority. While the adoption of the Canadian Charter of Rights and Freedoms transformed the Canadian system of government "to a significant extent from a system of Parliamentary supremacy to one of constitutional supremacy" (*Reference re Secession of Quebec*, [1998]

2 S.C.R. 217, at para. 72), democracy remains one of the unwritten
principles of the Constitution (Secession Reference, at paras. 61–69).
Recognizing that the elected legislature has specific consultation
obligations may constrain it in pursuing its mandate and therefore
undermine its ability to act as the voice of the electorate. (*Mikisew*
2018, para. 36)

In this fascinating paragraph, Karakatsanis makes an acrobatic effort to hold
on to the mythological truth of parliamentary supremacy.[8] I paraphrase:
Although it is subject to constitutional authority, parliament can make or
unmake any law it wishes. Moreover, democracy—given weight because it
is an unwritten constitutional principle (!)—means that parliament shall be
unconstrained so as to serve the people that elected it. This quixotic entanglement of constitutional and parliamentary commitments leaves much for a
reader to ponder over but lays bare the non-place of any truth of the autonomy
of parliamentary sovereignty (or constitutional sovereignty, for that matter).

Moreover, the justices pick and choose which unwritten constitutional
principles they want to privilege; in this case, democracy is the winner, and
nowhere do we hear a consideration of other unwritten principles, such as the
protection of minorities (*Secession*) or the honour of the Crown (*Little Salmon*), both arguably relevant to the Mikisew case. Are we to assume, then, that
there is an unspoken hierarchy to these unwritten principles? Or is it that the
lionized electorate that the court imagines is always already non-Indigenous?
At paragraph 42, the court admits that there are other relevant principles,
including the honour of the Crown, but this admission does not destabilize
the confidence of legal reasoning in support of parliamentary sovereignty.

Even other SCC members see the capricious reasoning in the majority
decision. Justice Brown writes a scathing critique of Justice Karakatsanis:

My colleague would, however, go further, raising—and then leaving
open—the possibility that legislation which does not infringe s.35
rights but may "adversely affect" them, might be found to be inconsistent with the honour of the Crown. (paras. 3 and 25). In so doing,
however, she undercuts the same principles which have led her to conclude that imposing the duty to consult would be "inappropriate" in
the circumstances of this case. Further, by raising the possibility (without, I note, having been asked to do so by any party to this appeal) that
validly enacted and constitutionally compliant legislation which has

not or could not be the subject of a successful s.35 infringement claim can nonetheless be declared by a court to be "not consistent with [the honour of the Crown,]" my colleague would throw this area of the law into significant uncertainty. Such uncertainty would have deleterious effects on Indigenous peoples, and indeed on all who rely upon the efficacy of validly enacted and constitutionally compliant laws. (*Mikisew* 2018, para. 104)

Here Brown criticizes Karakatsanis for not being severe enough in her insistence that this issue demands a clear separation of powers. He insists that the constitutional limits on the courts in this context (of legislative review) must be crystal clear both for the Mikisew and all future claimants. But where Brown sees confusion and pushes for clarity, I see confusion and argue that clarification is more obfuscation. The dilemma cannot be made clearer because it requires myth to hold its ground.

The Myth of Modern Law, or the Eternal Return of the Same

The fact that myth is required to ground the narrative of absolute sovereignty is not new to legal thinking. In his theory of the general will and its accompanying legal framework articulated in *The Social Contract* ([1762] 1997), Jean-Jacques Rousseau attempts to pinpoint how and where his imagined legislator sits. With great effort, he attempts to maintain a separation between his much-lionized autonomous sovereign will of the people and a lawmaker that would legislate on their behalf without influence, a distinction that he ultimately cannot hold. In the end, Rousseau invokes a theological spectre, "a superior intelligence," as the only legislator capable of enacting the revolutionary form of government, controlled by the will of the people, that he envisions. In short, the task of this legislator "would take gods":

> In order to discover the rules of society best suited to nations, a superior intelligence beholding all the passions of men without experiencing any of them would be needed. This intelligence would have to be wholly unrelated to our nature, while knowing it through and through; its happiness would have to be independent of us, and yet ready to occupy itself with ours; and lastly, it would have, in the march of time, to look forward to a distant glory, and, working in one century,

to be able to enjoy in the next. It would take gods to give men laws.
([1762] 1997, 60)

Fitzpatrick picks up on this passage of Rousseau in a 2003 article in the *Leiden Journal of International Law* titled "'Gods Would Be Needed . . .': American Empire and the Rule of (International) Law." Fitzpatrick's long-standing interest is the way in which occidental law denies its own theological impulses as it lays its claim to being objective, scientifically determined, and rational. In his germinal text *The Mythology of Modern Law*, he outlines how modern law garners its cloak of reasonability from its juxtaposition to an imagined "other"—through the figure of the Oriental, Indigenous, customary, and/or barbaric—law. In this work and others, he illustrates how legal thinkers like Rousseau and H. L. A. Hart make (theo)logical leaps in their attempts to draw out law's sovereign authority; his lasting contribution is to always see how Western law simultaneously relies on *and* denies these inheritances. This is not to suggest that Fitzpatrick is a righteous secularist—far from it. His point is not to dismiss the theological or the irrational but rather to point to its perpetual presence in occidental law, even as it is denied. And yet, although Fitzpatrick made these insights in 1992, colonial law's presumed authority continues to reign supreme.

More recently, John Borrows has taken up the problem with Western law's stories about itself. In *Recovering Canada: The Resurgence of Indigenous Law* (2002), he demonstrates how case law, although lionized and vaunted as unique, is at its core narrative. He uses this insight to claim that Indigenous law, although often dismissed as simple storytelling, could easily be invoked, like case law, in Canadian courts alongside common and civil case law to adjudicate more justly, not only for Indigenous individuals and communities, but for settlers as well. For him, law is a story and should be treated as such. In a similar vein, Stewart Motha claims in *Archiving Sovereignty* that "authority needs a story" (2018, 20). Where Borrows claims that law is made up of stories, Motha claims that all law requires fiction. According to Motha, "In the absence of a foundation, law requires a fiction that grounds its authority. This fiction also allows us to tell a story of law as absolutely autonomous, as objective and removed from questions of theology and literature" (96–97). Both Borrows and Motha point to the myth of law's rational, ordered autonomy, and yet this myth continues to hold much cultural sway. Indeed, the power of this myth continues to grant the Canadian settler-colonial government the state-backed authorization to retain control of Indigenous land, including all the benefits and resources that come with such ownership and the legal right to act as a paternalistic parent to Indigenous communities, holding the power to authorize funds and to infringe on rights and titles if deemed necessary.[9] And this state-enforced system of positive law takes its form through the enactment of jurisdiction.[10]

Jurisdiction lays at the heart of the maintenance of this legal authority. Although commonly attributed to a geographical or territorial demarcation, the term etymologically descends from the root words *juris* and *dictio* and translates from the Latin into "speaking the law." As Austin Sarat claims, jurisdiction "manifests law as performative through speech; it signifies not just a spatial demarcation of law's reach but also a staging of authority to make pronouncements that present themselves as being 'law'" (2013, 205). In this way, jurisdiction is more than space or territory; it is also its performative utterance. This "staging of authority" is what brings law into being and along with it, sovereignty.[11] Thus, jurisdiction invents law much like the signature invents the "people" in Jacques Derrida's work on constitutional authority. Here I substitute *law* and *jurisdiction* in Derrida's illuminating paragraph on the paradoxical relationship between signature and signer: "[Law] does not exist as an entity, it does not exist, before this declaration [of jurisdiction], not as such. If [law] gives birth to itself . . . this can only hold in the act of [jurisdiction]. [Jurisdiction] invents the [law]" (1986, 10).

Thinking about jurisdiction as an utterance, as a performance that inaugurates, renders bare the very tenuousness of law. This is why Jean-Luc Nancy refers to it as "jurisfiction": "The *persona* of the judge and his *edictum* are forged from the same *fictitious* gesture: right is said here of the case for which there can be no prior right, and which is *the case of right*" (Nancy 2003, 157).[12] This is not to say that such jurisfictions do not have real-world consequences. Shiri Pasternak's work with the Algonquin Nation at Barriere Lake shows that the state's power to subjugate comes precisely from a complex network of jurisdictions oriented to maintaining settler-colonial control of Indigenous land and resources and "erasing Indigenous law" (2017, 17). Further, the SCC's decision in *Mikisew* (2018) deploys a debate about jurisdictional boundaries (all under the assumption of *ultimate* jurisdiction) to retain sovereignty and prevent meaningful engagement with Indigenous communities on major legislative changes. And yet, dwelling on the concept of jurisdiction and its essence as an utterance, a staging of authority "makes visible a governing and productive instability in the law . . ." (Cormack 2009, 5). It is this instability that we must exacerbate at every opportunity and what I hope to have done in small part in this reading of *Mikisew*.

Conclusion

My point about the ultimate indeterminacy of the Crown's precise location or the tension between parliamentary and constitutional supremacy should not be mistaken as a relativistic argument. In this case, and more generally in approaching legal issues of decolonization, there is a strong discourse that asserts that prelegislative consultation with Indigenous communities is too complicated (see, for example, *Mikisew* 2018, 16–17). I want to be clear that it is not. Justices Abella and Martin, echoing Justice Hughes from the Federal Court, offer several simple legal answers. They suggest that "notice to affected parties and the opportunity to make submissions are hardly foreign to the law-making process" (*Mikisew* 2018, para. 92). Further, they note that the federal government's duty to consult during the law-making process is a "component of the Crown's overarching obligation to deal honourably with Indigenous peoples when regulating their rights" (para. 67) and, as such, is not confined to a particular time or place. Rather, "the honour of the Crown is always at stake in its dealings with Indigenous peoples . . ." (para. 56). Moreover, such an obligation has a precedent in *British Columbia Teachers' Federation v. British Columbia* (2016), and the court's duty to ensure this obligation is upheld has been set out in *Sparrow* (para. 93), *Haida Nation, Taku River,* and *Mikisew Cree* (2005; *Mikisew* 2018, para. 67). Finally, it is also worth noting that a mere victory for the right to consultation in the prelegislative stage does not mean (1) that Indigenous communities do not retain the right to continue to challenge the same legislation after is has been passed[13] nor (2) that Canada has fulfilled and exhausted its requirements owed to those communities.

In the process of writing this chapter, I learned the idiom "castles in the air," which is meant to refer to an unrealistic approach to a project, or something that lacks a strong foundation. For example, if you have no money, yet you plan to make a big purchase (i.e., buy a new car), you may be someone who is building "castles in the air." I was toying with the idea that Canadian law is like a "castle in the air," but it isn't in the air; its entire narrated existence as a well-ordered, rational, and therefore supreme law is built on an imagined, supposedly backward and customary, other. What I have tried to show here, in the footsteps of others, is how that narrative of superiority is created despite settler-colonial law's own logical leaps. While much Indigenous resistance and refusal happens at a distance to and in spite of the settler-colonial state, more work needs to be done by Canada's settler-colonial public—including legal practitioners and socio-legal scholars—to challenge the stories of Western legal superiority that animate our imaginations. We must make room for alternative narratives of justice and legal systems both within and without the contemporary settler-colonial state.

Notes

1 Socio-legal studies and post-colonial studies have long been in conversation. While the amorphous nature of both fields resists periodization, there is some scholarship devoted to drawing out the relationship. See Fitzpatrick and Darian-Smith (1996) and Harrington and Manji (2017). For more on the dilemmas of periodization and the assumption of disciplinary boundaries see Buck-Morss (2000).

2 The Federal Courts Act, section 2(2) is designed "to preclude judicial review of the legislative process at large" (*Mikisew* 2018, para. 18).

3 At paragraph 68, Justice Hughes agrees with the respondent, however, that this guide is a policy document that the government can change at any time and does not have to follow in linear fashion. Therefore, "for this court to instruct the Crown on which stages of the law-making process it must consult Aboriginal peoples would have the effect of constraining a process for which the government requires flexibility to carry out its duties" (*Mikisew* 2014, para. 68).

4 This suggests that planning can trigger the duty to consult and that the duty to consult can sometimes apply to non-executive action: "This obligation has also been applied in the context of statutory decision-makers that—while not part of the executive—act on behalf of the Crown (*Clyde River [Hamlet] v. Petroleum Geo-Services Inc.*, 2017 SCC 40, [2017] 1 S.C.R. 1069, at para. 29). These cases demonstrate that, in certain circumstances, Crown conduct may not constitute an 'infringement' of established s. 35 rights; however, acting unilaterally in a way that may adversely affect such rights does not reflect well on the honour of the Crown and may thus warrant intervention on judicial review" (*Mikisew* 2018, para. 25).

5 See, for example, Peter Russell's scathing critique of the state of Canada's democracy in the face of an increasingly centralized and ballooned Prime Minister's Office (2009). Russell also writes about the unchecked governmental power under majority governments with a strong whip system in Canada (2008).

6 Justice Major actually says at the beginning of this paragraph, "The separation of powers is not a rigid and absolute structure" (*Wells v. Newfoundland*, para. 54).

7 For a historical analysis of this "shape-shifting," see Paul McHugh and Lisa Ford's chapter "Settler Sovereignty and the Shapeshifting Crown," in *Between Indigenous*

and Settler Governance. They argue that the mid-nineteenth century to the early twentieth century saw "the rise of a new jurisprudence that both subordinated the will of the Crown to local settler legislatures and, at the same time, reasserted the Crown's non-justiciable prerogative power over indigenous affairs" (2012, 24).

8 I am indebted to Emilios Christodoulidis for this formulation of "acrobatic" (2016, 44).

9 There are many examples to provide as evidence, but one recent example is the infringement of rights guaranteed by section 35 of the Constitution Act (1982), articulated in *Tsilhqot'in Nation v. British Columbia*, in the name of the nation so long as the government shows that "(1) it complied with its procedural duty to consult with the right holders and accommodate the right to an appropriate extent at the stage when infringement was contemplated; (2) the infringement is backed by a compelling and substantial legislative objective in the public interest; and (3) the benefit to the public is proportionate to any adverse effect on the Aboriginal interest" (2014, para. 125).

10 For more on the integral connections among race, jurisdiction, and property see Bhandar (2018), Ford (1999), Harris (1993), and Keenan (2017).

11 For more on the performative utterance of jurisdiction as law, see Cormack (2009), Dorsett and McVeigh (2007), Matthews (2017), and Valverde (2009).

12 For more on Nancy's concept of "jurisfiction," see Leung (2012) and Matthews (2017).

13 See this point made in the employment context in *British Columbia Teachers' Federation v. British Columbia* 2015, para. 296.

References

Bhandar, Brenna. 2018. *Colonial Lives of Property: Law, Land, and Racial Regimes of Ownership.* Durham, NC: Duke University Press.

Borrows, John. 2002. *Recovering Canada: The Resurgence of Indigenous Law.* Toronto: University of Toronto Press.

Buck-Morss, Susan. 2000. "Hegel and Haiti." *Critical Inquiry* 26 (4): 821–65.

Christodoulidis, Emilios. 2016. "Public Law as Political Jurisprudence: Loughlin's 'Idea of Public Law.'" In *Public Law and Politics: The Scope and Limits of Constitutionalism*, edited by Emilios Christodoulidis and Stephen Tierney, 35–46. Aldershot, UK: Ashgate.

Cormack, Bradin. 2009. *Power to Do Justice: Jurisdiction, English Literature, and the Rise of Common Law.* Chicago: University of Chicago Press.

Derrida, Jacques. 1986. "Declarations of Independence." Translated by Thomas Keenan and Thomas Pepper. *New Political Science* 15:7–15.

Dorsett, Shaunnagh, and Shaun McVeigh. 2007. "Questions of Jurisdiction." In *Jurisprudence of Jurisdiction*, edited by Shaun McVeigh, 3–18. Oxford: Routledge.

Harris, Cheryl. 1993. "Whiteness as Property." *Harvard Law Review* 106 (8): 1710–91.

Harrington, John, and Ambreena Manji. 2017. "The Limits of Socio-legal Radicalism: Social and Legal Studies and Third World Scholarship." *Social & Legal Studies* 26 (6): 700–715.

Fitzpatrick, Peter. 1992. *Mythology of Modern Law*. London: Routledge.

———. 2003 "'Gods Would Be Needed . . .': American Empire and the Rule of (International) Law." *Leiden Journal of International Law* 16 (3): 429–66.

Fitzpatrick, Peter, and Eve Darian-Smith. 1996. Special Issue on Postcolonialism. *Social & Legal Studies* 5 (3): 291–447.

Ford, Richard T. 1999. "Law's Territory (a History of Jurisdiction)." *Michigan Law Review* 97:843–930.

Keenan, Sarah. 2017. "Smoke, Curtains and Mirrors: The Production of Race through Time and Title Registration." *Law and Critique* 28 (1): 87–108.

Leung, Gilbert. 2012. "Illegal Fictions." In *Jean-Luc Nancy: Justice, Legality and World*, edited by Benjamin Hutchens, 82–95. New York: Continuum.

Matthews, Dan. 2017. "From Jurisdiction to Juriswriting: At the Expressive Limits of the Law." *Law, Culture, and the Humanities* 13 (3): 425–45.

McHugh, Paul, and Lisa Ford. 2012. "Settler Sovereignty and the Shapeshifting Crown." In *Between Indigenous and Settler Governance*, edited by Lisa Ford and Tim Rowse, 23–34. New York: Routledge.

Motha, Stewart. 2018. *Archiving Sovereignty: Law, History, Violence*. Ann Arbor: University of Michigan Press.

Nancy, Jean-Luc. 2003. *A Finite Thinking*, edited by Simon Sparks. Stanford, CA: Stanford University Press.

Pasternak, Shiri. 2017. *Grounded Authority: The Algonquins of Barriere Lake Against the State*. Minneapolis: University of Minnesota Press.

Rousseau, Jean-Jacques. (1762) 1997. *"The Social Contract" and Other Later Political Writings*, edited and translated by Victor Gourevitch. Cambridge: Cambridge University Press.

Russell, Peter H. 2008. *Two Cheers for Minority Government*. Toronto: Emond Montgomery.

———. 2009. "The Charter and Canadian Democracy." In *Contested Constitutionalism: Reflections on the Canadian Charter of Rights and Freedoms*, edited by James B. Kelly and Christopher P. Manfredi, 287–306. Toronto: UBC Press.

Said, Edward. 1979. *Orientalism*. Vintage: New York.

Sarat, Austin. 2013. "Editorial." *Law, Culture, and the Humanities* 9 (2): 205.

Stern, Simon. 2017. "Wilde's Obscenity Effect: Influence and Immorality in the Picture of Dorian Gray." *Review of English Studies* 68:756–72.

Valverde, Mariana. 2009. "Jurisdiction and Scale: Legal 'Technicalities' as Resources for Theory." *Social & Legal Studies* 18 (2): 139–57.
van der Walt, Johan. 2005. *Law and Sacrifice.* London: Birkbeck Law Press.

Case Law

Beckman v. Little Salmon/Carmacks First Nation, 2010 SCC 53.
British Columbia Teachers' Federation v. British Columbia, 2015 BCCA 184.
British Columbia Teachers' Federation v. British Columbia, 2016 SCC 49.
Canada (Governor General in Council) v. Mikisew Cree First Nation, 2016 FCA 311.
Courtoreille v. Canada (Aboriginal Affairs and Northern Development), 2014 FC 1244.
Haida Nation v. British Columbia (Minister of Forests), [2004] 3 S.C.R. 511.
Manitoba Metis Federation Inc. v. Canada (Attorney General), 2013 SCC 14.
Mikisew Cree First Nation v. Canada, [2005] 3 S.C.R. 388.
Mikisew Cree First Nation v. Canada (Governor General in Council), 2018 SCC 40.
R. v. Sparrow, [1990] 1 S.C.R. 1075.
Reference re Secession of Quebec, [1998] 2 S.C.R. 217.
Taku River Tlingit First Nation v. British Columbia (Project Assessment Director), 2004 SCC 74.
Tsilhqot'in Nation v. British Columbia, 2014 SCC 44.
Wells v. Newfoundland, [1999] 3 S.C.R. 199.

Legislation

Bill 22, Education Improvement Act (BC).
Bill C-38, An Act to Implement Certain Provisions of the Budget Tabled in Parliament on March 29, 2012 and Other Measures (CAN).
Bill C-45, A Second Act to Implement Certain Provisions of the Budget Tabled in Parliament on March 29, 2012 and Other Measures (CAN).
Canadian Environmental Assessment Act, 1992.
Charter of Rights and Freedoms, 1982.
Constitution Act, 1867.
Constitution Act, 1982.
Federal Courts Act, 1985.
Fisheries Act, 1985.
Navigable Waters Protection Act, 1985.
Species at Risk Act, 2002.

Part II
Gendered Violence and Racial Subjugation

3 Making Terrorism
Security Practices and the Production of Terror Activities in Canada

Yavar Hameed and Jeffrey Monaghan

It was over forty years ago when Richard Ericson published his influential socio-legal text *Making Crime*, which provides a vivid account of the discretionary powers of detective practices in the "making" of crime. As Ericson suggested, "Based on the information work he has done, the detective decides whether the case can be made into a 'crime'; and, if he has a suspect, whether the suspect can be made into a 'criminal'" (1981, 7). In this chapter, we borrow from Ericson's insights on the construction of punishable subjects by analyzing the crime-making dynamics of the "war on terror" and the embeddedness of racialized constructions of menacing Islam in counter-terrorism practices. Providing a socio-legal reading of how the Anti-terrorism Act (ATA) produces a terrain of criminal liability for what are termed "terrorist activities," we explore how criminal justice practices in Canada have—to use Ericson's insights as a framing mechanism—decided what cases can be made into "terrorism" and, once suspects have been identified, made suspects into "terrorists."

Socio-legal scholarship can assist in deconstructing the crime-making dynamics that are embedded in the "war on terror." In concert with the insights from our colleagues featured in this volume, we employ socio-legal analysis to trace how social forces shape the contours of law; how race, colonialism, and domination structure the liberal norms of "justice." In producing a powerful social imaginary that presents the law as "neutral," socio-legal analysis can illustrate naturalized hierarchies of power in Western societies dominated by racism, sexism, the avarice of control, and the blunt hum of accumulation. While law's neutrality is often celebrated as a social fact in our public imaginary, socio-legal scholarship is well suited to articulate how the "genealogies of race and colonialism structure the epistemological and onto-logical foundations of law" (Murdocca, Vadasaria, and Bryan, chapter 1 in this volume). In examining aspects of what has transpired over the two decades of the "war on terror," counter-terrorism practices in Canada should be situated as part of what Rana describes as the "terror-industrial complex," representing "larger systems of structural violence that are normalized" through a net-work of material and immaterial workings that are "interwoven in Muslim life" (2016, 114–15). Examples of these expansive forms of violence extend from military wars and occupations, global mass surveillance, and drone operations abroad to a network of domestic institutions that operationalize anti-Muslim practices that are twinned to menacing notions of Islam. Much of the violence reproduced through these institutions—in policing, health care, social services, detention, and deportation regimes—is structured through neutral discourses of law, yet socio-legal theory and methods can trace how racial underpinnings of the "war on terror" animate these practices. Exist-ing scholarship has examined particular aspects of how the "war on terror" produces racialized socio-cultural logics (Kundnani 2014; Nagra 2017; Puar 2007) as well as policing practices (Monaghan and Molnar 2016), and our con-tribution here uses the examination of policing and criminal justice practices to contend that the process of making terrorism is contingent on racialized characterizations within contemporary counter-terrorism policing. We sug-gest that two powerful social logics help examine how the broad contours of police work produce what becomes labelled and prosecuted as "terrorism": (1) a logic of pre-emption that is focused on security actions against potential catastrophic futures (see Zedner 2007; also McCulloch and Pickering 2009, 2013; McCulloch and Wilson 2015) and (2) a logic that exceptionalizes Islam as an existential threat to Canadian society. As both these logics are knowledge practices grounded on speculative imaginings that produce the objects they aim to govern, they translate widely ranging incidents or events through a police-curated prism of the "war on terror" to make these instances legible as terrorism.

In this chapter, we examine some higher-profile terrorism cases, including the John Nuttall and Amanda Korody trial, the Aaron Driver case, and ele-ments of the "Toronto 18" plot. Using a socio-legal analysis of case judgments, media coverage, and contemporary legal scholarship, we focus on two fields of practice: first, how pre-emptive police work and especially police communications practices are constitutive of the spectacular character of (Islamic) terrorism cases; and second, how pre-emptive policing is translated into sentencing practices. Following Ericson's conclusions on police discretion—that "[the police] believe the ends justify the means, and their practices reflect this belief"—we show how pre-emptive police work produces terrorism cases as a special type of criminality, where terrorists are deserving of the exceptionalisms that animate the contemporary practices of making terrorism (1981, 7).

"Terrorism Activities" and the Making of Terrorism

Offences related to "terrorist activities" are a new area of criminal liability in Canada. Before the 2001 ATA, terrorism was addressed through traditional common law approaches dealing with issues of violence or criminal conspiracies. Under the ATA, "terrorist activities" include acts done for political, religious, or ideological gain with the intention of intimidating the public as well as providing a governmental process for labelling terrorist groups. Parliament and the courts have placed various provisos on the use (or potential use) of violence as well as some caveats regarding protesting that aim to craft the specific applicability of what constitutes terrorist activities. Moreover, the ATA itemizes a number of specific Criminal Code infractions through subsections that list various specific activities such as participation in a terror group, financing, support, and so on.

Though the content of the ATA in 2001 and amendments to it in 2015 (commonly known as Bill C-51) addressed specific acts of violence (in the United States, the attacks in New York and Washington in 2001, and in Canada, the attack at parliament in October 2014), the aims of the ATA are far broader. As described by one of the ATA's advocates, former Liberal justice minister Irwin Cotler, "One of the raisons d'etre for the Bill—having regard to the character of the transnational terrorist, existential threat—is organized around a culture of prevention and pre-emption, as distinct from reactive 'after the fact' law enforcement" (2001, 118). As Ericson (2007) has noted, it is precisely the need to move from a traditional "post-crime" logic toward what scholars have described as a "pre-crime" logic that defines the reorientation of security governance practices in the "war on terror." Given that Canada has little experience with terrorist events, the applicability of ATA powers and charges was immediately directed toward future threats and risks. In parallel with Ericson's description of ways in which risk-thinking has led to "treating every imaginable source of harm as a crime" (2007, 1), the ATA has functioned to translate the fear of terrorism into preventative and pre-emptive practices against future terrorists. Yet despite all these efforts to demarcate a specified juridical field of "terrorism," we suggest it is important to examine what activities have been demarcated as "terrorist" and who have been deemed as "terrorists." In doing so, we underline that the practices of "terrorism" are almost exclusively centred around Islam.

As a general characterization of ATA cases targeting Muslims, we underline four important, shared characteristics that shape what gets made into terrorism. First is the centering of Islam as the pre-eminent source of political violence in Canada. Examining ATA cases from 2004 (Khawaja) to June 2021, there have been sixty-six individuals charged with terrorism offences.[1] Of these cases, only thirteen have been against non-Muslims. Many of the hoax charges have been for low-level incidents (e.g., hoaxes, disruptions by left-wing activists), while two cases have been far-right instances of political violence. Both these far-right prosecutions have arisen subsequent to concerted public advocacy demanding that more visible far-right actors be prosecuted as—and made into—terrorists, particularly given the penchant of the Canadian security establishment to characterize far-right violence as a public order issue rather than terrorism. While we do not support the expansion of ATA securitization, the more recent turn toward prosecuting far-right actors evinces the terror-making powers of both police and prosecutors to transform incidents into terrorism but, more significantly, does not correct a fundamentally skewed legacy of ATA prosecutions targeting Muslims. This is particularly noteworthy given that white supremacist, misogynistic, and colonial violence are long-standing forms of political violence in Canada with no track record of being made into terrorism. Typically, attacks against Muslims, Jews, women, trans and queer communities, and racialized and Indigenous communities get classified as "hate crimes" (if they get prosecuted at all). And notwithstanding the recent inclusion of non-Muslim violence into ATA prosecutions, an overwhelming fifty-three of sixty-six ATA prosecutions have targeted Muslims who are alleged to have some connection with jihadist terrorism.

Stemming from this first characteristic, a second expression of the distinct place of terrorism embedded within the Canadian justice system is the reliance on a highly spectacular and punitive response to the events and people (pre-dominately Muslims) classified as terrorists. Unlike hate crimes prosecuted as a result of political violence from the right-wing actors, ATA trials have significantly higher penalties. Elsewhere, one of us has characterized this as a form of "terror carceralism" (Monaghan 2013) where the geopolitics of the "war on terror" is meted out against individuals deemed as terrorists in a highly punitive and spectacular form. Yet even with lower-level cases, the stigma produced by the highly mediatized charges and arrests—even for individuals who have been acquitted—is a long-lasting and punitive effect of counter-terrorism policing and communication powers (Monaghan 2020).

A third characteristic is the aspirational forms of the ATA cases. Only two of the ATA cases involving Muslims are based on physical acts of violence against civilians, one accused having been deemed not criminally responsible (NCR) and another with significant mental health issues but not deemed NCR by the courts. With the exception of more recent terrorism travel charges, the majority of the "terrorist activities" prosecuted in Canada have been aspirational and far-fetched plots. Most of the cases involve unreachable conspiracies under the scrutiny of police infiltrators. In many of the cases, particularly the "Toronto 18" and Nuttall/Korody cells, the plotters were delusional (and somewhat tragic) figures. These aspirational factors are also reflected in the fourth characteristic of the terrorism cases in Canada, which is that they are almost exclusively products of preventative governance. As events that are crimes based on future, aspirational actions, these cases all provide excellent examples of what scholars have described as a logic of "pre-crime" (Zedner 2007; see also McCulloch and Pickering 2009, 2013; McCulloch and Wilson 2015). As pre-emptive practices, pre-crime policing has significant impacts on the traditional post-crime procedural standards of criminal justice agencies.

McCulloch and Pickering warn that the shift from "post-crime" criminal justice to "pre-crime" national security practices demonstrates an "anticipatory logic [that] is the antithesis of the temporally linear post-crime criminal justice process" (2009, 632). Ericson describes these security practices as forms of "counter laws" or "laws against law" because they "erode or eliminate traditional principles, standards and procedures of criminal law that get in the way of pre-empting imagined sources of harm" (2007, 57). We contend that terrorism charges do not only arise from imagined sources of harm (potential future violence defined as terrorism) but the particular imagining of the identities of those associated with imagined harms. In practice, the making of terrorism involves both the creation of the legal-juridical category of "terrorism" and the imagining of who is a "terrorist."

While socio-legal scholarship calls attention to the forces that shape these legal practices, we underline how pre-emption and caricatures of Islam are shaped by the practices of police work. As Ericson and Haggerty (1997) have argued, police are increasingly "knowledge workers" who act as the primary conduit to communicate "risks" to the public. Risk communication practices, as Ericson and Haggerty explain, privilege police accounts of crime, risk, and insecurity as an organizing mechanism in contemporary society. Far from objective, Ericson (2007) has underlined that police communications are central in the prioritization of public knowledge and action about crime, particularly about security and terrorism. Police communications work is especially powerful in the "war on terror," where these practices of making terrorism are fundamentally racialized and characterizable by the four above-mentioned characteristics. Extending these insights on how police communications constitute and shape the social world, we detail how contemporary communications practices are highly spectacular and deeply influential in producing terrorism. Police work has embedded racialized and pre-emptive logics into the very conceptualization and application of terrorism charges. After detailing prominent examples of police work as making terrorism, we link these terror-making practices of policing to the sentencing practices. Doing so demonstrates how the police communications of terrorism are embedded in the broader criminal justice system.

Communication Practices: Terror Spectacles as Policing Strategy

We define communication practices as strategic discursive enactments by policing and security actors that attempt to frame what cases can be made into "terrorism" and, once suspects have been identified, who can be made into "terrorists." Equally influenced by securitization theory that shows how speech acts securitize social and political domains, we highlight how communication practices are deployed by state actors as strategic devices that advance a police narrative of events. These communication practices make terrorism and terrorists and enact a legitimizing narrative for greater police and surveillance powers against Muslim terrorists while producing narratives that shape criminal proceedings against "terrorists." By performing these practices, we suggest that the use of communications strategies designed to appeal to the imagination and vulnerability of society is an important component of what Kellner (2003) refers to as the "spectacle of terror." Kellner's analysis, which considers the way in which the rhetoric of state discourse under George W. Bush was amplified through popular US media culture in the wake of the 9/11 terror attacks, identified the role of a "media spectacle" as an instrument of propagating a Manichean binary of a "clash of civilizations" (2003). Within this media spectacle, a probing and contextual consideration of the background and motivation of a suspect is supplanted by a focus on the media-generated representations of the terrorist subject and the speculative horrors of the aspirational crime. The origins, criminal history, and social influences of the suspect are set aside under a narrative that is left vague and unchallenged. As Kinsman, Buse, and Steedman describe it, the discourse of national security is thus used as a "cutting out device" (2000, 283–84) to abstract the suspect from more complex social dynamics by sensationalizing the spectacularity of the crime and characterizing it as an attack on collective moral values (see also Kinsman and Gentile 2010). The effectiveness of the "terror spectacle" as a strategy thus rests upon the impact of the images that it captures and its deliberate omission of the facts surrounding the crime and its investigation. Below we highlight two prominent cases, that of Nuttall and Korody and Aaron Driver, to demonstrate how policing and police communications practices make terrorism, through their narration of exceptional terrorism subjects, deserving of exceptional pre-emptive action.

Manufacturing of Terror: The Case of Nuttall and Korody

John Nuttall and Amanda Korody were arrested on Canada Day (1 July) 2013 on terrorism charges related to a deadly plot to detonate improvised explosive devices on the grounds of the British Columbia Legislature. On 2 July 2013, the Royal Canadian Mounted Police (RCMP) held a national press conference that explained the arrest and provided details of the chilling plot. The press conference, which took place less than three months following the Boston Marathon bombings, was replete with colour photographs of seized items with evidence labels, including pressure cookers, rusted nails, and explosive substances. Though the RCMP underlined that there was no international connection to the conspiracy, the two accused were presented as being self-radicalized and inspired by Al Qaeda ideology (despite the RCMP emphasizing that they were not members of the organization). No details were provided about the personal background or history of the suspects or the context of the plot. Instead, the RCMP depicted a chilling image to the national media that conveyed a plot that had more potentially horrific consequences than the Boston bombing. According to the well-crafted narrative of the press conference, the plot was averted by effective police action and intelligence. Importantly, the RCMP made no mention of their use of the controversial Mr. Big-style undercover tactic (Keenan and Brockman 2010) or their role in educating, guiding, and convincing the two suspects of the necessity for as well as the time, place, and manner of staging a terrorist act. Because there was no explanation provided as to how the self-radicalization of the accused occurred or why they chose to proceed in the manner that they did, the only measure of protection in the face of inexplicable radical violence was strong police work and intelligence.

The police communications practice of holding press conferences to publicly explain the facts of an arrest is not a standard occurrence, but rather, it is a specifically coordinated and chosen event. Although rare, the staging of national press conferences is based on the anticipated political and public significance of an arrest as a culmination of a police operation and involves the discretionary release of otherwise confidential information. The decision to prioritize certain policing operations in the arena of national security is consistent with the decades-old practices associated with the subjective definitions of security (Kinsman, Buse, and Steedman 2000). Integral to this brand of policing is a blurring of the line between secret intelligence investigation and normal police investigation as a response to crime. Although historically, the deployment of state resources in support of intelligence investigation has enjoyed a special privilege and constant political currency without the need for public accountability and transparency, the construction of terrorist crimes has prompted an increased and deliberate effort by the state to justify the expansion of police powers to meet the perception of a new breed of crime.

Unlike the ex post facto media manipulation of critical discussion following a spectacular crime that has occurred, the communication of an aspirational or future criminal act requires an imagined conclusion. Indeed, in the case of Nuttall and Korody, part of the catastrophic portrait of the imagined crime rests upon the very real and gruesome reality of the Boston Marathon bombing. Photos of pressure cookers and rusted nails are, in themselves, not sinister—unless one extrapolates to imagine the damage that they could inflict upon innocent civilians. Likewise, the timing of the Nuttall and Korody attack is easily understood as constituting an archetypally "anti-Canadian" act in its anticipated plot, which was allegedly designed to be unleashed at the provincial legislature on Canada Day. However, the narrative that was drawn from these fragments at the RCMP press conference was grossly misleading. Not because the suspects were not involved in a plot to detonate improvised explosives in a public space on a national holiday, but because the nature of the criminal conduct, its urgency, manner of execution, timing, and setting were determined not by the accused themselves but by the police.

On 2 June 2015, almost two years after their arrest, Nuttall and Korody were convicted by a jury before the Supreme Court of British Columbia on two counts of terrorism-related offences for conspiracy to murder in association with a terrorist organization and possession of explosive substances with the intent to endanger life. Significantly, the terrorist organization responsible for the conspiracy was not Al Qaeda but the accused themselves. Their lawyers went on to raise a defence based on abuse of process by the Crown, also citing a violation of religious freedom of the accused and claiming that the police went too far in manufacturing the crime—that is, a defence of entrapment. On 29 July 2016, the defence of entrapment was founded for the first time in a Canadian terrorism case by the ruling of Madam Justice Bruce, which found that the RCMP had indeed manufactured the crime. In deciding to halt the prosecution of the charges, the presiding judge noted,

> There are no remedies less drastic than a stay of proceedings that will address the abuse of process. The spectre of the defendants serving a life sentence for a crime that the police manufactured by exploiting their vulnerabilities, by instilling fear that they would be killed if they backed out, and by quashing all doubts they had in the religious justifications for the crime, is offensive to our concept of fundamental justice. Simply put, the world has enough terrorists. We do not need the police to create more out of marginalized people who have neither the capacity nor sufficient motivation to do it themselves. (*R. v. Nuttall* 2016, para. 836)

The judge's ruling found that the RCMP exploited a vulnerable and marginalized couple who lacked the prerequisites to carry out a terrorist offence, resulting in the release of Nuttall and Korody after three years in custody. Yet the couple was dramatically rearrested by the police hours after their release on a terrorism peace bond. Rather than proceeding with hearing the peace bond application against the couple in July 2016, it was deferred by a provincial court judge pending a Crown appeal of the ruling that stayed their conviction. The Crown appeal was dismissed and the stay against conviction was upheld in December 2018, prompting the RCMP to withdraw peace bond proceedings against Nuttall and Korody.

However, this case has also left a gray cloud over the police. That the police now have a judicial record of manufacturing terror crime marks the worst possible critique for police terror investigations and serious confidence in public messaging relating to the urgency of anti-terror policing. Considering the 2 July 2013 press conference in retrospect, the RCMP did not lie to the media in suggesting that there was no international conspiracy and in identifying this attempted bombing as being "inspired" by Al Qaeda's ideology. However, the police communications failed to reveal anything about the social context of the accused—facts that would have played very badly for law enforcement in the media spectacle. These facts include (1) that the accused were unemployed methadone addicts who passed their time mainly by playing video games; (2) that there were serious and acknowledged issues relating to their mental health; (3) that the RCMP had used an undercover officer claiming to be affiliated with Al Qaeda as part of a five-month undercover operation, "Project Souvenir," to win the couple's trust, isolate them from their social circle, and coerce them into a plot to manufacture explosive devices for fear of being killed by Al Qaeda; (4) that the RCMP strongly urged the couple to adopt the Canada Day pressure-cooker plot as the most viable terrorist plot to pursue; (5) that the RCMP paid for the couple to attend a retreat to plan their crime but that the couple was unable to produce a viable plan without assistance, feedback, and coercive force applied by the RCMP; (6) that despite Nuttall's radical views, he did not have the ability, capacity, or penchant for violent activity nor the knowledge to create or conduct a violent terrorist plot; and (7) that the urgency and timing of the couple's plot to place improvised explosive devices on the grounds of the Victoria Legislature on Canada Day was the idea of the RCMP.

Based on what transpired at the 2 July 2013 press conference, it is evident that tightly presented media spectacles can unravel in the process of rigorous defence scrutiny and requisite obligations of disclosure on the part of the

Crown. Yet far before an incident goes before a court, policing and security agencies rely on communications practices to project an image of terror crime that pre-empts and shapes the public's opinion of the event. In using communications practices as a means of manufacturing terror spectacles, this approach is marshalled by claims of defending public safety by only revealing information that is for the good of the public.

Communications practices that seek to selectively present and omit details of alleged terrorism offences are not exclusive to the Nuttall and Korody case but have become an intrinsic aspect of the policing practices in the "war on terror." Police-choreographed communication practices deliberately control the flow of information through the media as a tool for influencing popular culture in favour of a strong social response toward fighting aspirational terror crimes. These practices have been evident throughout terrorism cases in shaping the public imaginary about diabolical Muslim terrorism, from Khawaja and his "hifi digi monster" to the case of the Toronto 18 (which we discuss below). Moreover, the sophistication of these communication practices appeared to be accelerated and amplified in the Nuttall and Korody case, as well as the case of Aaron Driver. It is thus instructive to consider the police communications strategies in relation to recent counter-terrorism events and their correlation with the legislative process. Here, we look at the Driver case and its relation to debates around the new ATA passed as Bill C-51.

Terror Spectacles and Selective Narrative: The Case of Aaron Driver

Aaron Driver was shot and killed by the RCMP outside of his home in Strathroy, Ontario, on 10 August 2016. Driver was identified as the subject in a martyrdom video, and a police tactical team surrounded his residence. Police intervention took place when Driver got into a taxi carrying a backpack that was suspected (correctly) to contain an explosive device. Driver proceeded to detonate the device on his person, which malfunctioned, instead releasing a cloud of white smoke. Wounded, Driver exited the vehicle, then police officers repeatedly shot and killed him.

In a unique performance of the terror spectacle, the RCMP coordinated a national news conference within twelve hours of Driver's death to screen a martyrdom video, reportedly received from the US Federal Bureau of Investigation (FBI), replete with a prepared press briefing. In the context of terrorism cases where disclosure of the source of international intelligence received by foreign agencies is subject to the most stringent legal protection and requires reciprocal diplomatic authorization for release, the video obtained through international intelligence-sharing was approved by US and Canadian governments to be strategically aired and served as the centrepiece of the Driver narrative. During the press conference, no details were released regarding the scope and nature of the national security investigation against Driver, dubbed "Project Sumo," apart from the fact that the investigation involved surveillance of Driver prior to his arrest under the terms of a terrorism peace bond. Additionally, no indication was given regarding the fact that a local London, Ontario, mosque was providing updates to the police on Driver and his views. Although the Canadian Security Intelligence Service (CSIS) was involved in Driver's file, no details have been provided regarding whether CSIS was involved in surveillance efforts that targeted him. And, no indication was given about the last RCMP meeting with Driver, whether he possessed a cell phone, how he had acquired a computer, and how he had managed to acquire components to build an explosive device.

The press conference and related information released by policing agencies have maintained significant gaps in explaining a chain of failures and inconsistencies in the management of the Driver case. A lack of explanation is particularly noteworthy given that Driver was detained under the terrorism peace bond provision of the Criminal Code, then released in February 2016 after agreeing to a series of onerous monitoring conditions and stipulations that prohibited him from using the internet or possessing a computer, laptop, or other device and banned his access to explosive materials. In providing only enough information to nourish and sustain the image of Driver as an ISIS-supporting monster, the media spectacle thrives on innuendo. Here, omitted and selectively controlled information operates to centre only the spectacular image of Driver and decentre the activities or inactivity of policing agencies. Within this vacuum of information, the RCMP maintains an implausible—if not worrying—position that between February and August 2016, Driver was not under surveillance. Although Driver's terms of release from prison required him to check in with the RCMP twice a month, senior RCMP officials emphatically repeated to the national media on 11 August 2016 that Driver was not under surveillance. The public has been left to conclude that there was no intelligence monitoring whatsoever to ensure that he was complying with ongoing conditions that he not have access to a computer, laptop, mobile device, explosives, or bomb-making components.

In the absence of any criminal proceedings, disclosure, or adversarial process to reveal the underpinnings of the police investigation into Driver's activities, we are left with a vacuum that has been filled by a selective narrative constructed by the police. This narrative suggests the need for more invasive policing powers to assist a worthy and highly vigilant struggle against a pervasive and uncontrolled phenomenon of Islamic terrorism. The police construction of Driver's crime also has profound implications for future policing efforts encouraging social expectations of permissiveness and supporting the pre-crime necessity of neutralizing the perceived Muslim purveyor of terrorist threats.

As particular ways of producing terrorism, communication strategies function on several levels. The RCMP press conferences from the Nuttall/ Korody and Driver cases are ideal examples of "cutting out devices" that simultaneously enact characterizations of terror monsters versus heroic police agents. During the Driver press conference, one journalist referred to the RCMP response to apprehend Driver as "a race against time" (MacCharles and Ballingall 2016), language that was adopted by the police, emphasizing the importance of maximizing the reach and efficiency of counter-terrorism policing powers. These communications reproduce what Aistrope calls the Muslim paranoia narrative: a deeply embedded system of representations that suggests young Muslims are both risky and at risk because of their susceptibility to a "paranoid and conspiracy-riven worldview, which is thought to thrive in alienated and disempowered communities" (2016, 183). As communications practices, the selective characterization of Muslim terrorists serves to reinforce augmented policing powers and foment a public desire to extend the "war on terror."[2] Yet these practices should also be understood as communicative strategies employed by policing and security agencies that are part of an ongoing, elite dialogue between law enforcement and the public. Considered communications practices, these police-controlled interventions are strategic interventions to shape the public's conceptions—and imaginations—of imminent Muslim terrorists. This dynamic was most evident during the rollout of the 2015 amendments to the ATA under Bill C-51, where the overwhelming weight of legal scholarship and analysis in response were squarely against both the necessity and legality of the proposed amendments.

Importantly, Bill C-51 was introduced following the 22 October 2014 attack in Ottawa by Michael Zehaf-Bibeau, and the parliamentary debates on C-51 were punctuated by the dramatic showing of Zehaf-Bibeau's martyrdom video. Although the shooting was quickly labelled as terrorism and used to justify the tougher security measures contained in the new ATA, the details of the video purporting to show the motivation and allegiance of the suspected shooter to ISIS was shown for the first time by the RCMP commissioner almost five months later, on 6 March 2015. At public deliberations before the Public Safety Committee reviewing Bill C-51, the occasion provided a highly dramatic—almost cinematic—revealing of the martyrdom video. In a national mediascape saturated with weeks of celebrating the heroism of the police and military in the wake of the attacks, the imagery of the now-dead Michael Zehaf-Bibeau pledging allegiance to ISIS was an archetype representation of the Islamic terrorist. From a strategically crafted backstage, the video was instrumentalized to support the enhancement of police powers in Bill C-51. Yet none of the amendments proposed by Bill C-51, according to then prime minister Harper, would impact or change the outcome of the Parliament Hill shooting. Nonetheless, the odious terror spectacle delivered with cinematic flare held important strategic significance. In his submission to the Public Safety Committee, Commissioner Paulson of the RCMP made a case for stronger measures to respond to terrorism crimes, including the adoption of lower thresholds to pursue terrorism peace bonds, which were adopted by the committee and included in the changes to the ATA. In a similar vein, the well-curated images of the Driver press conference diverted attention from police incompetence by alluding to broader debates on the need for more powers against encrypted telecommunications (Monaghan 2020). Such efforts shape public perceptions of imperfect policing strategies by suggesting the need for a more robust enabling environment for the proliferation of anti-terrorism powers. However, public opinion does not create terror crime in practice. The imagining of the perfect terrorist crime through selectively planned state communication strategies acts both as an expedient and necessary character foil that justifies a pre-existing political imperative for constructing better policing and legislative responses to terrorism crimes while facilitating the hegemonic and mutually reinforcing dialogue that defines terrorist crime in order to police it. As we further elaborate below, the police communications practices that make terrorism are instrumental in framing the criminalization practices that target specific individuals. By examining sentencing practices, we trace how courts reproduce logics of racialization and pre-emption against particular subjects who embody terrorism as an exceptional crime.

Making Terrorism: Sentencing Practices

With an increase in terrorism trials in Western countries, scholars have begun to detail sentencing practices associated with the "war on terror" (Aaronson 2013; de Goede, Simon, and Hoijtink 2014; de Goede and de Graaf 2013; van der Heide and Geenen 2015). De Goede and de Graaf have sketched how "the terrorist trial [is] a performative space where potential future terror is imagined, invoked, contested, and made real, in the proceedings and verdict, as well as through its wider media and societal echoes" (2013, 314). Underneath the imagination of future violence, what Chesney has called "anticipatory prosecution" (2007, 425), these trials focus on broader collections of rumours, statements, or musings captured by covert surveillance, associations, and aspirational plans. Cataloguing trials in the United States, Aaronson notes that of 508 cases from 2001 to August 2011, he "could count on one hand the number of actual terrorists . . . who posed a direct and immediate threat to the United States" (2013, 15). As authorities have aimed to infiltrate and disrupt potential terrorism plans at the earliest possible stages, all innuendos have become composites in the motives for an attack—with limited connection to the viability of such plots to become materialized. A divorce between aspirations and realizations was a key component of the Nuttall and Korody acquittals discussed earlier. Canadian courts, however, have accepted the anticipatory imaginings of terrorist violence in several other terrorism trials. We contend that these trials have been framed through police communications strategies that project the aspiring terrorists as highly organized, fanatical Muslims operating at the behest of a broader jihadist conspiracy that must be pre-empted before enacting unthinkable violence. To illustrate how racialized formations of the "war on terror" provide an exceptionalized treatment of future Islamic violence, we contract two case studies: the sentencing of Glen Gieschen and that of Toronto 18-member Saad Khalid.

Although little has been reported or written about Gieschen, he is among the most organized and well-trained would-be terrorists of the past two decades, though the case is less publicized than that of Corey Hurren (but highly similar). Gieschen was a member of the Canadian Armed Forces from 2008 to 2011 who then went on long-term disability (Slade 2014). Angered over compensation claims with Veterans Affairs Canada (VAC) regarding health care costs, he constructed a plan to attack a VAC office on the seventh floor of a downtown Calgary office tower. His plot was discovered after his wife, fearing he was suicidal, called the police. When the RCMP located Gieschen, he was sleeping in a utility shed, dressed in camo, with a .40 calibre semi-automatic handgun (ibid.). The RCMP found a significant cache of restricted combat weapons, explosives, and prohibited devices, including a .308 calibre semi-automatic rifle, body armour, several loaded magazines, a ballistic range-finder scope for shooting long distances, a laser sight for shooting at close range, night-vision binoculars, smoke grenades, one thousand rounds of ammunition, and components from which he would be able to construct fifteen metal pipe bombs as well as a potentially lethal chemical bomb (Graveland 2015a; Slade 2014). The cache of weaponry found under Gieschen's control easily eclipsed arms found in any other cases where individuals have been charged under the ATA in Canada. Moreover, evidence that was found included detailed plans of the office building and elaborate reconnaissance videos and photographs. Gieschen's attack was laid out, step by step, in a written plan on his laptop that included killing guards, setting off explosives and chemical bombs, stealing computer data, and escaping via a train yard where he would use explosives to rupture chemical-carrying rail cars, set-off an adjacent gas line, and rupture a gas pump station (Slade 2014). Reports underlined that Gieschen was upset with the VAC over his claim that he developed multiple sclerosis because of a flu shot while in the military.

Our purpose is not to call for more punitive measures toward Mr. Gieschen but to highlight disparities in treatment between those who have been made into terrorists and those, like Mr. Gieschen, who escape the terrorism-making practices of the police and security establishment. Gieschen's trial illustrated that his aspirational and sophisticated plans, his military training, and his possession of high-powered weaponry and explosives all pointed toward a clearer potential for carrying out political violence. Yet the trial proceedings against Gieschen are fundamentally different from what we detail against Khalid and others charged under the ATA. For example, despite the plans, weaponry, and motives, Gieschen was not charged with ATA terrorism offences. He was never labelled as a potential terrorist by police, and there were no press conferences, no national media attention, and no police representations to parliament demanding more tools and resources. During the trial, Gieschen was similarly never labelled a potential terrorist by the Crown. Despite his willingness to engage in political violence, the Crown did not make Gieschen a terrorist, demonstrating a lenience toward him not evident in other trials against would-be terrorists.

Lenience and compassion toward Gieschen were particularly evident in his sentencing. Not contesting the details of his plan or his political motives, Gieschen pled guilty to three charges: possession of a firearm, possession of a prohibited weapon, and possession of a weapon. Four other weapons and explosives charges were dropped. Unlike terrorism trial defendants who have often received life sentences, Gieschen was only sentenced to four months, with an eighteen-month credit for time served. No restrictions were placed on parole eligibility, although he is subject to a lifetime firearms ban.

Despite restraining from characterizing Gieschen's plot as terrorist violence, the court nonetheless engaged in an imaginative future that represented it for its catastrophic potential. Justice Sean Dunning claimed, "If Mr. Gieschen had followed through with all or part of his plan, the results would have been catastrophic for those working in the Bashaw building and for first responders who would have come upon a nightmare of death and destruction" (Graveland 2015c). Dunning noted Gieschen's political motivations, suggesting that Canada is not accustomed to individuals "seeking to avenge perceived slights to advance their political agenda" (ibid.). Adding that this was a "very serious" case that was "chilling in its meticulous planning," Dunning nonetheless believed Gieschen's remorse (ibid.). Gieschen was presented as an empathetic figure who recognized his wrongdoings and was given a sentence at the lowest end of the four to six years requested by the Crown.

Sympathy and lenience from the courts and the Crown were matched in the local media coverage, which included sympathetic headlines like "Ex-soldier Who Plotted Deadly Attack on Calgary Veterans Affairs Office Apologizes in Court" (Martin 2015). Media emphasized Gieschen's "emotional" apology (ibid.), underlined how he was regretful for his actions, and repeated a claim from his defence that he did not intend to carry out the plot. In contrast to many of the ATA trials where subjects were exposed to lengthy periods of intimate surveillance, Gieschen's trial did not include long dissections of his motives or politics. During terrorism trials in Canada, as well as in other jurisdictions, intensive surveillance campaigns produced large volumes of anecdotal and inchoate evidence about the politics, character, personal beliefs, and often odd social mannerisms of the subjects—all of which were magnified and extensively scrutinized. This scrutiny extended not only to an examination of potentially "radical" Islamic beliefs but also to a scrutiny of the subjects' social norms and identities. Not possessing a pre-crime identity that is subject to national security surveillance, Gieschen's motives and personal character was spared the unrelenting scrutiny of constant surveillance. Despite large volumes of evidence regarding his capabilities and motives, the absence of intimate surveillance changes the focus of a trial setting, allowing for more empathetic punishment. In addition to having a defendant with an identity that solicits public sympathy—that of a damaged military veteran—Gieschen's treatment at trial presents a hard contrast to the treatment of Saad Khalid.

Khalid was a member of the Toronto 18 plot and, at nineteen years old at the time of his arrest, occupied a subordinate role within the cell. Receiving extensive media coverage, in large part because of the communication practices associated with media-coordinated arrests, the Toronto 18 plot included far-fetched ideas but limited resources and little capacity to carry out mass explosions. Nonetheless, Khalid was arrested when trying to purchase the ammonium nitrate needed for their ambitious idea of building three one-tonne explosives. Unlike Gieschen, the Toronto 18 had no military training or access to sophisticated arms and explosives and only sought them once they were infiltrated—and somewhat encouraged—by undercover operatives.[3] Not having any specific sources for acquiring materials, the plotters googled to find providers, which led them to an RCMP gotcha site. After making arrangements with the covert RCMP officers to purchase the fertilizer, Khalid and his associate Saad Gaya put on their custom-made "Student Farmer" T-shirts and drove a rented truck into a SWAT-style takedown that was video recorded and released to the Canadian media. Khalid and Gaya did not carry any weapons and did not have access to, or any specific knowledge of, means to transform the fertilizer into explosives.

Although the courts recognized that Khalid (and Gaya) were subordinates to the cell leaders who had specific details about the potential targets and technical details about bomb making, Khalid received no sympathy nor reduced moral blameworthiness. The courts rejected Khalid's attempt to reduce his level of moral culpability based on his lack of detailed knowledge about the plot, suggesting that "wilful blindness is the same as knowledge in the eyes of the criminal law" (R. v. Khalid 2010, para. 3). Despite the overall lack of operationalization of the Toronto 18's plot, as well as Khalid's limited knowledge of plot details, he was nonetheless classified as a terrorist and sentenced under a much more punitive regime than the usual for mere explosives charges. Originally sentenced to fourteen years, the Crown appealed to have the sentence increased. On appeal, the court reasoned that the original sentence was gravely insufficient and raised the penalty to twenty years with an order under S.743.6(1.2) of the Criminal Code to require half the sentence be served before he was eligible for full parole.

In similar ways to Gieschen's and other terrorism trials, the sentencing relied on a speculative imagining of potential future actions. Underlining the need to be punitive toward the imagined catastrophe, Khalid's sentencing decision quotes from the trial of the Toronto 18 leader, Amara (*R. v. Amara* 2010): "[The plot] would have caused catastrophic damage . . . killing or causing serious injuries to people in the path of the blast waves and force" (*R. v. Khalid* 2010, para. 11). However, unlike Gieschen, the speculated futures invoked for the Toronto 18 required an imagining of the destructive capacities of the explosive as well as an imagining that the plotters possessed a capacity to acquire the resources needed to actualize the attack. Again, quoting from *Amara* (para. 201), the court stressed,

> There is *no dispute* that what would have occurred was multiple death and injuries. On the timetable indicated in the facts with detonation occurring at 9 a.m., the impact would have been magnified as workers arrived for work. With one ton bombs at each location, the results would have been catastrophic. What this case revealed was spine-chilling. I agree with Mr. Lacy that the potential for loss of life existed on *a scale never before seen in Canada*. It was *almost unthinkable* without the suggestion that metal chips would be put in the bombs. Had the plan been implemented it would have changed the lives of many, if not all Canadians forever. (emphasis added)

The court was unequivocal: there was no dispute that Khalid represented a materialization of a spine-chilling terrorist who is fully capable of carrying out almost unthinkable violence on a scale never "seen" in Canada. Unlike Gieschen, who received sympathetic understanding, Khalid was no mere subordinate, or wayward youth, or citizen facing a difficult life or emotional experiences. By foregrounding only the speculative and spectacular possibilities of his plot, the court suggests he is nothing short of a moral monster, a heartless terrorist that must be interpreted via the "war on terror."

A key distinction for the construction of a terrorist is the place of Islam. The motive for his political violence was featured prominently in the Toronto 18 trials because of the extensive surveillance campaign and the ability of police work to frame the criminal proceedings. The court proceedings underlined that the roots of Khalid's moral depravity were religious. It was framed as Islamic terrorist violence through a lens of clashing civilizations and, more specifically, Islam's irrational hatred of the West. In raising the length of his prison sentence, the court repeated Khalid's psychological assessment: "His motivation does not flow from anti-sociality, impulsivity or psychopathy, but rather from his religious beliefs, his sympathy toward the extreme Muslim cause and his perceived need to take steps to stand up against the Western world, and to influence change" (R. v. Khalid 2010, para. 20). Moreover, the politics of Muslim religiosity are framed as a distinct set of political motives—motives that highlight Khalid's antitheticality to Canadian identity. Invoking the soil in a typically dramatic representation of nationhood, the court writes, "Fuelled by his religious and ideological convictions, he was prepared to engage in the mass murder of innocent men, women and children on Canadian soil" (para. 35). Framed as Islam's violent orientation against the West, Khalid's criminal blameworthiness is not understandable through other explanations of crime. It can only be understood as terrorism's irrational hatred. In contrast, political violence was categorized as a traditional crime in Gieschen's trial, where personal problems and poor decisions were at play, and therefore humanized the plotter. Despite Khalid's limited knowledge of the plot, his expressions of remorse, and the plot's general non-operationalizability, the court suggests that Khalid's part was not a "mere mistake" and should only be understood as a "diabolical plot . . . fuelled by fanatical beliefs" (para. 50). While Gieschen's violent plot was constructed as horrendous, his remorse was deemed authentic, and various mitigating circumstances were accepted to lessen the punitive sanctions imposed. For Khalid and other terrorism trial defendants, expressions of remorsefulness were rejected, and mitigating circumstances presented to lessen their punishments were re-intercepted as evidence of further riskiness.

In sentencing, Khalid's treatment was thoroughly embedded in racialized discourses of the "war on terror." Despite several mitigating factors, Khalid was spared no lenience. The court listed Khalid's mitigating circumstances, noting that he was young, a first-time offender, had expressed remorse, had rejected radical views, was supported by his family, and was considered to have a high likelihood of rehabilitation. Yet all mitigating factors were rejected. The court speculated that "youthful first offenders present as attractive recruits to sophisticated terrorists," and therefore the court advocated for a "more punitive approach" against Khalid and other would-be (Muslim) terrorists

(*R. v. Khalid* 2010, paras. 46–47). Sentencing terrorists, the court reasoned, must be appreciated because "terrorism is a crime unto itself" (para. 32), thereafter outlining how "terrorism is a unique crime and why we believe it must be treated differently from conventional crimes" (paras. 32–34). Despite the Crown asking for eighteen to twenty years, the court suggested Khalid was deserving of twenty to twenty-five years (and imply he could have received a life sentence). Taking the high end of the Crown's request, Khalid was sentenced to twenty years and deemed ineligible for parole until he had served at least half his sentence. Concluding with highly moralistic claims toward Islamic violence, the court stated, "Stern sentences in that range are meant to send a clear message—those who chose to pursue deadly terrorist activities from or in Canada will pay a very heavy price" (para. 56). In many ways, the contrast between the Gieschen and Khalid cases are ideal to illustrate how making terrorism is driven by crude depictions of Islam that have endured through the "war on terror." While orientalist discourses of irrational violence in Islam predate 9/11 (Stampnitzky 2013), the "war on terror" has dramatically intensified how police and criminal justice systems exceptionalize Muslims who have been framed as terrorists. Through the differential treatment in the cases of Khalid and Gieschen, one man is made into a remorseless and irredeemable terrorist, while the other is viewed as a sympathetic and wayward Canadian. In other words, it is not the actions themselves but how the individuals are reconstructed through associations, identities, and political categories—a reconstitutive imaginary that accords (or does not) with the prefabricated identities of terrorism and the terrorists of the "war on terror."

As the case studies of Khalid and Gieschen demonstrate, a focus on sentencing practices is important for tracing how police practices and the criminal justice system engage in making terrorism. Ericson (1981) noted that policing practices represent a central function in making terrorism, and yet we also wish to highlight how socio-legal analysis can shed light on the broader imaginaries of race and how pre-emption can shape what (and who) gets made into terrorism (and terrorists). Furthermore, an analysis of sentencing practices is revealing of how we make terrorism precisely because of the idealized role of sentencing within the criminal justice system. The general characterization of sentencing is that it operates as an objective, disembodied process based on the weighing of risks and mitigations as well as a careful assessment of the facts. Yet the speculative character and normative discourses that are common in terrorism trials lay bare how the normative environment produced in the "war on terror" functions as a racialized system where "terrorism" is almost exclusively applied to Muslims with extreme punitiveness and police-mediated fanfare.

Discussion and Conclusion(s)

In this chapter, we selected case studies to illustrate how police communication and sentencing practices are performed to decide what activities can be made into "terrorism" and what individuals are made into "terrorists." The case studies are illustrative of the racialized character of terror-making and the pre-emptive policing practices of the "war on terror." Using a socio-legal analysis that emphasizes how race, religion, and police practices shape the character of criminalization, we stress that these examples are not outliers but emblematic of the racialized construct of terrorism in the "war on terror." Terrorism cases almost exclusively abide by the characteristics that we detailed at the outset of the chapter—they almost exclusively target Muslims, they exhibit a highly punitive and spectacular dimension, and they address almost exclusive "aspirational" plots where the security practices themselves are embedded in logics of pre-emptive governance.

Securitization practices continue their expansion, now entering a third decade of the "war on terror." A notable area of expansion has been the inclusion of far-right violence into the counter-terrorism efforts by the policing and security establishment. However, while some efforts are harnessed to expand the reach of security powers toward non-Muslim entities, the vast majority of counter-terrorism resources remain directed toward Muslims. More importantly, the deeply embedded anti-Muslim racism within the security establishment will not be ameliorated by expanding security and policing efforts. While addressing that forms of violence and harm are of the utmost importance, there remains a broad array of tools to govern social harms that are far more effective than punitive policing and, at the same time, do not risk rationalizing increasingly illiberal surveillance and social control powers that have become central mechanisms of national security policing.

And yet with the expansion of security governance practices and resources, there have been no efforts to expand—let alone maintain—democratic oversight or accountability of policing and security agencies. In fact, we contend that systems of oversight in the Canadian context have dramatically withered under the intense proliferation of security governance practices. Outside of costly and largely ineffective litigations, accountability systems are virtually non-existent. While the formal processes of oversight accountability have been left to degrade, we contend that the normalization of pre-emptive practices presents an even more ominous threat to liberal standards of democracy. As security practices become increasingly routinized, their abilities to self-rationalize and self-proliferate outside any domain of the social become further entrenched. Moreover, as we have demonstrated with police communication and sentencing practices, these efforts to produce terrorism are deeply political. Although policing and security agencies often represent themselves as neutral or apolitical, these practices inscribe a politics onto the world—a politics that amplifies and spreads the pre-crime imaginary onto the world. As Huysmans notes, "Security is a political practice by virtue of always bringing into play and being connected to certain conceptions of politics" (2014, 13). As a technique of security, the production of terrorists and terrorism is a specific technique of governance that cannot be separated from the "war on terror." It is also a politics that is revealing itself as fundamentally racialized and discriminatory. In constructing certain crimes as "terrorism" or individuals as "terrorists," the politics of the "war on terror" are played out on specific denizens. As security governance continues to embed pre-crime imaginaries into an expanding range of social practices, the likelihood of those agencies becoming unbound from democratic or moral anchors increases. Likewise, the probability that the rights of vulnerable or racialized communities become liminal or suspendable increases.

Notes

1 This figure is our calculation based on triangulating case records, media accounts, and government sources.
2 On 16 August 2016, five days following the national media conference, the Canadian Association of Chiefs of Police passed a resolution calling for suspects to hand over digital passwords during a police investigation.
3 Toronto 18 defendants attempted an entrapment defence but were unsuccessful (see R. v. Ahmad 2009).

References

Aaronson, Trevor. 2013. *The Terror Factory: Inside the FBI's Manufactured War on Terrorism*. Brooklyn, NY: Ig.

Aistrope, Tim. 2016. "The Muslim Paranoia Narrative in Counter-radicalisation Policy." *Critical Studies on Terrorism* 9 (2): 182–204.

CBC. 2016. "Aaron Driver's Cabbie Plans Legal Action Against Police." CBC News online, 18 August 2016. http://www.cbc.ca/news/canada/windsor/aaron-driver -taxi-bombing-1.3726701.

Chesney, Robert. 2007. "Beyond Conspiracy? Anticipatory Prosecution and the Challenge of Unaffiliated Terrorism." *Southern California Law Review* 80 (3): 425–502.

Cotler, Irwin. 2001. "Thinking Outside the Box." In *The Security of Freedom: Essays on Canada's Anti-terrorism Bill*, edited by Ronald J. Daniels, Patrick Macklem, and Kent Roach, 111–29. Toronto: University of Toronto Press.

de Goede, Marieke. 2015. "Speculative Values and Courtroom Contestations." *South Atlantic Quarterly* 114 (2): 355–75.

de Goede, Marieke, and Beatrice de Graaf. 2013. "Sentencing Risk: Temporality and Precaution in Terrorism Trials." *International Political Sociology* 7 (3): 313–31.

de Goede, Marieke, Stephanie Simon, and Marijn Hoijtink. 2014. "Performing Pre-emption." *Security Dialogue* 45 (5): 411–22.

Ericson, Richard. 1981. *Making Crime: A Study of Detective Work*. Toronto: University of Toronto Press.

———. 2007. *Crime in an Insecure World*. London: Polity.

Ericson, Richard, and Kevin Haggerty. 1997. *Policing the Risk Society*. Toronto: University of Toronto Press.

Graveland, Bill. 2015a. "Sentence Delay for Former Soldier Who Planned Attack on Veterans Affairs Office." Estevan Mercury, 30 January 2015. http://www .estevanmercury.ca/sentence-delay-for-former-soldier-who-planned-attack-on -veterans-affairs-office-1.1748067#sthash.t6Y2eLLG.dpuf.

———. 2015b. "Glen Gieschen Gets 4 Years for Firearms, Explosive Charges." CBC News, 24 February 2015. http://www.cbc.ca/news/canada/calgary/glen-gieschen -gets-4-years-for-firearms-explosive-charges-1.2970194.

———. 2015c. "Ex-soldier Gets 4 Years for Planned Attack on Veterans Affairs Office." MacLeans.ca, 25 February 2015. http://www.macleans.ca/news/canada/ex -soldier-gets-4-years-for-planned-attack-on-veterans-affairs-office/.

Huysmans, Jef. 2014. *Security Unbound: Enacting Democratic Limits*. New York: Routledge.

Keenan, Kouri, and Joan Brockman. 2010. *Mr. Big: Exposing Undercover Operations in Canada*. Halifax, Nova Scotia: Fernwood.

Kellner, Douglas. 2003. *Media Spectacle*. New York: Routledge.

Kinsman, Gary, and Patrizia Gentile. 2010. *The Canadian War on Queers: National Security as Sexual Regulation*. Vancouver: UBC Press.

Kinsman, Gary William, Dieter K. Buse, and Mercedes Steedman. 2000. *Whose National Security? Canadian State Surveillance and the Creation of Enemies*. Toronto: Between the Lines.

Kundnani, Arun. 2014. *The Muslims Are Coming! Islamophobia, Extremism, and the Domestic War on Terror*. New York: Verso.

MacCharles, T., and A. Ballingall. 2016. "Race Against Time Stopped Terror Attack: RCMP Fatally Confront Ontario Daesh Sympathizer Bent on 'Dreadful' Carnage." *Toronto Star*, 12 August 2016.

Martin, Kevin. 2015. "Ex-soldier Who Plotted Deadly Attack on Calgary Veterans Affairs Office Apologizes in Court." CTV News, 11 February 2015. https://www.ctvnews.ca/canada/ex-soldier-who-plotted-attack-on-veterans-affairs-office-apologizes-1.2232315.

McCulloch, Jude, and Sharon Pickering. 2009. "Pre-crime and Counter-terrorism: Imagining Future Crime in the 'War on Terror.'" *British Journal of Criminology* 49 (5): 628–45.

———, eds. 2013. *Borders and Crime: Pre-crime, Mobility and Serious Harm in an Age of Globalization*. New York: Palgrave Macmillan.

McCulloch, Jude, and Dean Wilson. 2015. *Pre-crime: Pre-emption, Precaution and the Future*. New York: Routledge.

Monaghan, Jeffrey, and Adam Molnar. 2016. "Radicalisation Theories, Policing Practices, and 'the Future of Terrorism?'" *Critical Studies on Terrorism* 9 (3): 393–413.

Monaghan, Jeffrey. 2013. "Terror Carceralism: Surveillance, Security Governance and De/Civilization." *Punishment and Society* 15 (1): 3–22.

———. 2020. "Preforming Counter-terrorism: Police Newsmaking and the Dramaturgy of Security." *Crime, Media, Culture: An International Journal* 18, no. 1. https://doi.org/10.1177/1741659020966370.

Nagra, Balgit. 2017. *Securitized Citizens: Canadian Muslims' Experiences of Race Relations and Identity Formation Post-9/11*. Toronto: University of Toronto Press.

Neal, Andrew. 2012. "Normalization and Legislative Exceptionalism: Counterterrorist Lawmaking and the Changing Times of Security Emergencies." *International Political Sociology* 6:260–76.

Pratt, John. 2007. *Penal Populism*. New York: Routledge.

Puar, Jasbir. 2007. *Terrorist Assemblages: Homonationalism in Queer Times*. Durham, NC: Duke University Press.

Rana, Junaid. 2016. "The Racial Infrastructure of the Terror-Industrial Complex." *Social Text* 34 (4): 111–38.

R. v. Ahmad. 2009. CanLII 84788 (ON SC).

R. v. Amara. 2010. ONSC 441.

R. v. Khalid. 2010. ONCA 861.

R. v. Nuttall. 2016. BCSC 1404.

Slade, Daryl. 2014. "No Publication Ban for Man and His Family in Weapons Case." *Calgary Herald*, 27 November 2014. http://calgaryherald.com/news/local-news/no-publication-ban-for-man-and-his-family-in-weapons-case.

Stampnitzky, Lisa. 2013. *Disciplining Terror: How Experts Invented "Terrorism."* Cambridge: Cambridge University Press.

van der Heide, Liesbeth, and Jip Geenen. 2015. "Preventing Terrorism in the Courtroom–the Criminalisation of Preparatory Acts of Terrorism in the Netherlands." *Security and Human Rights* 26 (2–4): 162–92.

Zedner, Lucia. 2007. "Pre-crime and Post-criminology?" *Theoretical Criminology* 11 (2): 261–81.

4 Law, Gendered Violence, and Justice

Critically Engaging #MeToo

Emily Lockhart, Katrin Roots, and Heather Tasker

Law's engagement with sexual violence has been a topic of debate, critique, and advocacy for over five decades, with efforts largely focused on securing arrests and convictions against perpetrators. What has been asked more recently are questions around what acts are positioned as sexual harms, which of these harms are legible to the law, and who has to perpetrate and be victimized by this violence for the law to be propelled to act (see Cossman 2021; Hannem and Schneider 2022). #MeToo has drawn attention to abuses and harms that have previously been ignored or failed to spark action. In demanding attention from legal actors and the general public, feminists working to advance the politics of the #MeToo movement have helped secure arrests, trials, and convictions of celebrities long accused of sexual violence and harassment and have positioned gendered abuse as an issue central to social justice advancements.

The achievements of #MeToo have not gone unchallenged, nor have they resulted in unequivocal social good. While celebrity cases draw attention and demand media coverage, a myriad of other modes of violence continue to be unseen by and remain unintelligible to the law. In this chapter, we examine the evolution and impact of #MeToo and the ways the movement reiterates both earlier feminist activism and critiques of alignment with formal law. We argue that #MeToo, while commendable and necessary, at times contributes to both neoliberal and carceral feminist frameworks. In effect, the #MeToo movement has not meaningfully challenged the structural and economic conditions that give rise to gendered violence in the first place. Our goal here is not to undermine the strides that have been made by the #MeToo movement in drawing much needed attention to the issue of sexual violence and in starting the process of addressing, at least in policy, some issues that urgently need to be addressed. Instead, our aim is to encourage change that has systemic impacts rather than only technical developments and the transitory satisfaction of celebrity accountability. We demonstrate how the contemporary #MeToo movement and the resulting legal responses to sexual violence and abuse show similarities to earlier feminist efforts to engage the law in response to gender-based violence. Through this historicization, we draw out the processes that make law's recession and active occlusion of some violent acts possible and examine the means through which these are invisibilized as acts of violence by law.

This chapter uncovers the discursive and ideological overlap between second-wave feminist activism and the current #MeToo movement. We begin by describing the #MeToo movement and exploring its politics, potentials, and limitations. We then advance some central critiques related to liberal feminism's continued reliance on the criminal legal system and how this contributes to whitewashing gendered and sexual violence.[1] Finally, we move to a discussion of how this approach divorces gendered violence from intersecting oppressions related to race and poverty, resulting in the invisibilization of the law's own victims. Our argument is not that #MeToo has not contributed to advancements against gendered violence, but rather that these developments remain narrow in defining what is read as violence and who are read as victims and perpetrators and fails to capture the violence built into the law itself. We argue that the hypervisibility of online and broadly publicized activism, while undoubtedly serving a purpose, does not apply equally to all survivors of sexual violence. Any legal developments that emerge as a result of targeted activist efforts do not universalize this progress as an enactment of justice for all. Indeed, what has happened with #MeToo is a clear example of the politics of liberal feminism, reiterating similar patterns and processes we saw in relation to intimate partner violence and sexual violence in the 1970s and '80s. The spectacularism attached to cases related to the #MeToo movement has served to stand in for sexual harm broadly; the attention these events receive is powerful in mobilizing limited legal responses, but in drawing the eye to spectacular and individual cases, the everyday experiences and executions of violence—including violence committed by and through law—remain routinized and invisibilized, and, when seen, are barely read as violence at all.

Critical Feminist Engagement with #MeToo

We are living in a moment of fourth-wave, digital feminism, defined by its ability to traverse global boundaries, with activists mobilized within networked communities. This wave is largely ridden by young millennial and Generation Z women. A desire to carve out a space for new expressions of online feminist activism characterizes this fourth-wave political project, with social media opening spheres of political participation for young women (Kim and Ringrose 2018). Young feminists are increasingly using social media technologies to develop their feminist identities and employing online platforms to assert themselves in the political landscape (Keller 2016). Online feminist activism can be influential, connective, and contagious in enabling activism offline and leading to material changes. A recent example is the "We Need Consent" campaign created and led by Canadian teenagers Tessa Hill and Lia Valente. This online campaign and petition to challenge rape culture in sexual education curricula was embraced by the Ontario government and used to reform provincial health curriculum in 2015 (Ostroff 2016). Of course, not all e-petitions or hashtag campaigns lead to these types of policy changes, but this is an example of the transformative potential of digital activism in the era of fourth-wave feminism. Feminist activists have used social media to forge global campaigns and connect people around the world, uniting around shared goals of challenging and transforming the sexist cultural norms that continue to contribute to sexual and gender-based violence. The ability to create change, both social and legal, in regard to sexual harassment with the help of digital means is worth serious attention. The most famous example of a movement of this nature is #MeToo.

#MeToo has fuelled the trendiness that was already beginning to surround feminism, with celebrities and politicians embracing the identity and media campaigns calling for individual women to rise up and call out sexism. Yet some scholars have argued that this emphasis on individual action ignores the structural and economic conditions that contribute to sexual and gender-based violence in the first place (Gash and Harding 2018; Rottenberg 2019). As Catherine Rottenberg writes, "Neoliberal feminism helps reify White and class privilege as well as heteronormativity, thereby lending itself to neo-conservative and xenophobic agendas" (42). From its popular emergence on social media as a powerful movement, #MeToo has continued to attract intense media attention, which helps to sustain its visibility. However, what is also clear is that this media attention and sustained visibility is largely held up by white, cis-gendered celebrity women that have come forward (Hannem and Schneider 2022; Rottenberg 2019). According to JoAnn Wypijewski (2020), while sex is a complicated and complex subject, the media coverage of #MeToo put forward one set of stories and one type of explanation about the subject. Wypijewski argues that the dominant discussion of #MeToo has been driven by white, middle-class feminists whose liberal politics do not consider intersecting operations of oppression. This is not to say that the potential of #MeToo necessarily must be limited to this discourse; indeed, one of the strengths of emerging movements and the democratization of feminist engagement is that they open some space for diverse perspectives and outcomes. However, this does not in itself mitigate the continued tendency to position white women and liberal approaches as representative of sex-based discrimination and violence. The individualistic tendencies of the movement that celebrate the *me* in #MeToo are not successful in creating structural change or making collective political demands for systemic change, "ultimately atomising each person who uses the hashtag" in a process that is symptomatic of liberal and neoliberal feminism (Rottenberg 2019, 45). By failing to centre a structural critique, the movement continues to leave behind those who are often most vulnerable to violence—sexual or otherwise—such as immigrants; migrant workers; domestic workers; low-income, racialized, queer, and sex working women; and non-binary folks.

The original iteration of the #MeToo movement was started by civil rights activist Tarana Burke in 2006. The aim of this grassroots activism was to help and support women and girls (mainly of colour) who had survived sexual violence. Fast-forward eleven years to 2017, and the movement looked very different. On October 15, 2017, after the *New York Times* (Kantor and Twohey 2017) released a story detailing allegations of sexual abuse against well-known Hollywood producer Harvey Weinstein, actress Alyssa Milano took to Twitter with Burke's phrase, calling on anyone who had experienced sexual harassment or abuse to use social media and come together under the hashtag (#) "MeToo." In the tweeting age, Milano's prominence as a white, wealthy, attractive celebrity was a vehicle to make women's rights advocacy more palatable and instantly accessible to millions. Milano's tweet quickly caught on, rapidly reaching other women and being retweeted nearly half a million times over a twenty-four-hour period. #MeToo generated vast media attention as cases picked up across the political spectrum. Headlines about sexual assault and harassment allegations against wealthy men in powerful positions continued to emerge. Harvey Weinstein was charged and, on March 11, 2020, sentenced to twenty-three years in prison for rape and sexual assault.[2] After Weinstein was called to account for his sexually violent behaviour in October 2017, it seemed that the flood gates on social media had opened, and over the span of a few months, multiple men in power were making headlines for sexual assault and harassment allegations. #MeToo hypervisibilized the popular trials of powerful men such as Harvey Weinstein, Bill Cosby, Larry Nasar, and Jeffrey Epstein, which captured public attention, served as household entertainment, and became etched into the cultural memory. Nasar pled guilty to twenty counts of first-degree sexual assault against minors and was sentenced to 40–125 years in prison (Barr and Murphy 2018). Epstein was first sentenced for procuring a minor for prostitution but was released on house arrest. He was later charged and convicted of sex trafficking and was sentenced to a New York State jail where he died by suicide (BBC News 2019). Cosby was tried and convicted in 2018 for drugging and sexual assault. While the conviction was initially upheld on appeal, it was overturned in June 2021 by the Pennsylvania Supreme Court. In a move indicative of the fallibility of legal progress in sexual violence cases, the court found that the district attorney had an obligation to honour his predecessor's promise not to charge Cosby (Dale 2021; for discussion of the trial and media coverage, see Hannem and Schneider 2022). These cases are the tip of the iceberg in the #MeToo movement,[3] as many powerful men faced legal action for sexual abuse and workplace sexual harassment.

Prior to the rise of #MeToo, there was the Canadian case of Jian Ghomeshi, a famous media personality whose sexual misconduct was well known within the show business community but who for years was not held accountable for it. In November 2014, Ghomeshi was charged with four counts of sexual assault and one count of overcoming resistance by choking against three complainants. In January 2015, he was charged with an additional three counts of sexual assault, but by May of the same year, two of the charges were dropped by the Crown attorney. The controversial trial ended in Ghomeshi's acquittal on the remaining five charges as the judge found that the complainants were not credible (Johnston, Coulling, and Kilty 2020). Although the case predated the #MeToo movement and resulted in a verdict that differed from those of Weinstein, Epstein, and others, it nonetheless embodies the typical #MeToo scenario and fuelled public discussion about sexual assault, consent, and carceralism, contributing to a rise in activism against sexual violence (for discussion, see Hannem and Schneider 2022).

The celebrations of convictions in most of these cases can be understood as reaffirming the legitimacy of law in establishing what is a harm. Brenda Cossman notes that the critique around the absence of law coming from feminist commentators is itself "symptomatic of the broader role of law in legal regulation of sexual violence: Law has long been the arbiter of sexual violence both defining harms and deciding whether that harm has occurred. Even in its apparent absence, law is, it is argued, deeply present" (2019, 19). Through this process, harms against certain people are pushed to the forefront and come to characterize sexual violence in our current time. The legal response to Weinstein, Nasar, and Epstein sent a message that no amount of wealth and power can shield sexual predators. The cases that were brought forward and ultimately resulted in convictions relied as much on the identity and credibility of the victims as on the facts. Of the dozens of women levelling accusations against the above-named abusers, only a handful were represented in court based on the details of their particular experiences, the dates of the assaults, and the perceived reliability and consistency of the survivors' stories. This particular construction and presentation of victimhood legitimizes the experiences of this harm and identifies these acts as violence, in part because they have been committed against someone who fits society's image of the "ideal victim" of sexual assault: one who is young, vulnerable, and does not inhabit spaces of risk (Gotell 2008). Most of these cases expose sexual assault and harassment against young (mostly white) women. Importantly, many of the victims/survivors in these popular trials were actors, models, directors, Olympic and US gymnasts, high school students, and so on. These young women fit the standards of good victimhood, which, according to Lise Gotell, is "built on exclusions that draw on race and class-based ideologies'" (867). Their abusers were men in positions of power, which facilitated the exploitation and control over the victims/survivors. The sexual assault trials allowed a reaffirmation of the law's power to define criminality but also victimhood. Through this performance of the law's power, violence against those who do not fit within the scope of legibility to a tweeting and hashtagging public and who are not positioned as "ideal victims" is invisibilized. The insidious nature of invisibilization serves to hide the countless operations of violence inflicted. Law asserts its power to define harm through the recognition of certain victims and by proceeding with some cases; this selectivity comes to represent the violence that is most meaningful or most egregious to the public. In this process, we see a reassertion of the same hierarchies and exclusions that feminists have drawn attention to for over fifty years.

Historically, where legal advancements in the area of gender-based and sexual violence are concerned, not all women have benefited equally, with poverty, race, sexual orientation, gender-identity, (dis)ability, and age being important factors (Bakht 2012; Crenshaw 1991; Levine and Meiners 2020; Lindberg, Campeau, and Campbell 2012). Changes to sexual assault laws that took place in the 1980s and 1990s failed to challenge cultural narratives of rape. This is particularly so in relation to Black women, who are often depicted as savage, promiscuous, and sexually aggressive (Crenshaw 1991; Irwing 2008; Manatu-Rupert 2000), and Indigenous women, who continue to be charac-terized by degrading references such as "squaw, Indian princess and sexually available brown woman" (Hunt 2013, 87). Such stereotypes often influence police decision-making around charging and the case-building strategies of defence and Crown attorneys in sexual assault cases (Bakht 2012; Irwing 2008; Lindberg, Campeau, and Campbell 2012). In Canada, Indigenous women are three times more likely to suffer violence when compared with white women and are significantly more likely to be killed (Palmater 2016). Despite the stereotypes insisted on by conservative politicians and lawmakers that this violence is inflicted by Indigenous men, Indigenous women are less likely to be killed by an intimate partner than other women in Canada (ibid.) Consider, for instance, the findings of Human Rights Watch (2013), which documented numerous human rights violations committed against Indigenous women and girls by police in British Columbia, including "young girls pepper-sprayed and Tasered; a 12-year-old girl attacked by a police dog; a 17-year-old punched repeatedly by an officer who had been called to help her; women strip-searched by male officers; and women injured due to excessive force used during arrest." Human Rights Watch also reported on numerous instan-ces of Royal Canadian Mounted Police (RCMP) officers sexually assaulting Indigenous women and girls. In one such case, officers took a woman outside her town, sexually assaulted her, and threatened to kill her if she told any-one (Human Rights Watch 2013). Letters sent by the Legal Services Board of

Nunavut in spring 2020 confirm this, detailing thirty cases of abuse experienced by Inuit women perpetrated by RCMP officers (Rohner 2020).

These abuses are compounded by police failure to protect Indigenous women and girls from other modes of violence. The issue of violence against Indigenous women is severe and systematic enough to meet the threshold of genocide, according to a report by the National Inquiry into Missing and Murdered Indigenous Women and Girls (2019). Law's refusal to recognize victims it was not formulated to see is perhaps the most damning example of law's violence: women and girls being disappeared from their communities, raped and killed across the country for decades without a systematic and formal inquiry or intervention, their cases treated as aberrations or the fault of the victims, crimes against them attributed to their "lifestyle" rather than the deeply woven intersections of racism and misogyny predicating violence against them and the continued violence of the law in refusing to see them. For these reasons, racialized women, queer and trans women, sex workers, and single mothers often opt out of reporting abuse in the first place (Levine and Meiners 2020)

Rather than bringing attention to gendered violence as systemic, and patriarchal practices as operating distinctly on different bodies, #MeToo presents a supposed universality contradictorily predicated on individualism. While critiques of unequal gender relations certainly play a central role in many #MeToo discussions, the emphasis on necessary political and cultural changes remains sharply liberal: more regulations, clearer policies, the need to convict bad men, no means no, and so on. Concealed state-based violence that both permits and inflicts harms on women, particularly marginalized women, positions the state and law as being sometimes neglectful but also as holding the possibility for reform and allyship: if more women were in power, if we had better laws, and so on, then sexual violence would cease to be a problem. While #MeToo has led a call to action, shining light on the magnitude of sexual abuse and harassment perpetrated across a myriad of spectrums, there is little evidence to suggest that the movement has meaningfully addressed systemic discrimination based on race, class, gender, and sexuality and the structural, cultural, and material conditions that contribute to the experiences of marginalized women. As noted above, there is glaring evidence that marginalized women continue to experience violence, including that perpetrated by criminal legal actors and the police. Such cases have never been the subject of livestreamed trials, nor can hashtags capture the complexity of colonialism, racism, misogyny, and transphobia intersecting to produce these tragic outcomes. This, in itself, is not an indictment of #MeToo: movements do not have to be all things to all people. It is, however, important to challenge the illegibility of victimhood produced not only by individual violence but by the complicity and refusal of the law to act in response to certain forms of violence, especially when the violence is committed against particular individuals/groups. The explanation for the diversion of media attention toward prominent and famous (American) cases of sexual violence is deceptively simple: Who and what will prompt clicks, and how much ad revenue will this generate? Indigenous, Black, and queer women experiencing brutal violence, often perpetrated by state actors, do not elicit the same attention from the public, in turn giving the law permission to continue to look away. It is not exclusion alone that is the problem here; more law or more legal attention will do little for those who are considered less human within a nation-state predicated on their eradication and continued refusal of rights codified in both national and international law. As we discuss below, if one is not legible as a victim because they are always and already positioned as unworthy of care and support, it is difficult to correct this through applications of laws that were not created in their image (see also Coulthard 2014).

Feminist responses to #MeToo reveal the continued tensions between legal feminists who demand further state intervention to address gendered violence and see criminal law as necessary and critical legal feminists who critique the reliance on the criminal legal system to resolve these problems. The mistrust of law held by critical legal feminists stems from previous attempts to engage with the law to address gendered violence and a general perception that law is a blunt and reactive tool that does little to address the root causes of crime, help address offending behaviours, or support the needs and experiences of survivors (Bernstein 2012, 239; Comack and Balfour 2004; Snider 1990). Furthermore, the criminal legal system negatively impacts already marginalized communities and often creates further harms for survivors (Smart 1989; Taylor 2018). For example, legal amendments made to Canada's sexual assault laws in the 1980s and 1990s, among other developments, made it possible to charge both men and women with sexual assault, removed the doctrine of recent complaint, and placed limitations on the use of women's sexual history at trial (Comack and Balfour 2004, 113; Doe 2003). However, these legal amendments have not stopped legal actors, including judges themselves, from violating rape shield provisions (Craig 2018, 2020).[4] While few feminists would have anticipated legal reforms to be incorporated into practice without resistance, the degree of abusive comments in sexual assault cases by judges leading to acquittals or reduced sentences has been significant, even in recent years (ibid.).

Yet feminist activism is never a single discrete project, and it is clear that renewed emphasis on the rights of sexual violence survivors has led to at least some accountability outcomes in Canada. For example, in 2016, former Alberta Federal Court justice Robin Camp underwent a disciplinary hearing for comments made to a seventeen-year-old rape survivor normalizing painful sex and blaming her for the assault (Heidenreich 2018). Similarly, an independent review was carried out following statements by Nova Scotia Provincial Court judge Gregory Lenahan regarding drinking and consent during his acquittal of Bassam Al-Rawi for sexual assault (Mulligan and Tattrie 2018). In rejecting the appeal brought by the accused in *R. v. Goldfinch* (2019),[5] in which he had previously successfully argued to have his former sexual relationship with the complainant admitted into evidence, the Supreme Court of Canada released a statement warning judges that rape shield provisions must be upheld (*R. v. Goldfinch*). Despite these advancements, Lenahan was cleared of wrongdoing (Craig 2020; Mulligan and Tattrie 2018). Camp lost his appeal to remain a judge but won his bid to be reinstated as a practicing lawyer in 2018 (Heidenreich 2018). These outcomes demonstrate that although there is some progress in accountability for legal actors, the project of securing zero tolerance for violations of *Criminal Code* section 276, "rape shield" provisions, is still far from being complete.

Feminist efforts have seen similar advancements and challenges in relation to laws around intimate partner violence that have undergone a number of changes since the 1980s. For example, in 1982, the federal government implemented a mandatory charging policy making it compulsory for police to charge the perpetrator in every case of intimate partner violence brought to their attention (Johnson and Connors 2017). Similar to the legal changes enacted in relation to sexual assault, this "zero tolerance policy" led to indignation among defence counsel. To subvert the legal changes, defence counsel used intentional tactics to protest what they perceived to be a politically motivated law by creating a distinction between intimate partner violence and "real violence" (Comack and Balfour 2004, 163), thus undermining the severity of the issue. The mandatory charging policy has also been critiqued for assuming that women are a homogenous group with the same needs and issues and failing to take into account factors such as class, race, immigration status, and so on (Crenshaw 1991). For poor women, immigrant women, and racialized women, it is not enough to address gender violence alone; the intersecting forms of oppression that make women vulnerable in the first place—including poverty, racial discrimination in employment, and housing practices—must also be considered and acted upon (1246). For instance, immigrant women are often reluctant to report abuse and leave their abuser due to possible complications with their immigration status and fears of being deported, therefore zero tolerance policies would do very little to help this group of women (ibid.; see also Levine and Meiners 2020).

In light of lessons learned from these and other feminist efforts to engage the law, anti-carceral[6] feminists argue that the invitation for state intervention reinforces law's power, pointing out that the overvisibility of marginalized groups to law has profound negative consequences for poor, racialized, immigrant, and Indigenous 'folks (Bernstein 2010; Comack and Balfour 2004; Smart 1989; Snider 1990). Anti-carceral feminists have expressed concern over the possibility and, indeed, the likelihood that the contemporary #MeToo movement risks becoming yet another issue to be "solved" through increased intervention of the legal system and the targeting of the usual suspects—racialized and immigrant men (Taylor 2018; Terweil 2019). Recognizing these concerns, we argue that law's variegated history with gender violence coupled with the silencing effects that the movement has on marginalized voices are important to consider when analyzing the impact of #MeToo. These tensions, which are currently playing out in the #MeToo movement, around the utility of law and how we should or should not dismantle violence against women continue to be unsettled. The contemporary #MeToo movement encompasses a number of socio-legal changes, including evidence of increased reporting, reliance on formal law, legal responses equated with justice, and an emphasis on *visibility*. These advancements are a victory for some feminist activists; others remain cautious that while increased legal attention to sexual violence may do something important for certain people, it may also contribute to continued lack of visibility to and normalization of other modes and victims of violence, including law's own violence.

As discussed above, some victims are further silenced through neoliberal responses to sexual violence that encourage individual women to speak up against their abuse. It is also possible that an increased focus on the power of the state to respond to these situations will negatively impact communities that are already overpoliced and overrepresented in the criminal legal system, posing a risk for racialized men in particular. As noted in the introduction to this book, the targeting of racialized men by the criminal legal system is part of a larger trend of slow violence that includes oversurveillance and police violence toward this group of people in the United States and Canada (Davis 2017a, 2017b; Maynard 2017; Alexander 2012; Chan and Chunn 2014; Jeffries 2011; Collins 2004; James 2012; Duru 2004). For example, in 2020, Black Americans made up 13 percent of the total population in the United States and 37.9 percent of the prison population, demonstrating the over representation of Black Americans among prison populations (US Federal Bureau of Prisons 2020). To understand the severity of this, consider that there is now a larger percentage of Black Americans incarcerated in the United States than there was in South Africa "at the height of apartheid" (Alexander 2012, 6). Loïc Wacquant explains that in the United States, the prison system "has been elevated to the rank of main machine for 'race making,'" where "the massive over-incarceration of Blacks [sic] has supplied a powerful common-sense warrant for 'using colour as a proxy for dangerousness'" (2002, 56). For these reasons, some Black women choose not to report sexual crimes committed against them by Black men (Crenshaw 1991).

Unlike in the United States, where the racial dynamics of criminal legal engagement with racialized people are well known and widely documented, in Canada, they often remain veiled under the mythology that Canada is multicultural and therefore a tolerant and accepting nation (Cole 2020; Glasbeek, Alam, and Roots 2019; Glasbeek, Alam, and Roots 2020; Maynard 2017). Canadians often define themselves as being in opposition to the explicit racism and discrimination occurring in the United States and elsewhere (Maynard 2017, 3). Yet race-based criminalizing trends tell a different story, as seen in the incarceration of Indigenous groups in Canada (David and Mitchell 2021). According to the Department of Justice in Canada (2019), between 2015 and 2016, Indigenous adults made up around 3 percent of the Canadian population, while Indigenous men accounted for 26 percent of the provincial and territorial male prison population, and Indigenous women made up 38 percent of those admitted to provincial and territorial prisons (see also Chartrand 2019; Balfour 2008). Indigenous people in prisons are also disproportionately overrepresented in maximum security classifications, segregated at higher rates, and more likely to become the subjects of use-of-force interventions, all of which extend their prison terms (Chartrand 2019, 69).

There are also alarming overincarceration rates of Black populations in Canada. According to a 2013 annual report by Canada's Office of the Correctional Investigator the number of Black inmates in Canada's federal prisons increased every year, growing by nearly 90 percent between 2003 and 2013 (during the same time period, the number of white inmates actually declined by 3 percent). In 2010–11, for instance, Black Canadians "made up 9.2 % of the federally incarcerated population, an increase of 50 % from 2000" (Warde 2013, 462; Crawford 2011). The overincarceration of racialized people signals a need for caution around any initiative that supports carceral interventions.

Criminal legal pursuit and incarceration of racialized individuals, particularly Black men, is uniquely contentious in relation to sexual crimes, particularly when committed against white women. The narrative of Black men's sexual desire of white women is one that can be traced back to the Jim Crow era, when it became the avenue for controlling Black men, who were viewed as "prematurely freed from the civilizing influences of slavery" (Collins 2004, 166). The trope of the "Black man as rapist" has functioned in powerful ways to validate racism and the segregation of Black men based on the suggested need to protect white women (Maynard 2017, 41; Walker 2010). After the abolition of slavery in the United States, the practice of lynching appeared as a way to control the Black population and especially to control the Black man's uncontrollable desire for a white woman (Duru 2004). Lynchings—the illegal hangings, stabbings, shootings, and burnings of most commonly Black men by mobs—were justified by the idea that the recently freed Blacks would become "lawless bands of savages" who needed to be controlled (ibid., 1326) were used to protect white women from the uncontrollable sexuality of the Black man. That most lynching victims had not been accused of sexual assault, but were instead attacked for a myriad of other reasons, had little to do with the need to control "Black man's mythic sexual savagery" (ibid., 1327).

While Canadians generally tried to avoid the American-style racism associated with lynchings, the trope of Black men's sexual savagery continued to operate in less overt ways during the nineteenth century. For instance, the need to protect white women was relied upon to justify the continued use of capital punishment as a sentence for rape and to exclude Black people from settlement (Maynard 2017, 41; Walker 2010). As Robyn Maynard contends, "The intensive focus on rape in this era cannot be understood outside of its racial context and should not be mistaken for a genuine societal attempt to end sexual violence against White women (or any women)" (2017, 43). The deployment of the "Black men as rapists" trope continues through the images of the prototypical Black "pimp," sexual predator (Collins 2004), and most recently, the human trafficker (Roots 2023). The racism embedded within criminal legal institutions is not merely a technical issue of poor training and improperly applied policies and regulations. Rather, the oppression and inequality circulating through these institutions can be read as built into law itself, which derives authority from the threat, veiled or explicit, of legitimately enacting violence. Law has been constructed as a mode of social control and governance aimed at regulating society for select populations rather than as a protective and benevolent force for all (see Sarat and Kearns [1993] 2009).

This history provides us with ample reason to be, at the very least, concerned about the possibility of expanded law enforcement efforts potentially fuelled by the #MeToo movement. Anti-carceral feminists have pointed out that feminist support for punitive policies against sexual and gender-based violence have contributed to increased incarceration (Bumiller 2008; Davis 2003; INCITE! 2001). As Anna Terweil explains, "Feminist prison abolitionists have expressed concern that the #MeToo movement could also have the undesirable effect of increasing support for prisons as 'solutions' to sexual violence. Taking sexual violence seriously, they point out, all too often means supporting more or harsher punishments for perpetrators" (2019, 2; Davis 2003). She highlights that these "tough on crime" policies have been passed in order to protect women. Instead of reducing gendered violence, however, such policies result in expanded punishments that affect, first and foremost, racially and economically marginalized people (2). We can identify this as another way that hypervisibilization of certain cases involving white, powerful men and celebrities serve to further invisibilize law's violence toward racialized folks, in a reiteration of the historical violence discussed in this chapter. While there has been a cultural backlash to #MeToo and a panic around "false" allegations against powerful white men, we have not seen the same level of critical concern about the multitudes of racialized men imprisoned unjustly and/or falsely/mis-accused.

In Canada, there is limited information on the demographics of those accused and convicted in sexual assault cases[7]—a notable and troubling information gap. In the absence of this data, we can look to the United States for information on who is being charged and convicted of sexual assault. While there are some marked differences in the operation and approach of the US and Canadian legal systems, data from the United States can provide us with some important context on the racialization of sexual assault suspects in North American cultures. For instance, according to the US National Registry for Exonerations, Black people are eight times more likely than white people to be falsely convicted of rape (Gross et al. 2022, iii). African American sexual assault exonerees also received significantly longer sentences compared to their white counterparts and spent on average nearly four-and-a-half years longer in prison before being exonerated. Thus, "it appears that innocent Black sexual assault defendants receive harsher sentences than Whites if they are convicted, and then face greater resistance to exoneration even in cases in which they are ultimately released" (iii). In support of this, research by Daniel Filler (2004) found that Black Americans are disproportionately represented on public sexual offender registries.[8] That the overrepresentation of Black people on sexual offender registries and the significant collateral consequences this registration brings are issues that are underresearched in academia and underaddressed in the media and by public officials demonstrates the kind of hyperinvisibilization and slow violence that exists in relation to the criminalization of racialized bodies. Without increased emphasis on this issue, we are concerned that #MeToo will not fundamentally challenge the way carceral violence perpetuates structural racism and indeed risks bolstering it.

In addition to the overwhelming targeting of Black men under sexual violence laws, the limited research that does exist in the Canadian context demonstrates that Indigenous men are also disproportionately targeted for prosecution regarding sexual offences. As Bruckert and Law note, one in four individuals serving sentences in Canadian jails for sexual assault are Indigenous (2018; see also Benoit et al. 2015). This is supported by 2008/2009 data from the Correctional Service of Canada, according to which a significant proportion of Indigenous offenders were serving prison sentences for sexual offences compared with non-Indigenous persons. In contrast to constructions of the Black man as the sexual predator, Indigenous men are seen as perpetrators due to their alcohol abuse and subsequent "tolerance to violence while drunk" (Comack and Balfour 2004, 81). The legacies of colonialism that led to these challenges and constructions have been subverted by neoliberal individualism and the consequent need to protect society from these troubled and violent individuals. #MeToo activists should actively incorporate the practice of decolonization into their advocacy, especially given that not only do Indigenous men face state violence, but Indigenous women face the highest rates of interpersonal violence and are routinely excluded from state protection.

The impact of marginalization on criminal legal outcomes applies to victims and survivors as well as those labelled as perpetrators. When victims and survivors are racialized, queer, and/or work in the sex trade, we routinely see lower sentences for perpetrators. According to Open Society Foundations, "Black defendants who victimize Whites tend to receive more severe sentences than . . . Blacks who victimize other Blacks" (Kansal 2005). In the context of sexual assault convictions in Canada, Bruckert and Law (2018) found that sentences for sexual assault offences are more lenient in cases where the victim is racialized. These cases remind us that legislative changes resulting from #MeToo and other well-intended movements are still operationalized by a criminal legal system embedded in inequality and injustice. They caution us from putting too much faith in the law as an apparatus for systemic change.

Conclusion

Feminist engagement with law has a long and contentious history premised on noble intentions that don't always lead to as noble of outcomes. Continued feminist efforts to engage the law and the state in order to address gender-specific issues have come under criticism. Here, we see increased recognition that legal change does not always or even often lead to changes in lived experiences. In this chapter, we have relied on the anti-carceral feminist framework to discuss the most recent iteration of these feminist efforts in the form of the #MeToo movement, which has gained significant public attention in recent years. The movement has made a notable impact and led to a number of powerful men being held accountable for their sexually predatory behaviour. And while the #MeToo movement seems different from previous efforts to engage the public on issues of gendered violence through its success in bringing down a number of influential men, caution toward overoptimism should be exercised.

The law has not been constructed to recognize or act on the systemic discrimination woven into the fabric of settler-colonial states, and so action by criminal law can only serve to address individualized harms suffered. The hypervisibilization of a few high-profile cases of sexual assault and harassment does not negate the simultaneous invisibilization of the law's own violence against racialized people through overincarceration, unjust sentences, the dehumanization of victims, and police violence. These processes instead serve to undermine the transformative potential of movements designed to shine light on violence and abuses of power. For these to be truly effective, law's own violence must no longer be allowed to operate in the shadows. Through marginalizing law's authority to determine the nature and legitimacy of harms suffered, space may be opened to consider gendered violence in a historically contextualized and collective way, reorienting violence prevention and redress to community-oriented practices of social justice.

Notes

1 Rather than using the term *criminal justice system*, we will be using the term *criminal legal system* throughout this paper in order to disrupt the assumption that the system achieves justice.

2 In April 2021, Weinstein's lawyers filed an appeal with the New York State Supreme Court arguing that the conviction should be reversed because his first trial was tainted due to a biased judge and a biased juror (BBC News 2021).

3 In addition to all the allegations against powerful men, other interesting socio-legal changes have occurred. For example, several states throughout the United States have passed laws prohibiting the use of non-disclosure agreements in sexual misconduct cases. Additionally, the Time's Up Legal Defense Fund that has seen a number of celebrity contributors, including Taylor Swift, Jennifer Aniston, and Reese Witherspoon, was created to help women access legal representation for sexual misconduct cases. In 2018, the US House of Representatives and the Senate passed new regulations on sexual harassment in Congress.

4 "Rape shield" is a term applied to legal amendments preventing the admission of the sexual history of sexual assault complainants as evidence of the accused's innocence. It also limits the amount of blame or responsibility that can be levelled against the complainant for their assault. In Canada, these provisions are covered in section 276 of the Criminal Code.

5 Goldfinch was acquitted in his original trial but was later convicted on appeal. It was the conviction that he appealed at the Supreme Court, the decision of which found that the evidence of previous sexual contact should not have been allowed in the original trial.

6 "Carceral feminism" is a term coined by Elizabeth Bernstein (2010; 2012) to describe and critique the reliance on the law and the criminal legal system—including police, prosecution, and the prison system—to resolve problems of gender violence.

7 Canadian police services do not typically collect race-related data. The exception now is the Toronto Police Service, which began collecting race-based data in January 2020 as a part of a new initiative to identify and eliminate race-based discrimination.

8 These sex offender registries were brought about with Megan's Law. The law was enacted in 1996 after seven-year-old Megan Kanka was raped and killed by a known child molester who had moved across the street from the family. The aim of the law is to warn the community of known sex offenders living in their areas. All states in the United States now have some form of Megan's Law (http://MegansLaw.ca.gov).

References

Ackerman, Alissa R., and Meghan Sacks. 2018. "Disproportionate Minority Presence on U.S. Sex Offender Registries." *Justice Policy Journal* 16 (2): 1–20.

Alexander, Michelle. 2012. *The New Jim Crow: Mass Incarceration in the Age of Colorblindness*. New York: New Press.

Bakht, Natasha. 2012. "What's in a Face? Demeanour Evidence in the Sexual Assault Context." In *Sexual Assault in Canada: Law, Legal Practice and Women's Activism*, edited by Elizabeth Sheehy, 591–612. Ottawa, ON: University of Ottawa Press.

Balfour, Gillian. 2008. "Falling Between the Cracks of Retributive and Restorative Justice: The Victimization and Punishment of Aboriginal Women." *Feminist Criminology* 3 (2): 101–20.

Barr, John, and Dan Murphy. 2018. "Larry Nassar Thinks Sentence for Sexual Abuse Too Harsh." ABC News, 25 July 2018. https://abcnews.go.com/Sports/larry-nassar -thinks-sentence-sexual-abuse-harsh/story?id=56812588.

Batacharya, Sheila. 2010. "Hootchies and Ladies: Race, Gender, Sexuality and 'Girl Violence' in a Colonial White Settler Society." In *Reena Virk: Critical Perspectives on a Canadian Murder*, edited by Mythili Rajiva and Sheila Batacharya, 35–49. Toronto: Canadian Scholars.

BBC News. 2019. "Jeffrey Epstein: The Financier Charged with Sex Trafficking." 16 November 2019. https://www.bbc.com/news/world-us-canada-48913377.

———. 2021. "Harvey Weinstein Appeals against Conviction for Sex Crimes." 5 April 2021. https://www.bbc.com/news/world-us-canada-56642644.

Benoit, Cecilia, Leah Shumka, Rachel Phillips, Mary Clare Kennedy, and Lynne Belle-Isle. 2015. *Issue Brief: Sexual Violence Against Women in Canada*. Commissioned by the Federal-Provincial-Territorial Senior Officials for the Status of Women. https://refugeeresearch.net/wp-content/uploads/2017/05/ Benoit-et-al-2015.-Issue-brief-Sexual-violence-against-women-in-Canada.pdf.

Bernstein, Elizabeth. 2010. "Militarized Humanitarianism Meets Carceral Feminism: The Politics of Sex, Rights, and Freedom in Contemporary Antitrafficking Campaigns." *Journal of Women in Culture and Society* 36 (1): 45–71.

———. 2012. "Carceral Politics as Gender Justice? The 'Traffic in Women' and Neoliberal Circuits of Crime, Sex and Rights." *Theoretical Sociology* 41:233–59.

Brock, Deborah. 1998. *Making Work, Making Trouble: Prostitution as a Social Problem*. Toronto: University of Toronto Press.

Bruckert, Christine, and Tuulia Law. 2018. *Women and Gendered Violence in Canada: An Intersectional Approach*. Toronto: University of Toronto Press.

Bumiller, Kristin. 2008. *In an Abusive State: How Neoliberalism Appropriated the Feminist Movement Against Sexual Violence*. London: Duke University Press.

Chan, Wendy, and Dorothy Chunn. 2014. *Racialization, Crime and Criminal Justice in Canada*. Toronto: University of Toronto Press.

Chartrand, Vicki. 2019. "Unsettled Times: Indigenous Incarceration and the Links Between Colonialism and the Penitentiary in Canada." *Canadian Journal of Criminology and Criminal Justice* 61 (3): 67–89.

Chunn, Dorothy, Susan B. Boyd, and Hester Lessard. 2007. "Feminism, Law and Social Change: An Overview." In *Reaction and Resistance: Feminism, Law and Social Change*. Vancouver: UBC Press.

Cole, Desmond. 2020. *The Skin We're In: A Year of Black Resistance and Power*. Toronto: Doubleday Canada.

Collins, Patricia Hill. 2004. *Black Sexual Politics: African American Gender and the New Racism*. New York: Routledge.

Comack, Elizabeth, and Gillian Balfour. 2004. *The Power to Criminalize: Violence, Inequality and the Law*. Halifax, Nova Scotia: Fernwood.

Correctional Service of Canada. 2013. "The Changing Federal Offender Population: Aboriginal Offender Highlights 2009." 18 July 2013. http://www.csc-scc.gc.ca/research/092/ah2009-Aboriginal_Highlights-2009-eng.pdf.

Cossman, Brenda. 2019. "#MeToo, Sex Wars 2.0 and the Power of Law." In *The Asian Yearbook of Human Rights and Humanitarian Law*, vol. 3, edited by Javaid Rehman, Ayesha Shahid, and Steve Foster, 18–37. https://doi.org/10.1163/9789004401716_003.

———. 2021. *The New Sex Wars: Sexual Harm in the #MeToo Era*. New York: NYU Press.

Coulthard, Glen Sean. 2014. *Red Skin, White Masks: Rejecting the Colonial Politics of Recognition*. Minneapolis: University of Minnesota Press.

Craig, Elaine. 2014. "Person (s) of Interest and Missing Women: Legal Abandonment in the Downtown Eastside." *McGill Law Journal/Revue de droit de McGill* 60 (1): 1–42.

———. 2018. *Putting Trials on Trial: Sexual Assault and the Failure of the Legal Profession*. Montreal and Kingston: McGill-Queen's University Press.

———. 2020. "Sexual Assault and Intoxication: Defining (In)Capacity to Consent." *Canadian Bar Review* 98:70–108.

Crawford, Alison. 2011. "Prison Watchdog Probes Spike in Number of Black Inmates." CBC News, 15 December 2011. http://www.cbc.ca/news/politics/story/2011/12/14/crawford-black-prison.html.

Crenshaw, Kimberlé. 1991. "Mapping the Margins: Intersectionality, Identity Politics, and Violence Against Women of Colour." *Stanford Law Review* 43 (6): 1241–99.

Dale, Maryclaire. 2021. "Bill Cosby Freed from Prison, His Sex Conviction Overturned." AP News, 30 June 2021. https://apnews.com/article/bill-cosby -conviction-overturned-5c073fb64bc5df4d7b99ee7fadddbe5a.

David, Jean-Denis, and Megan Mitchell. 2021. "Contacts with Police and the Over-representation of Indigenous Peoples in the Canadian Criminal Justice System." *Canadian Journal of Criminology and Criminal Justice* 63 (2): 23–45.

Davis, Angela. 2003. *Are Prisons Obsolete?* New York: Seven Stories.

———. 2017a. "Introduction." In *Policing the Black Man*, edited by Angela Davis. New York: Pantheon.

———. 2017b. "The Prosecution of Black Men." In *Policing the Black Man*, edited by Angela Davis. New York: Pantheon.

Department of Justice Canada. 2019. *Spotlight on Gladue: Challenges, Experiences, and Possibilities in Canada's Criminal Justice System*. Last modified 12 April 2019. https://www.justice.gc.ca/eng/rp-pr/jr/gladue/p2.html.

Doe, Jane. 2003. *The Story of Jane Doe: A Book About Rape*. Toronto: Vintage Canada.

DuBois, Teresa. 2012. "Police Investigation of Sexual Assault Complainants: How Far Have We Come Since Jane Doe?" In *Sexual Assault in Canada: Law, Legal Practice and Women's Activism*, edited by Elizabeth Sheehy. Ottawa, ON: University of Ottawa Press.

Duru, Jeremi N. 2004. "The Central Park Five, the Scottsboro Boys, and the Myth of the Bestial Black Man." *Cardozo Law Review* 25:1315–65.

Filler, Daniel. 2004. "Silence and the Racial Dimension of Megan's Law." *Iowa Law Review* 89:1535–1775.

Gash, Alison, and Ryan Harding. 2018. "#MeToo? Legal Discourse and Everyday Responses to Sexual Violence." *Laws* 7 (21): 1–24.

Glasbeek, Amanda, Mariful Alam, and Katrin Roots. 2019. "Postcolonialism, Time, and Body-Worn Cameras." In "Decolonizing Surveillance." Special issue, *Surveillance and Society* 17 (5): 743–46.

———. 2020. "Seeing and Not-Seeing: Race and Body-Worn Cameras in Canada." *Surveillance and Society* 18 (3): 328–42.

Gotell, Lise. 2008. "Rethinking Affirmative Consent in Canadian Sexual Assault Law: Neoliberal Sexual Subjects and Risky Women." *Akron Law Review* 41 (4): 865–98.

Gross, Samuel R., Maurice Possley, and Klara Stephens. 2017. *Race and Wrongful Convictions in the United States*. National Registry of Exonerations. Irvine: University of California Irvine. http://www.law.umich.edu/special/exoneration/ Documents/Race_and_Wrongful_Convictions.pdf.

Gross, Samuel R., Maurice Possley, Ken Otterbourg, Klara Stephens, Jessica Paredes, and Barbara O'Brien. 2022. *Race and Wrongful Convictions in the United States 2022*. National Registry of Exonerations. Irvine: University of California Irvine. https://www.law.umich.edu/special/exoneration/Documents/Race%20Report %20Preview.pdf.

Hannem, Stacey, and Christopher J. Schneider. 2022. *Defining Sexual Misconduct: Power, Media and #MeToo*. Regina, Saskatchewan: University of Regina Press.

Heidenreich, Phil. 2018. "'Knees Together' Judge Robin Camp Wins Bid to Be Reinstated as Lawyer in Alberta." Global News. 23 May 2018. https://globalnews .ca/news/4227215/knees-together-judge-robin-camp-law-society-alberta/.

Human Rights Watch. 2013. "Those Who Take Us Away: Abusive Policing and Failures in Protection of Indigenous Women and Girls in Northern British Columbia, Canada." 13 February 2013. https://www.hrw.org/report/2013/02/13/ those-who-take-us-away/abusive-policing-and-failures-protection-indigenous -women.

Hunt, Sarah. 2013. "Decolonizing Sex Work: Developing an Intersectional Indigenous Approach." In *Selling Sex: Experience, Advocacy, and Research on Sex Work in Canada*, edited by Emily van der Meulen, Elya M. Durisin, and Victoria Love. Vancouver: UBC Press.

INCITE! Women of Color Against Violence. 2001. "Statement on Gender Violence and the Prison Industrial Complex (2001)." https://incite-national.org/incite -critical-resistance-statement/.

Irwing, Toni. 2008. "Decoding Black Women: Policing Practices and Rape Prosecution on the Streets of Philadelphia." *NWSA Journal* 20 (2): 100–120.

James, Carl E. 2012. "Troubling Role Models: Seeing Racialization in the Discourse Relating to 'Corrective Agents' for Black Males." In *Troubled Masculinities: Reimagining Urban Men*, edited by Kenneth James Moffatt. Toronto: University of Toronto Press.

Jeffries, Michael. 2011. "Thug Life and Social Death." In *Thug Life: Race, Gender, and the Meaning of Hip-Hop*, edited by Michael Jeffries. Chicago: University of Chicago Press.

Johnson, Holly, and D. E. Connors. 2017. *The Benefits and Impacts of Mandatory Charging in Ontario: Perceptions of Abused Women, Service Providers and Police*. Ottawa: University of Ottawa. https://ruor.uottawa.ca/bitstream/10393/37546/1/ MCP%20Report%20Final%20EN%2014072017.pdf.

Johnston, Matthew, Ryan Coulling, and Jennifer Kilty. 2020. "Digital Knowledge Divides: Sexual Violence and Collective Emotional Responses to the Jian Ghomeshi Verdict on Twitter." *Annual Review of Interdisciplinary Justice Research* 9:167–205.

Kansal, Tushar. 2005. *Racial Disparity in Sentencing*. Open Society Foundations, January 2005. https://www.opensocietyfoundations.org/publications/racial -disparity-sentencing.

Kantor, Jodi, and Megan Twohey. 2017. "Harvey Weinstein Paid Off Sexual Harassment Accusers for Decades." *New York Times*, 5 October 2017. https://www .nytimes.com/2017/10/05/us/harvey-weinstein-harassment-allegations.html.

Keller, Jessalyn. 2016. "Making Activism Accessible: Exploring Girls' Blogs as Sites of Contemporary Feminist Activism." In *The Politics of Place: Contemporary Paradigms for Research in Girlhood Studies*, edited by Claudia Mitchell and Carrie Rentschler. New York. Berghahn.

Kim, Crystal, and Jessica Ringrose. 2018. "'Stumbling upon Feminism' Teenage Girls' Forays into Digital and School-Based Feminisms." *Girlhood Studies* 11 (2): 46–62.

Levine, Judith, and Erica R. Meiners. 2020. *The Feminist and the Sex Offender: Confronting Sexual Harm, Ending State Violence*. London: Verso.

Lindberg, Tracey, Priscilla Campeau, and Maria Campbell. 2012. "Indigenous Women and Sexual Assault in Canada." In *Sexual Assault in Canada: Law, Legal Practice and Women's Activism*, edited by Elizabeth Sheehy. Ottawa, ON: University of Ottawa Press.

Lober, Brook. 2018. "(Re)Thinking Sex Positivity, Abolition Feminism, and the #MeToo Movement: Opportunity for a New Synthesis." Abolition Journal, 26 January 2018. https://abolitionjournal.org/rethinking-sex-positivity-abolition -feminism-metoo-movement-opportunity-new-synthesis/.

Manatu-Rupert, Norma. 2000. "Media Images and the Victimization of Black Women: Exploring the Impact of Sexual Stereotyping on Prosecutorial Decision Making." In *The System in Black and White: Exploring the Connections Between Race, Crime and Justice*, edited by Michael W. Markowitz and Delores D. Jones-Brown. Westport, CT: Praeger.

Maynard, Robyn. 2017. *Policing Black Lives: State Violence in Canada from Slavery to the Present*. Halifax: Fernwood.

Mendes, Kaitlyn, Jessica Ringrose, and Jessalyn Keller. 2018. "#MeToo and the Promise and Pitfalls of Challenging Rape Culture through Digital Feminist Activism." *European Journal of Women's Studies* 25 (2): 236–46.

Miller, Reuben J., and Forrest Stuart. 2017. "Carceral Citizenship: Race, Rights and Responsibility in the Age of Mass Supervision." *Theoretical Criminology* 21 (4): 532–48.

Muhammad, Khalil Gibran. 2010. *The Condemnation of Blackness: Race, Crime, and the Making of Modern Urban America*. Cambridge, MA: Harvard University Press.

Mulligan, Preston, and Jon Tattrie. 2018. "Here's Why Judge Lenehan Was Cleared in 'Drunk Can Consent' Sex-Assault Case." CBC News. 4 April 2018. https://www .cbc.ca/news/canada/nova-scotia/judge-gregory-lenehan-1.4604983.

National Inquiry into Missing and Murdered Indigenous Women and Girls. 2019. *Reclaiming Power and Place: The Final Report of the National Inquiry into Missing and Murdered Indigenous Women and Girls*. Ottawa, ON: Canada Privy Council.

Office of the Correctional Investigator. 2013. *Annual Report of the Office of the Correctional Investigator 2012–2013*. https://www.oci-bec.gc.ca/cnt/rpt/annrpt/ annrpt20122013-eng.aspx.

Ostroff, Joshua. 2016. "Teen Consent Activists Tessa Hill and Lia Valente Win Toronto Women of Distinction Award." Huffington Post Canada, 8 March 2016. https://www.huffpost.com/archive/ca/entry/teen-consent-activists-tessa-hill-and -lia-valente-win-toronto-wo_n_9411044#:~:text=consentconsent%20culture -,Teen%20Consent%20Activists%20Tessa%20Hill%20And%20Lia%20Valente %20Win%20Toronto,when%20women%20work%20for%20women.%22.

Owens Patton, Tracey, and Julie Snyder-Yuly. 2007. "Any Four Black Men Will Do: Rape, Race, and the Ultimate Scapegoat." *Journal of Black Studies* 37 (6): 859–95.

Owusu-Bempah, A., and S. Wortley. 2014. "Race, Crime and Criminal Justice in Canada." In *The Oxford Handbook of Ethnicity, Crime, and Immigration*, edited by S. Bucerius and M. Tonry. 281–320. New York: Oxford University Press.

Özsu, Umut. 2020. "Genocide as Fact and Form." *Journal of Genocide Research* 22 (1): 62–71.

Palmater, Pamela. 2016. "Shining Light on the Dark Places: Addressing Police Racism and Sexualized Violence Against Indigenous Women and Girls in the National Inquiry." *Canadian Journal of Women and the Law* 28 (2): 253–84.

Razack, Sherene H. 2002. "Gendered Racial Violence and Spatialized Justice: The Murder of Pamela George." In *Race, Space and the Law: Unmapping a White Settler Society*. Toronto: Between the Lines.

———. 2016. "Gendering Disposability." *Canadian Journal of Women and the Law* 28 (2): 285–307.

Rohner, Thomas. 2020. "Inuit Women in Nunavut Suffer 'Unnecessary Violence,' Racism from RCMP, Legal Aid Board Says." CBC, 8 June 2020. https://www.cbc.ca/ news/canada/north/inuit-nunavut-rcmp-allegations-violence-racism-1.5599557.

Roots, Katrin. 2023. *Domestication of Human Trafficking: Law, Policing and Prosecution*. Toronto: University of Toronto Press.

Rottenberg, Catherine. 2019. "#MeToo and the Prospects of Political Change." *Soundings* 71:40–49.

Rotenberg, Cristine, and Adam Cotter. 2018. "Police-Reported Sexual Assaults in Canada Before and After #MeToo, 2016 and 2017." Statistics Canada, 8 November

2018. https://www150.statcan.gc.ca/n1/pub/85-002-x/2018001/article/54979-eng
.htm.

R. v. Goldfinch, 2019 SCC 38.

Sarat, Austin, and Thomas R. Kearns, eds. (1993) 2009. *Law's Violence*. Ann Arbor:
University of Michigan Press.

Sheehy, Elizabeth A. 2012. *Sexual Assault in Canada: Law, Legal Practice and
Women's Activism*. Ottawa: University of Ottawa Press.

———. 2014. *Defending Battered Women on Trial: Lessons from the Transcripts*.
Vancouver: UBC Press.

Smart, Carol. 1989. *Feminism and the Power of Law*. London: Routledge.

Snider, Laureen. 1990. "The Potential of the Criminal Justice System to Promote
Feminist Concerns." *Studies in Law, Politics and Society* 10:143–72.

Symonds, Alexandria. 2017. "How to Break a Sexual Harassment Story." *New York
Times*, 15 October 2017. https://www.nytimes.com/2017/10/15/insider/sexual
-harassment-weinstein-oreilly.html.

Taylor, Chloë. 2018. "Anti-carceral Feminism and Sexual Assault—a Defense a
Critique of the Critique of the Critique of Carceral Feminism." *Social Philosophy
Today* 34:29–49.

Terweil, Anna. 2019. "What Is Carceral Feminism?" *Political Theory* 48 (4): 1–22.

Thuma, Emily. 2015. "Lessons in Self-Defence: Gender Violence, Racial
Discrimination and Anticarceral Feminism." *Women's Studies Quarterly* 43 (¾):
52–71.

US Federal Bureau of Prisons. 2020. "Inmate Race." Last updated May 2020. https://
www.bop.gov/about/statistics/statistics_inmate_race.jsp.

Wacquant, Loïc. 2002. "From Slavery to Mass Incarceration." *New Left Review* 13.
https://newleftreview.org/issues/ii13/articles/loic-wacquant-from-slavery-to-mass
-incarceration.

Walker, Barrington. 2010. *Race on Trial: Black Defendants in Ontario's Criminal
Courts, 1858–1958*. Toronto: University of Toronto Press.

Warde, Brian. 2013. "Black Male Disproportionality in the Criminal Justice Systems
of the USA, Canada, and England: A Comparative Analysis of Incarceration."
Journal of African American Studies 17:461–79.

Wortley, Scott. 2006. *Police Use of Force in Ontario: An Examination of Data from
the Special Investigation Unit Final Report*. Toronto: African Canadian Legal
Clinic.

Wypijewski, JoAnn. 2020. *What We Don't Talk About When We Talk About #MeToo:
Essays on Sex, Authority, and the Mess of Life*. New York: Verso.

5 Through Different Lenses

Legality, Humanitarianism, and the Western Gaze

Heather Tasker

In 2008, the United Nations High Commissioner for Refugees (UNHCR) initiated a project called Do You See What I See? (DYSWIS).[1] The project documented stories by young refugees through photography, and the results were shared with viewers from other places and backgrounds. The objective was to build connections and foster unity between various refugee youth while simultaneously presenting refugee voices and stories to a global community. DYSWIS provided twenty-four youth living in the Kharaze refugee camp in Yemen and the Osire camp in Namibia with cameras, a two-week training course taught by a professional photographer, and encouragement to move through the camp and visually document important elements of their lives. The photos were organized into exhibitions in Yemen and Namibia and later re-edited and exhibited at the UNHCR headquarters in Geneva.[2]

By drawing on the DYSWIS as a case study, this chapter explores the politics, potentials, and limitations of photography as a medium for advancing humanitarian concerns and agendas while questioning how the figure of the refugee child is positioned and mobilized as a depoliticized subject. I employ a socio-legal approach to spatiality and critical humanitarianism to question the role and representation of the camp as a liminal space both territorially and within international law. Through these discussions, questions of law's power circulate: How does law contribute to subject formation? How does the simultaneous presence and absence of law within refugee camps serve to reinforce law's power through determining its subjects?

Conceptualizing Law and Globality

Globality within socio-legal studies is a relatively new but vibrant area of scholarship concerned with the ways law and legality operate beyond state-based boundaries and institutions. Eve Darian-Smith (2013) argues that much of socio-legal studies has historically been focused on Western law and norm production, often removed from global processes and movements that occur beyond and across national borders. To fill this lacuna, Darian-Smith calls for a deprovincialization of the field so that all legal research, including that which examines national processes, considers the larger geopolitical influences at work. Darian-Smith ultimately calls for a rethinking of what law means in a global world and how our basic assumptions may be destabilized when we begin to think about global impacts on legal arrangements.

In taking Darian-Smith's observation seriously, I consider not only doctrinal law but also systems of regulation that serve to shape lives and social relationships that may constitute positivist law. The role of international institutions in reproducing legal power must be considered for its impacts on producing legal subjects and normative orderings. Susan Silbey's (2010) discussion on legality is central here. The notion of legality expands beyond formal law to consider regulative normativity—how we come to be disciplined subjects of law without the direct action of law itself. The United Nations engages in sustained processes of cultural translation of resolutions and policies for incorporation into different legal systems and community norms. While these policies are not necessarily encoded in formal law, the international pressure that is exerted for their adoption and their potential for transformation and legislation within national contexts demonstrates the ways that organizations of power work across state-based jurisdictions to enforce understandings of normativity. Relatedly, Saskia Sassen's (2008) work on global assemblages is concerned with cross-border networks developed for furthering specific aims and that sometimes serve to shift the loci of power from state-based governance to transnational organizing. We see here how conceptions of the centrality of formal power are changing and sometimes become diluted in our increasingly interconnected world. This does not mean, however, that these are necessarily democratic processes. Indeed, violence and environmental destruction can often be wrought by these assemblages, with hegemonic power relations being further solidified. Rather, the importance of this method of tracing cross-border connections serves to uncover emerging and existing relationships that form and are maintained across state borders and that may influence law and policy in multiple jurisdictions. Human rights campaigns, for example, are often organized between multiple countries in hopes of affecting law and policy in the country that the abuses are recognized in as well as in the activists' home nations.

While DYSWIS is not itself a legal project, the status of refugees is discussed in multiple places within international law, as refugee camps follow systems of governance and have their own internal sets of law-like practices. Refugees are also subjects within international humanitarian law. Further, international humanitarian law is concerned with normativity—with what should be and what is considered appropriate within and between states as pertaining to armed conflict. As such, humanitarian logics are both moralistic and norm-making, influencing legislation and regulations outside of doctrine. Following this, my chapter extends conceptions of the law beyond national legislation to examine how the UNHCR has attempted to forge connections across space by making material the experiences of refugee youth. In this, refugee youth, whose status designates them as having been marked by encounters with legal systems, share stories that cross state borders to be interpreted within the locations where the images are viewed. By examining how global forces intersect with localized processes of subject production, the project underscores the interrelatedness of space, images, and legality. My process is not one that minimizes the direct impacts of law but rather demonstrates the elusiveness of law's power: even when not formally invoked, law influences and shapes relations and subjectivities through its normative influence.

Humanitarian Projects

The UNHCR describes their core mandate as follows:

> ... to ensure the international protection of 31.7 million uprooted people worldwide. It promotes the basic human rights of refugees and that they will not be returned involuntarily to a country where they face persecution. It helps them to repatriate to their homeland when conditions permit, integrate into states of asylum or resettle in third countries. UNHCR promotes international refugee agreements, helps states establish asylum structures and acts as an international watchdog over refugee issues. (UNHCR n.d.)

This emphasis on protectionism, the intrinsic rights of humans, and the status of refugees as primarily legal resonates with how many would normatively understand the role of the UNHCR. Over the last couple of decades, however, persuasive critiques have been generated within anthropology, political science, refugee/migration studies, and sociology regarding the ways that refugees are represented and understood by the UNHCR and like-minded humanitarian agencies as voiceless, passive victims, the seminal critique questioning whether refugees must be represented by a third party at all (Malkki 1996). In recent years, new initiatives by the UNHCR appear to take notice of these criticisms by offering new opportunities for self-authorship and self-presentation to a potentially global audience.

DYSWIS, the project undertaken by the UNHCR, is one such initiative. It positions a relatively new figure of the refugee within humanitarian storytelling, one that departs in significant ways from the voiceless, agentless subject that has been a focus of significant critique. The project is indicative of the UNHCR's attempt to reallocate unequal enactments of power by providing opportunities for refugee youth to present their stories to a global audience, marking an important turn in humanitarian storytelling. It is evidence of the UNHCR trying to move beyond the neocolonial paternalism that accompanied most attempts at garnering support for refugees (Razack 2007). DYSWIS provided opportunities for youth to present their own stories, with the caveat that the stories remain within the confines of what is legible in liberal, humanitarian citizenship. Ultimately, in attempting to correct previous harms, DYSWIS legitimizes the experiences of refugee youth when they fall within the mandate of its humanitarian logics and politics.

Humanitarian agencies operate based on three core tenets: humanity, impartiality, and neutrality (Nyers 2006). This presupposes the separation of humanitarianism from politics, constructing the two as mutually exclusive. Didier Fassin explains that humanitarianism serves as "both a moral discourse (based on responsibility toward the victim) and a political resource (serving specific interests) to justify action considered to be in favour of others . . . action taken in the name of a shared humanity" (2010, 239). In this way, the presented apoliticism of humanitarianism in fact masks the political engagement and priorities of humanitarian actors (Slim 2015). Malkki explains how humanitarian agencies represent refugees, speaking for groups of displaced people and silencing refugee voices through the volume of humanitarian speech (1996). Malkki writes that "humanitarian interventions tend to be constituted as the opposite of political ones" (378). This separation, she argues, is often taken for granted, and the effects of this process serve to essentialize and dehistoricize those labelled as refugees, effectively silencing them. It appears that the representation of refugees by agencies that purportedly subscribe to apolitical and moral objectives has the effect of depoliticizing and dehistoricizing the very category of "refugee." Those who fall within this legal status are constructed as neutral and impartial through this seemingly inescapable connection with the humanitarian agencies they are represented by.[3]

From the perspective of the UNHCR, DYSWIS was ultimately a photography project. Designed and constructed to give refugee youth an opportunity to express their views about life in camps, the final product was an exhibition meant to share these perspectives with a broader viewing public. In DYSWIS, the humanitarian principles and logics guiding the project elicit sympathy from and forge some connection with viewers, which may compel action (McEntire et al. 2015). It is important to query why a visual, realist medium such as photography was chosen. What are the sensibilities that place precedence on visual imagery—on seeing as a source of truth? What is the value imposed on these photographs by exhibitors and viewers—what truths are they believed to express?

Photography, Politics, and the Scopic Drive

In explaining the appeal and perceived artistic merit of photography, Pierre Bourdieu writes that photography captures "an aspect of reality which is only ever the result of arbitrary selection" (1999, 164). The social uses for which it has been designed and that it is expected to fulfill are to be realistic and objective. Photography, then, can appear to be an objective recording of the world. In this understanding, however, Bourdieu argues that "society is merely confirming itself in the tautological certainty that an image of the real which is true to its representation of reality is really objective" (164). In considering DYSWIS then, it becomes apparent that the representations of the refugee camp depicted in the photographs are selections of the reality of the camp, but because the selections are captured and materialized through film (and their authority is again reasserted through inclusion in the exhibition), the reality that is portrayed is taken as a real, objective, and true representation. This would not be understood in the same way if the youth produced drawings or poetry. The choice of photography as a medium is based around the ideas that seeing is believing and a photograph is worth a thousand words: such idioms demonstrate the faith and importance placed on visual imagery in presenting human conditions. As such, DYSWIS is considered an artistic endeavour but is more legible as a documentation project presenting the lived realities of refugee youth. Here the photograph is understood as evidence. The project design makes clear that photographs were chosen to affirm the experiences and thoughts of the youth participants while also uncovering the truth of their lives.

Bourdieu (1999) further discusses the technical and aesthetic qualities of photographs, what can be photographed, and what should or must be photographed. This distinction appears to be particularly relevant in the assessment of the photographs for inclusion in the exhibitions. The aesthetic sensibilities, likely informed by humanitarian prerogatives, of those who arranged the exhibit would determine what photographs must or should be seen by the viewing public rather than what could be seen. Bourdieu states, "Because it presupposes the uniqueness and coherence of a system of norms, such an aesthetic is never better fulfilled than it is in the village community. Thus, for example, the meaning of the pose adopted for the photograph can only be understood with relation to the symbolic system in which it has its place" (1999, 166). In organizing the exhibit and selecting photographs for display then, one must consider that which the "village community" will relate to based on the system of norms that have been established for the purpose and ease of interpretation. Who is the "village community" for a project like DYSWIS? Is it those living in the camp who gain insight into the experiences and perceptions of their neighbours? Or is it humanitarian workers, politicians, and interested others viewing from a place of relative privilege and power? A political orientation informed by adherence to humanitarian principles guides who chooses to visit these exhibits, while the project write-up explains that compassion and a humanitarian orientation informed many of the choices youth made about their photographs subjects: "They saw photographing as a way of expressing this compassion and concern for those more needy among them."

Most of the seventy-five photographs included in the final exhibit can be grouped into three categories—everyday life in the camps: a man carrying a goat, women preparing food, children's families or houses; the deprived conditions of the camps: piles of garbage, hungry children, amputees; or aspirational settings: classrooms and maps with captions explaining children's goals to travel and have successful careers. The most shocking photographs within the Namibia and Yemen collections did not make it into the final exhibit: a "crazy woman," as the caption describes, laying on the ground and grasping a board and one of a boy holding what looks like a makeshift knife to the throat of a younger child in the Osire camp in Namibia and a child on an operating table overseen by doctors the Kharaze camp in Yemen.

The photographs that DYSWIS chose for the final exhibit are in some ways demonstrative of what Homi Bhabha (1983) explains as the processes of subjectification made possible and plausible by stereotypical, colonial discourse through his "scopic drive" concept. He argues that stereotypes based on colonial relationships allow people to relate to and derive pleasure from viewing the other and that this pleasure and understanding is based on a set of accessible tropes developed through colonialism (Bhabha 1983). Similar critiques have been levied by feminist researchers arguing that descriptions of spectacular, brutal sexual violence serve to resolidify power differentials, thus positioning white women as saving Black and Brown women from Black/Brown men (Spivak 2003; Sa'ar 2005; Lewis 2021). The project differs in some ways from these concerns as the youth themselves chose the subjects and the orientation of the photographs. Nevertheless, the training they received came from a particular orientation and had a humanitarian sensibility, and the project had clear goals in mind; it was not youth-designed or led. Concerningly, nowhere in the project description is the relative participation of the photos' subjects discussed. Given the extremely vulnerable positions of many of the individuals pictured, it is uncomfortable to think they may not have freely given consent to have their photographs taken or may not know that some images are freely accessible online. For a project intending to empower the youth photographers, it is unclear why the subjects of the photographs are not also discussed as agentic individuals with the right to determine if and how their images should be shared.[4]

Gender inequality and the constrictive hopelessness of the camp is expressed in the exhibit, allowing Western viewers to reaffirm their stereotypes of the unfortunate circumstances of the "other" while also feeling connected to their struggles. We witness fifteen-year-old girls performing domestic chores: "I am preparing lunch for the family. The children are coming home soon" (Hodhan, fifteen years old, Kharaz refugee camp, Yemen; image caption; Redden 2008). And a young girl who enjoys football despite her gender: "Something about myself. I look like my family and I do wash the plates. And I like to play football even if I am a girl. I feel nice when I am with my mother . . . And I want to do a job of being a doctor or nurse" (Ishimewe, eleven years old, Osire refugee camp, Namibia; image caption; Redden 2008). Here, viewers may question where "the children" are that Hodhan is not. School? Out with friends? And we hope that Ishimewe can accomplish her goal of becoming a nurse or doctor, laudable in most societies. Here my critique is not of the images nor the captions, and it is certainly not with the girls who produced the images. Rather, it is to highlight the imperative within the project of positioning girls in a state of relative deprivation for viewers to consider and sympathize with. This highlights the problematic in the relationship between seeing and being seen, evident in the DYSWIS project:

> In order to conceive of the colonial subject as the effect of power that is productive—disciplinary and "pleasurable"—one has to see the surveillance of colonial power as functioning in relation to the regime of the scopic drive. That is, the drive that represents the pleasure in "seeing" which has the look as its object of desire, is related both to the myths of origins, the primal scene and the problematic of fetishism and locates the surveyed object within the "imaginary" relation. (Bhabha 1992)

In relation to DYSWIS then, there is an interesting tension between seeing, the presentation of what is to be seen, and the regime of the scopic drive. While the content is related to the experiences and images by refugee youth, this is juxtaposed with the pleasure derived by the viewing public, which includes those who visited the exhibit at the UNHCR head office in Geneva or saw the excerpts of the exhibit that were available online.

According to project organizers, DYSWIS was intended to empower the refugee youth who took part in the initiative. It is reasonable to assume it was also intended to garner compassion from the viewing public. In her study of responsibility and photography, Sliwinski (2004) relays an anecdote by a man who never understood the horror of the war he lived through until he saw photographs of the atrocities in a museum. In this case, his experiences were muted and pushed aside until he encountered visual evidence of what the people of his country suffered. This was a politicizing experience that led to his personal engagement with questions of war and peace with which he may not have otherwise grappled. This mode of engagement is the hope behind many photoethnography (Wright 2018) and humanitarian photography projects (Fehrenbach and Rodogno 2015). In DYSWIS, however, the photographs capture neither the refugees' journeys to the camp nor the conditions that turned them into refugees. They are telling stories not of violence or suffering related to contextual and political realities but of everyday life in the camp. This alone does not negate the political potentials of similar projects; storytelling can be a deeply political act, including through the medium of photography, and the challenges, joys, and violence of everyday life are important topics to explore. The challenge arises in the filtering of the stories: when photographs are developed within and presented by organizations that emphasize their apoliticism and neutrality, what is the likelihood that youths' stories are included if they insist on a different version of political citizenship?

In considering the relationship between humanitarian logics and the emphasis on photography as truth telling, it is useful to consider the ways that photography can be mobilized to reaffirm white superiority under the guise of neutrality. Razack (2007) focuses on the images of violence and pain designed to elicit outrage and action. Rather than having this effect, however, Razack states that all too often these images are simply consumed rather than acted upon. Instead of inspiring solidarity or a sense of common humanity, these images serve to reinforce the superior position of white, Western audiences over "others." The subjects of the images are reduced to and characterized by their pain and suffering, thus their humanity is not represented or recognized. In her discussion of disembodied universality, Razack (2007) states that the people being depicted are construed as objects, while those viewing the images are moral subjects who are separate and apart from the photographic content they are viewing. This division places the viewer on a higher moral level than the object being viewed. In most cases where the objects are racialized as non-white and the viewing subjects as white, Razack proposes that a form of race pleasure emerges in which "white superiority is confirmed through images of the suffering of black bodies" (378).

Szorenyi (2006) offers a similar critique of representations that present refugees as static, desperate, and without agency. Szorenyi examines refugee coffee-table books that receive high praise for the photographers who have captured these images of struggle and suffering, but in all cases, she finds there is little contextualization of the images or engagement with the people who are being presented. Szorenyi queries the real point of these images that are marketed to Western consumers: Are they intended to inspire compassion, sympathy, and action? Are they collected for the aesthetic value of the photos themselves? Szorenyi emphasizes the importance of the presentation of suffering and, citing Butler (2004), acknowledges the importance of visibility in helping "victims of atrocity and injustice." For Szorenyi, the issue seems to lie more with the motivations behind the production and marketing of the books, as well as with the lack of perceived agency and individuality of the subjects—or, as they are presented, objects—of the pictures.

If we are to draw on Szorenyi's insights, DYSWIS can also be viewed as attempting to integrate the force of these critiques by shifting the focus from the refugee as a decontextualized, passive, voiceless object to a viewing, agentic subject. Brendan Bannon, the photographer who delivered the training workshop explains that "this project gave refugee children a chance to explore the totality of the refugee experience; to show the world both the differences and similarities of their lives" (Redden 2008). He goes on to describe the project as affording the young people new opportunities: "They explained themselves to each other, and became closer in the process. Together, they gave a clear idea of their lives—lives rich in experience, emotion, history, fantasy, humour and compassion" (ibid.). DYSWIS then raises an interesting tension between the lack of political engagement publicly recognized by the UNHCR in the refugee camps and the self-authorship enacted by the youths who took the photographs. Photography is an agentic activity that deploys power over what is included in the shot, how the composition of the photograph will impact the viewer's understanding of the content, and what is excluded from the picture. Placing the camera in the hands of refugee youth, then, serves to recognize and support the decision-making capabilities of the photographers to express their personal realities and to construct their narratives for presentation. This appears as an acknowledgement of the political capabilities of the youth, and one could assume that the intended outcome of this project would be to educate and perhaps inspire action from the viewers of this exhibit. However, critical visual studies has shown that the purpose of projects such as DYSWIS is more expository than action-oriented (Fehrenbach and Rodogno 2015). Photography projects such as this often seem to express the belief that seeing, in and of itself, is important and valuable, that through viewing suffering or adversity we become aware and educated, that seeing is enough to impart empathy or sympathy, and that affect alone can make a difference (Sliwinski 2004). DYSWIS does not appear to differ in this regard. Any actions, feeling, or demand for structural change that is elicited through DYSWIS is still within the humanitarian scope and thus does not challenge its mandate or principles. As such, these outcomes are also impartial and neutral.

Legality, Liminality, and the Camp

Viewers' inspiration to demand formal, systemic change based on DYSWIS does not unsettle the context and space, either physical or relational, of the camp. The stories occupy a temporary and conditional space of usefulness to the humanitarian model, reaffirming the importance of places such as refugee camps while simultaneously demonstrating their insufficiencies and shortcomings. In this there is little space for challenging the political realities and global power relations that led to children living in refugee camps and few opportunities to create alternatives to the refugee camp model of temporary settlement.

Importantly, while refugees themselves are classified and fall under the purview of international humanitarian law in the 1951 Convention of the Refugee and 1967 Refugee Protocol, nowhere in international law are refugee camps addressed (Janmyr 2016). As such, camps operate in a legally liminal space, and their governance and management vary significantly. Janmyr emphasizes that the confinement and detention exhibited in many camps is similar to that of justice and state-run institutions often contested within international law, but refugee camps remain unconsidered. Refugee camps, then, operate in a space of liminality on two registers—both in the sense that they are simultaneously inside and outside of nation-states and that their inhabitants are considered within international law but the spaces they live in are not. The exceptional state of refugee camps has been explored at length elsewhere,[5] but what is important for our consideration of DYSWIS is that experiences occurring in spaces marked by uncertainty, liminality, and temporariness are made intelligible through assertions and recessions of law. NGOs and agencies such as UNHCR provide aid, services, and legal support to refugees in camp settings and also may provide oversight and monitoring to draw attention to and prevent human rights abuses. Foucault discusses the regulative power of forces operating through the "mythicized state" (2003). In this, Foucault is not discounting the influence of the notion of sovereignty but rather drawing attention to the multiple operations of governance outside formal state power. We can see this operation within refugee camps: positioned as simultaneously inside and outside a nation-state, regulated and governed by quasi-legal actors, without formal provisions or consideration within international law. This liminality is necessarily precarious and positions refugees within camp settings as subjects to the laws that define their status within a space unseen by law. In this, we might consider law's recession as an act of its power: without formal law to define or operate in refugee camps, law is refusing a recognition of subjecthood to refugees. Their status is determined by legal and quasi-legal actors, such as the UNHCR and other international institutions, during or after migration and through resettlement. Their liminality and precarity is re-emphasized and reinforced, though, through the refusal of law within the camps.

As the editors state in the introduction of this volume, law is not only violence; it is also a polyvalent force working to construct, regulate, and produce subjectivity in mutually constitutive and historically specific ways. Law can be violence, but it can also contribute to creative and productive projects, ones that may shape subjectivities and subjects through their relation to law. Law's slow violence can be felt, however, through a turning away of legal protections and governance, a feeling made palpable within some of the stark photographs depicting the violence of children going hungry and disabled people sitting alone and apart from others. In the case of DYSWIS, refugee youth are defined as refugees through their legal positioning as having been forcibly displaced from their homes, and their subjectivities in relation to this category were mined for the project. DYSWIS does not grapple with the intricacies of international law pertaining to refugees, and yet we can read through the images the simultaneous presence and absence of law alongside the ambiguity and liminality within the photographs.

The DYSWIS camps are presented as facts, and their legitimacy is not challenged by the project presenting these spaces as uncontested reality. From the photos and the captions, we are struck by the quasi-carceral life in the camp. While several photographs highlight the relative deprivation and feelings of being trapped in the camp, the depoliticization and decontextualization of humanitarian logics driving the project limit opportunities to challenge the governance of these spaces. For example, in one image we see a pair of small hands grasping a chain-link fence. It may be difficult to interpret were it not for the caption, "Prison. I dreamt I was in prison" (image caption; Redden 2008). It is largely through the pairing of the words with the imagery that feelings of empathy, confinement, and sympathy are developed. Indeed, after viewing the photographs, one is left with a feeling of sadness that youth live in these conditions, but there is limited space available to question how they came to be there, where they are going, or how the camp system could be reimagined. Instead, we are left with a sense of suspension, the feeling that there is a moral imperative to engage, but how to do so and with what political objective in mind is as undefined by the project as the space itself is within law. By visually capturing only the present moment in the camps and providing no historical context, understanding of and relating to the youth becomes limited to only that which is immediately visible.

Shane McGrath (2005) argues that refugees are subject to a "politics of compassion," which can have positive effects for those who may benefit from these outcomes but may also serve to prioritize a Western subjectivity and subjectification upon those who come under the scope of the compassionate viewer. In this project, the youth, and the subjects in their photographs, were presented in a way that caused reception to their stories to be shaped by humanitarian sensibilities and the politics of compassion and sentimentality. This effectively limited the self-authorship potential of DYSWIS. Further, Szorenyi (2006) shows that the separation between those who feel compassion and those who are the recipients of that compassion serves to reinforce inequalities, once again solidifying the disparate relationship between refugees and those who consume and react to their stories.

Conclusions and Future Directions

Projects such as DYSWIS offer applied insight into the implementation of humanitarian prerogatives in ambiguous spaces, providing the opportunity for established conceptions to be re-evaluated and reimagined in a way that may allow for new relationships to develop between refugees and the agencies representing them. DYSWIS arose out of humanitarian traditions and responses to critiques of the mandate and effects of humanitarianism. Its organization around refugee subjects in refugee camps positioned the project in spaces marked by liminality, both with regard to the territory of the camp and their legal position. The final output was a photography exhibition in which the objective reality and truth of the refugee youth experience was purportedly presented, and yet there remains outstanding issues with the prioritization of visual representations of "truth" and the limits of political engagement and potential both in the photographs themselves and for those viewing them. Questions and considerations of politicization, contextualization, subjectification, and seeing/being are all relevant to my consideration of DYSWIS. In advancing legal subjectivity in diffuse ways, non-state forces are advancing notions of liberal normativity through processes that are deeply implicated in how youth experience and engage with international institutions. In analyzing a project such as DYSWIS, it is important to look at the sensibilities and knowledges that lead to its development and implementation, the spatial and political location of the project, and the continuing influences of its existence. It is not easy to criticize a project intended to empower refugee youth and support them in telling their stories; nowhere herein do I intend to take away from the positive elements and intentions behind the project. However, it is imperative to engage with projects and initiatives aiming to do good; this is how we better understand entrenched power relations and open space to consider how even noble intentions are often limited in their outcomes, to uncover where these limitations originate from and to what effect, and to find out how these reinforce rather than effectively challenge Global North–South hierarchies.

If we consider the value of photographs to be relational rather than objective, then we can begin to break down the binary of seeing/being seen and at a minimum remain cognizant of the discrepant power relations that accompany it. The issue remains, however, that the engagement in DYSWIS moves away from the authors of the images and texts and instead becomes refocused on the UNHCR, which is in current ownership of the exhibition. It seems plausible that the connections made are not with the youth in camp spaces but rather with the agency that implemented the project. This is where DYSWIS differs from other photoethnography projects. The exhibition is more strongly associated with the UNHCR than with the youth, or with either camp. By claiming ownership over the photographs and authoring the exhibition that is accessible to the public, the UNHCR minimizes the political voice from the photographers and reroutes the potential for relationality and connections that could have been established from the youth to the organization.

Similar to what I have attempted to do in this chapter, socio-legal studies creates space to bring together different bodies of research and literature in order to examine how law and normative ordering impacts social relations and sense of place. In this, we are able to look at the intersections, creative opportunities, and political potential of challenging dominant configurations of power through nuanced studies of the ways they operate and circulate in varied sites around the world and come to be reproduced even within projects designed to challenge them. In the case of DYSWIS, we may be left with a sense that colonial power relations are hegemonic and near impossible to rupture. Indeed, the nature of hegemony is that it seems inescapable in its dominance and as a mode of truth that cannot easily be undone (Gramsci 1971). By working with the methods put forward by socio-legal studies, we can gain an in-depth understanding of how these relations are codified, both in doctrinal law and in numerous other scripted ways, and how these texts influence understandings of and relationships to people both near and far. By offering ways to understand not just local contexts but the ways that international organizations and institutions operate across state borders, space is opened for exploring how the most influential bodies, such as the UN, are complicit in processes that legitimize imposed depoliticization and fetishization of the human experience. Through this we can start to pull the threads that may ultimately serve to unravel the configurations of domination that continue to exist through insidious racialization and othering.

Since my initial analysis of this project, DYSWIS has been implemented in refugee camps in Syria and Jordan, with photographs and brief testimonials available on a designated site for the project (UNHCR 2015). While a full consideration of the more recent iterations of the project has not been completed at this time, preliminary investigation shows that the updated site offers more opportunity for context and has videos as well as still photographs. The site itself does not provide details about specific political realities that create conflict and displacement, nor does it host detailed stories from project participants. From the website, however, it does appear that photo exhibitions are held in project refugee camps as well as online. This is a positive development, as opportunities for shared experiences are positioned in locales where they arise instead of in decontextualized spaces.

Photography projects such as DYSWIS offer important opportunities for marginalized young people to present their experiences and point the camera at what is interesting or important in their lives. Self-authorship mitigates some critiques of disempowering narratives that present refugees only as victims. The medium of photography is not neutral however, nor is the training, the curation behind putting together an exhibit, or how the photographs are viewed by differently positioned audiences or humanitarian projects writ large. Through these processes, law's presence and absence can be felt simultaneously: the violence and deprivation depicted in some photographs can be interpreted as demonstrating lawlessness, a lack of protection. And yet the subjectification of refugees within international law makes their presence within the liminal spaces of the camps necessarily legal. This emerges in tension with the concreteness of the moments captured on film, raising more questions than answers about how youth's lives are governed, where and when the turning away or refusal of law acts as violence, and how humanitarianism, as purportedly apolitical and impartial, is positioned to grapple with these challenges.

Notes

Acknowledgements: This chapter is an adaptation of my master's research, which benefited immensely from Dr. Anna Pratt's supervision and her commitment to critical scholarship. Thank you to the editors of this collection—Mariful Alam, Pat Dwyer, and Katrin Roots—for their support, keen edits, and thoughtful suggestions.

1 The UNHCR has made DYSWIS an ongoing project and has conducted photography workshops in a number of other camps in different countries, including Jordan and Syria. This paper only considers the original iteration of the project, but the analyses and critiques within may also apply to the later versions. I offer a brief discussion of more recent developments in the conclusion of this chapter.
2 The photographs were previously accessible online through the UNHCR. Unfortunately, during the production of this book, the online exhibit was removed from the UNHCR site. See Redden 2008 for a sample of the photographs. Additionally, a few of the photographs are included in this video about the project: https://www.youtube.com/watch?v=V-KV4bpdnfY. I have decided not to reproduce the images discussed in this paper. I did not attempt to obtain copyright permission to have the photos printed in this chapter, as I do not want to further reproduce the same processes that I am critiquing. I have chosen to include the captions and narratives written by the youth, as this is the way they made sense of the images they created.
3 International law itself is borne of colonialism, a history that remains embedded in international relations and includes the actions and interactions of agencies such as the UNHCR. This legacy has yet to be reconciled, and its impacts are the subject of numerous works of post and anti-colonial scholarship. Please see Anghie (2007), Baxi (2006), Mbembe (2001), and Rajagopal (2003).
4 It is possible that there was a photo release process that was not shared in the description; however, the number of children pictured with no adults seemingly present and the woman presented as suffering from serious mental health challenges, for example, raises doubts as to how and whether consent was obtained.
5 See Edkins (2000), Gregory (2006), and Turner (2005).

References

Agamben, Giorgio. 1998. *Homo Sacer: Sovereign Power and Bare Life*. Stanford, CA: Stanford University Press.

Anghie, Antony. 2007. *Imperialism, Sovereignty and the Making of International Law.* Cambridge: Cambridge University Press.

Baxi, U. 2006. "What May the 'Third World' Expect from International Law?" *Third World Quarterly* 27 (5): 713–25.

Bhabha, Homi K. 1994. "The Other Question: Stereotype, Discrimination and the Discourse of Colonialism." In *The Location of Culture,* 125–51. London: Routledge.

———. 1992. "'The Other Question': Stereotypes and Colonial Discourse." In *The Sexual Subject: A Screen Reader in Sexuality,* 312–23. London: Routledge.

Bourdieu, Pierre. 1999. "The Social Definition of Photography." In *Visual Culture: The Reader,* edited by Jessica Evans and Stuart Hall, 162–80. Thousand Oaks, CA: SAGE.

Butler, Judith. 2004. *Precarious Life: The Powers of Mourning and Violence.* New York: Verso.

Darian-Smith, Eve. 2013. *Laws and Societies in Global Contexts: Contemporary `Approaches.* Cambridge: Cambridge University Press.

Edkins, Jenny. 2000. "Sovereign Power, Zones of Indistinction, and the Camp." *Alternatives: Global, Local, Political* 25 (1): 3–25.

Fassin, Didier. 2010. "Inequality of Lives, Hierarchies of Humanity: Moral Commitments and Ethical Dilemmas of Humanitarianism." *In the Name of Humanity: The Government of Threat and Care,* edited by Ilana Feldman and Miriam Ticktin, 238–56. Durham, NC: Duke University Press.

Fehrenbach, Heide, and Davide Rodogno, eds. 2015. *Humanitarian Photography.* Cambridge: Cambridge University Press.

Foucault, Michel. 2003. *Society Must Be Defended: Lectures at the Collège De France, 1975–76.* Translated by David Macey. New York: Picador.

Gramsci, Antonio. 1971. *Selections from the Prison Notebooks.* London: Lawrence and Wishart.

Gregory, Derek. 2006. "The Black Flag: Guantanamo Bay and the Space of Exception." *Human Geography* 88 (4): 405–27.

Janmyr, Maja. 2016. "Spaces of Legal Ambiguity: Refugee Camps and Humanitarian Power." *Humanity: An International Journal of Human Rights, Humanitarianism, and Development* 7 (3): 413–27.

Khosravi, Sharham. 2010. *"Illegal" Traveller: An Autoethnography of Borders.* London: Palgrave MacMillan.

Lewis, Chloé. 2021 "The Making and Re-making of the 'Rape Capital of the World': On Colonial Durabilities and the Politics of Sexual Violence Statistics in DRC." *Critical African Studies* 14 (1): 1–18.

Malkki, Liisa H. 1995. "Refugees and Exile: From 'Refugee Studies' to the National Order of Things." *Annual Review of Anthropology* 24:495–523.

———. 1996. "Speechless Emissaries: Refugees, Humanitarianism, and Dehistoricization." *Cultural Anthropology* 11 (3): 377–404.

Mbembe, Achille. 2001. *On the Postcolony*. Berkeley: University of California Press.

McEntire, Kyla Jo, Michele Leiby, and Matthew Krain. 2015. "Human Rights Organizations as Agents of Change: An Experimental Examination of Framing and Micromobilization." *American Political Science Review* 109 (3): 407–26.

McGrath, Shane. 2005. "Compassionate Refugee Politics?" *M/C Journal* 8, no. 6. https://journal.media-culture.org.au/index.php/mcjournal/article/view/2440.

Nyers, Peter. 2006. *Rethinking Refugees: Beyond States of Emergency*. New York: Routledge.

Rajagopal, Balakrishnan. 2003. *International Law from Below: Development, Social Movements and Third World Resistance*. Cambridge: Cambridge University Press.

Rajaram, Prem Kumar. 2002. "Humanitarianism and Representations of the Refugee." *Journal of Refugee Studies* 15 (3): 247–64.

Razack, Sherene. 2007. "Stealing the Pain of Others: Reflections on Canadian Humanitarian Responses." *Review of Education, Pedagogy, and Cultural Studies* 29 (4): 375–94.

Redden, Jack. 2008. "World Refugee Day: In a New Exhibition, Refugee Children Photograph Their Own Lives." Do You See What I See? UNHCR project. http://www.unhcr.org/485b7df4a.html.

Rygiel, Kim. 2012. "Politicizing Camps: Forging Transgressive Citizenships In and Through Transit." *Citizenship Studies* 16 (6): 807–25.

Sa'ar, Amalia. 2005. "Postcolonial Feminism, the Politics of Identification, and the Liberal Bargain." *Gender & Society* 19 (5): 680–700.

Sassen, Saskia. 2008. "Neither Global nor National: Novel Assemblages of Territory, Authority, and Rights." *Ethics & Global Politics* 1 (1–2): 61–79.

Silbey, Susan. 2010. "Legal Culture and Cultures of Legality." *Handbook of Cultural Sociology*, edited by Laura Grindstaff, Ming-Cheng M. Lo, and John R. Hall, 470–79. London: Routledge.

Slim, Hugo, 2015. *Humanitarian Ethics: A Guide to the Morality of Aid in War and Disaster*. Oxford: Oxford University Press.

Sliwinski, Sharon. 2004. "A Painful Labour: Responsibility and Photography." *Visual Studies* 19 (2): 150–61.

Spivak, Gayatri Chakravorty. 2003. "Can the Subaltern Speak?" *Die Philosophin* 14 (27): 42–58.

Szorenyi, Anna. 2006. "The Images Speak for Themselves? Reading Refugee Coffee-Table Books." *Visual Studies* 21 (1): 24–41.

Turner, Simon. 2005. "Suspended Spaces-Contesting Sovereignties in a Refugee Camp." *Sovereign Bodies*, edited by Thomas Blom Hansen and Finn Stepputat, 312–32. Princeton, NJ: Princeton University Press.

UNHCR. n.d. "Legal Protection." United Nations High Commissioner for Refugees. https://www.unhcr.org/legal-protection.html.

———. 2012. "Global Report." United Nations High Commissioner for Refugees. https://www.unhcr.org/51b1d6180.pdf.

———. 2015. Do You See What I See? https://www.un.org/en/exhibits/exhibit/voices -wind/do-you-see-what-i-see.

Wright, Christopher. 2018 "Photo-Ethnography." In *The International Encyclopedia of Anthropology*, edited by Hilary Callan, 1–5. Hoboken, NJ: Wiley-Blackwell.

Part III
Resistance and Social Transformation

6 Practicing Freedom of Information as "Feral Law" and Advancing Research Methods in Socio-legal Studies

Alex Luscombe and Kevin Walby

Research methods in socio-legal studies deserve more attention. As Banakar and Travers have noted, the "absence of methods texts" (2005, x) in socio-legal studies creates challenges for scholars and limits creativity. The lack of development of specific research methods in socio-legal studies stands in contrast to criminology and criminal justice studies, where research methods texts abound (also see Martel, Hogeveen, and Woolford 2006). In this chapter, we attempt to foster more attention toward research methods in socio-legal studies in Canada. To do so, we reflect on how to use access to information (ATI) and freedom of information (FOI) laws as part of socio-legal studies. In the field of socio-legal studies, ATI/FOI laws are increasingly used as research techniques to generate disclosures about the inside workings of government. As we argue, ATI/FOI data can be incorporated into socio-legal research projects and triangulated with other data types (e.g., public documents, interviews, field observations). Used as such, ATI/FOI requests can enhance the "openness" of government, a partial and mediated window into the practices of governing (Walby and Larsen 2012; also see Cordis and Warren 2014; Nam 2012; Hazell and Worthy 2010; Shepherd, Stevenson, and Flinn 2010).

Using ATI/FOI law to conduct research can be difficult. Because the spirit and principles of ATI/FOI can be undermined by government agencies to protect and reproduce dominant political structures, such as those in place for state surveillance (Roberts 1999, 2002, 2005), scholars must devise creative ways of navigating the "games that bureaucrats play" (Katz 1969, 1261). Efforts to break through government structures of opacity via ATI/FOI are frequently undermined through loopholes and state secrecy provisions in the law. Agencies can also pre-emptively block any transparency effect from an FOI disclosure by limiting the contents of disclosure or disclosing the record in a format that's difficult to work with (e.g., an unsearchable PDF file, or a printed and poor-quality scan of a spreadsheet). At its worst, ATI/FOI operates less as a legal-democratic right for rendering government more open and more as a means by which government can claim the legitimating effects of having an ATI/FOI regime while undermining any real democratizing social change (Brownlee and Walby 2015; Duncan, Luscombe, and Walby 2022; Luscombe and Walby 2017).

Contributing to debates in socio-legal scholarship on research methods (Banakar and Travers 2005), activism, and legal expertise, we theorize the prospects of ATI/FOI for justice as well as the twists, turns, and drawbacks of ATI/FOI by advancing the notion of "feral lawyering." Although the efficacy of an ATI/FOI regime is mostly outside the user's hands, we argue that some barriers to meaningful disclosure can be overcome through use of creative feral lawyering strategies. Rather than succumb to the seemingly indisputable expert decisions of ATI/FOI offices, practicing ATI/FOI law in this way helps the researcher creatively push back using a more adversarial approach to gain access to government records.[1] We advance the notion of feral lawyering not as a way of characterizing some essential form that exists in the world but as an ethos that can be adopted by new ATI/FOI users, particularly for those already engaging in this kind of research as a means of rendering their work intelligible. In the latter respect, the concept of feral lawyering serves as a more precise way of accounting for the scrappy brokering work many ATI/FOI users are required to engage in and thus of ATI/FOI law in action.

Throughout this chapter, we use the term *feral* in a double sense. On the one hand, the word *feral* is meant to conjure an image of a wild and untamed animal that cannot be controlled and domesticated. Socio-legal researchers that adopt a feral lawyer mentality in their use of ATI/FOI refuse to be subdued by the expert claims and appeals to state authority of ATI/FOI coordinators. On the other hand, an animal can also *become* feral, as in the sense of a domesticated animal being released and allowed to run wild. In practicing ATI/FOI as feral lawyers, users refuse to take a submissive "lay citizen" role by demanding and negotiating rather than asking for information from their governments. ATI/FOI users that practice feral lawyering not only refuse to be tamed by government laws, official discourse, and the presumed expertise of coordinators, but they also actively reconstitut their relation to the state, breaking free from their docile, lay-citizen bodies. By adopting this more active, creative, and adversarial approach to ATI/FOI, users help level the playing field, becoming more like professional lawyers (broadly understood) than lay citizens. Feral lawyers demand, negotiate, and challenge, upholding a *will* and *proficiency* to know rather than the more passive and contained "right to ask" or "right to know" that government discourse encourages.

Most academic and socio-legal researchers using ATI/FOI are not acting in the capacity of professional lawyers (and may not hold law degrees), yet through creative brokering, they can often learn to mimic bargaining, argumentation, and appeal practices familiar to professional lawyers. We argue that feral lawyering captures this dynamic by shrinking the practical and epistemic gap assumed between professional practitioners of law and users of ATI/FOI. Our chapter attempts to reframe orthodox assumptions in popular legal discourse about who can be a skilled user of law. We begin with reflections on the development of socio-legal studies and how we situate our approach in this developing field. Next, we contrast our understanding of practicing ATI/FOI law in action, conceptualized as feral lawyering, with the official ATI/FOI narrative promoted by government. Finally, we elaborate on the notion of feral lawyering and provide examples from our ongoing research on public police agencies in Canada.

Why Socio-legal Studies? And How?

There has been considerable discussion about what socio-legal studies is and where it is headed (see Travers 2001; Thomas 1997). These discussions have often started with reflection on doctrinal legal scholarship. As Alan Hunt (1981) once pointed out, traditional legal studies has had trouble accepting theoretical and critical work. Doctrinal analyses of case law are still taught as producing a kind of truth in law schools. Hunt (1981) argued that the importance of a sociology of law is that it allows for theoretical and critical work in ways that doctrinal analyses exclude. Cotterrell (1998) similarly argued for a social and theoretical understanding of law, to guard against the reductionism of pure doctrinal approaches. Yet, even the sociological turn in law and the subsequent development of a sociology of law has limits. One limit is that the sociology of law has not been multidisciplinary and has tended toward more abstract conceptual interventions, including the notion of society itself (Fitzpatrick 1995). In the past two decades, the field of socio-legal studies has flourished. In socio-legal studies, a greater diversity of research methods and theoretical perspectives are now drawn on, an even greater diversity than Hunt and Cotterrell even imagined (see Hudson 2006; Leonard 1995; Kline 1994). Mariana Valverde (2016) has argued that socio-legal studies is marked by its focus on law in action—that is, studying the consequences, the impacts, and the offshoots of law by examining how it works, not simply settling for how the law says it works. Feenan (2009) similarly argues that socio-legal studies examines law in context. In other words, socio-legal studies draws on a diversity of methods and theories to disrupt the self-referential nature of law and its authority.

Beyond the focus on law in action, Valverde (2016) notes that socio-legal studies cannot afford to be overly philosophical or theoretically obtuse. The trouble with some critical socio-legal work is that the analytical schemes developed are so dense that they do not help advance the mission of analyzing law in action (also see McKnight 2015; Jabbari 1998; Kagan 1995). As Valverde puts it, "Neither legal philosophy nor grand European sociology of law are particularly helpful, and in many respects these traditions constitute obstacles to concrete analyses of legal processes" (2016, 172). Taking this claim as our point of departure, our conceptualization and practical approach to feral lawyering is influenced by literature in social studies of science (Callon 1984; Latour 1987; Law 2009; Mol 2010). It has been argued that social studies of science offers a unique and useful approach to the study of law and legal knowledges "in the making" (Cloatre 2015; Rooke, Cloatre, and Dingwall 2012; Cowan and Carr 2008; Lévi and Valverde 2008).[2] The language and approach of social studies of science informs our conception and study of feral lawyering and is consistent with the emphasis of socio-legal studies on legal processes.

In social studies of science, the emphasis is on empirically documenting social life "in action" (Latour 1987). Socio-legal phenomena are messy and precarious configurations constructed by heterogeneous actors in motion (Law 2009). The approach highlights empirical questions of how actors and their material counterparts work together in a coordinated effort to achieve some goal or outcome. Objects (e.g., texts), as much as people, have the capacity to shape social outcomes. *The law* and its *power*, therefore, are never predetermined conditions but achievements, network effects, and the outcomes of a successful "translation" (Callon 1984). A social studies of science approach is consistent with a socio-legal approach for four reasons.

First, a social studies of science approach and a socio-legal approach both focus on the minutiae of daily practices. Second, both undermine the presumably unassailable authority and universality of truth and knowledge, in one case science and the other case law. Third, both perspectives strive to use theory in a way that is still in contact with the empirical world or, better yet, based on empirical observation. Comparative, empirical inquiry is a core focus in contemporary socio-legal studies (Creutzfeldt, Kubal, and Pirie 2016). Fourth, both social studies of science and socio-legal studies view the researcher as an active participant in the research process, preferring methodologies that are open, messy, and reflexive. Informed by social studies of science, below we develop a mentality and guiding conceptual framework through which to theorize, practice, and analyze law—ATI/FOI law specifically—that does not ignore the letter of the law but instead requires a full immersion in law as a way of studying it in action. The concept and mentality of feral lawyering elaborated below does just that.

Going Beyond Official Legal Discourse

The Government of Canada's website section on "how access to information and personal information requests work" presents the ATI Act as providing "Canadian citizens, permanent residents and any person or corporation present in Canada a right to access records of government institutions that are subject to the Act" (Canada 2017). As the web page explains, each federal agency has an "Access to Information and Privacy Coordinator." "The coordinators are responsible for ensuring that any access to information or personal information requests received by the institution are responded to in accordance with the Acts" (2017). The web page continues on to say that while citizens have a right to ask, not all information can be released. The coordinators review the information and determine what can and cannot be released: "Some information needs to be withheld to protect other important democratic values, such as national security considerations, or to protect the privacy of personal information" (2017). Some of these exemptions are required by law; others are determined at the discretion of the public body (2017). If the requester is not "satisfied" with how their request was processed or with the contents of the disclosure, they can "make a complaint" to the Office of the Information Commissioner of Canada (2017). One finds a similar framing in government websites on FOI at the provincial level.

The government's official discourses on ATI/FOI frame the process through the language of legal rights (the right to ask), expert decision-making (requests are reviewed by expert bureaucrats), national interests (information is only inaccessible when its disclosure would undermine "other important democratic values"), and customer satisfaction (the right to "complain" when "dissatisfied" with the process or outcome). Lay citizens are encouraged to make requests for information under ATI/FOI laws, await the decision of expert coordinators, and then accept or "complain" about the outcome. This official narrative and the framing of ATI/FOI are not only simplistic and inaccurate but seek to constitute the requester in a particular way in relation to the state. Official discourse around ATI/FOI positions the requester, as lay citizen, in relation to the coordinator, as expert bureaucrat, and in this way seeks to enact a power relation wherein requesters submissively take what they get. The law, national interests, and democratic values are presented as the core mechanisms through which information is disclosed or withheld. Other more questionable considerations that might block or mediate the contents of a disclosure—for example, understaffed ATI offices, personal quarrels, an interest in avoiding political scandal—are not assumed to figure into the equation.

Legal studies literature on ATI/FOI tends to reproduce this dichotomy, treating ATI/FOI law as a special knowledge. For example, Kazmierski's (2016) work on ATI/FOI is reflective of a doctrinal approach and sticks to case analysis or application of the Charter and constitutional tests to ATI/FOI law (also see Kazmierski 2009, 2013, 2014). Focus on the letter of the law and official legal and administrative mechanisms are also primary focuses of literature on FOI and public policy (Cordis and Warren 2014; Hazell and Worthy 2010; Shepherd, Stevenson, and Flinn 2010). Of course, this approach is much needed to track changing precedents. The problem with such a doctrinal approach alone, however, is the analysis often stops with the letter of the law. We want to theorize and analyze ATI/FOI law and practice in a way that is consistent with socio-legal studies, and we want to study law in a way that moves with it. That is, we want to analyze ATI/FOI law and practice using a method that can examine the making of law, the letter of the law, but also, crucially, law in action.

Below, reflecting on the work required to successfully file an ATI/FOI request for academic research in Canada, we present an alternative approach to conceptualizing ATI/FOI in action. We call this approach feral lawyering, a notion we introduce to highlight both the variance of ATI/FOI regimes in practice (within and between organizations, countries, etc.) as well as the creative strategies required for requesters to effectively gain access to useful information in government. It is indeed a form of lawyering insofar as the ATI/FOI user works with legal knowledges, processes, and resources to leverage information from the government, yet it is feral in the sense that the ATI/FOI user can be more creative, collaborative, investigative, and subversive in their work than those employed within the constraints of the formal legal system. The goal of reconceptualizing the work of ATI/FOI requesting as feral lawyering is not to suggest that requesters are equivalent to professional lawyers or that requesters receive professional training as lawyers (though this would be helpful). There remain crucial differences between professional and feral lawyers, not the least of which is the specialized training received by professional lawyers, the access to resources, and the role of the courts, which can (but rarely) figure into ATI/FOI processes in Canada (see Yeager 2006). Still, to be successful, ATI/FOI requesters are required to adopt many of the same negotiation, argumentation, and appeal practices familiar to professional lawyers. Rather than ask and wait as lay citizens, the ATI/FOI user as feral lawyer must adopt an active, creative, sometimes obtrusive approach to navigating the wild and variable legal regime that is ATI/FOI (on creativity and law, see Lefebvre 2008).

Feral Lawyering

In addition to challenging official discourse on ATI/FOI, there are two further benefits for socio-legal studies literature to researching and practicing ATI/FOI as feral lawyering. First, it pushes socio-legal scholarship to explore those areas of social life, in which law is constituted and legal subjects are produced, that otherwise lie outside of the expert services and formal arenas (in particular, the courts) of trained legal professionals. ATI/FOI matters rarely make it to the courts and, except in rare moments of journalistic frustration, are not widely publicized. When viewed through the terms set forth by government's official discourse, it is easy to overlook the extent to which regular users of ATI/FOI are involved in lengthy disputes that involve them operating as quasi-professional lawyers despite usually receiving no formal legal training.[3] Not unlike jailhouse lawyers who train themselves to use law as a tool, feral lawyers using ATI/FOI for socio-legal research educate themselves on laws, legal modes of argumentation, effective strategies for brokering access, and avenues for challenging seemingly "closed" decisions such as formal appeal with Information and Privacy Commissioners (IPCs).

Second, feral lawyering involves complex and lengthy processes of negotiating with coordinators, arguing, and appealing decisions, and insofar as the feral lawyer extensively documents these, they make ATI/FOI *processes*—not just the letter of law or surrounding official narratives—into researchable subject matter for socio-legal studies scholars. Everything from the writing of the request to the interactions with the coordinator can be extensively documented. True to a social studies of science approach, this can also entail keeping track of non-human as much as human actors involved at every stage. When feral lawyering, ATI/FOI users are, for example, "acted on" by a variety of legal and bureaucratic texts that shape their actions, and these can be reflected on in detailed field notes for later analysis (see also Prior 2008). By keeping detailed field notes of everything from the initial request to the negotiations with coordinators, feral lawyering is something that can be reflected on in a subsequent analysis of how ATI/FOI law works in action. Such analyses are often overlooked in socio-legal scholarship on ATI/FOI, where the focus tends to be on the disclosure outcome. Feral lawyering requires that the workings of ATI/FOI law in action are well documented.

Brokering Access, Strategies of Argumentation, and Appeal

ATI/FOI starts with the filing of a request for records with a government agency. This can be anything from a corpus of emails to a series of internal reports, a Memorandum of Understanding, or any other bureaucratically generated text unique to the organization the researcher is interested in. Drafting the requests requires careful consideration of the file structure of the agency records in question. The ATI/FOI user should do their homework on the agency, their personnel, their records, and so on, to inform the wording of the request. This might entail looking at the wording of other similar requests and asking colleagues or journalists for feedback. Once an ATI/FOI request has been filed with a government agency in Canada, the user will often receive a phone call from a coordinator. Sometimes the user will receive an official letter first, acknowledging receipt of the request, but it is this first informal contact by telephone that for feral lawyers constitutes the first moment of negotiation with the government over access to data. The moment the user answers the telephone from a (typically) "private" number, the coordinator will usually start the exchange by seeking to "clarify" the wording of the request, sometimes also asking why the information is being sought. Once the requester has supplemented their written request with a verbal explanation of the information they are after, it is typical for coordinators to encourage them to reduce the scope of the request by presenting claims about high fees and lengthy time delays due to the large amount of work that would allegedly be required to process a request. When acting as feral lawyers, ATI/ FOI users tend not to give in blindly to the coordinator's recommendations (which usually entail dropping or limiting the scope of the disclosure) but use this as an opportunity to "broker access" to the records they are after (Larsen and Walby 2012). There may be a discussion of costs for larger disclosures that occurs, though an early mention of cost by an ATI/FOI coordinator during the brokering process may be an attempt to dissuade the user. The feral lawyer needs to be shrewd during these conversations and negotiations and be prepared to challenge exorbitant fee estimates if necessary.

ATI/FOI requests present users with numerous opportunities to employ creative and legalistic styles of argumentation to broker access to information. When feral lawyering, ATI/FOI users may mimic styles of argumentation popular in their understanding of professional law (which will vary from person to person). For example, one strategy that we commonly use, particularly in large comparative research projects involving multiple identical ATI/FOI requests on multiple agencies, is to argue precedent. When a coordinator seems hesitant to release information or informs us that they will be heavily redacting it, we inform this coordinator when possible that other agencies—particularly nearby ones or agencies in their same province—have released this information already without applying the same sections of law to severe it. Coordinators will rarely if ever ask about your requests with other agencies, but as feral lawyers, we usually offer it. By sharing the response and disclosure package of other agencies, these agencies sometimes reconsider their own proposed approach to framing the disclosure. This is evidence that, although they often present their rationales as indisputable, there is no "natural" or "inherent" connection between the information being asked for and the sections of the law that prevent that information from being disclosed in the interests of the state. Challenging their rationales through tactics like this one is proof that the seemingly impenetrable legal arguments put forth by coordinators to justify their decisions are not set in stone.

One request we submitted to the Abbotsford Police Department (APD) in British Columbia provides a case in point (see Luscombe, Walby, and Lippert 2017). For a larger comparative research project on user-pays policing (i.e., companies hiring public police for private ends, for example, crowd control, event security), we submitted requests for internal police records logging the names of businesses that had hired members of the APD between 2012 and 2015. Having filed this same request with ninety police departments across Canada, we encountered varying degrees of openness and ease of access to records. For reasons unknown, the APD was the one agency that sought to block us. After receiving an incomplete and highly redacted version of the documents we requested, we demanded that the coordinator provide us with a written explanation of their rationale and legal justification, something they had not initially provided with the disclosure package. As the coordinator explained to us by email,

> I understand what you are asking for, however, that is not information that we will be providing and is not in the public interest. We have provided you with the financial information which indicates what the Abbotsford Police have received in recouped expenses for callout services provided. If the Abbotsford Police were to hire an outside company to provide a service, then yes, we would release that information as it would be the taxpayers' right to know where the money is going. However, when we are hired by another organization/company to provide a service for them (on a cost recovery basis only), it is not our place to release information on the specifics of that organization and how they spend their money. As a public body, not only do we release information, we also have a responsibility to protect the personal information of individuals and private companies. If you have any other questions, please feel free to contact me again.

The passage above evinces many of the elements of ATI/FOI official discourse that we have discussed so far. By requesting that the coordinator explain their reasoning in writing, we were able to obtain the basic necessary information to construct a counter-argument and initiate an appeal. First, note the tone of the explanation, written in a seemingly unchallengeable, expert, and authoritative way. Rather than state that they did not *believe* the information to be in the public interest, a view that ran contrary to our own, the coordinator stated that the information "is not in the public interest." And rather than the information being something that they *wished* or *preferred* not to provide, it was presented as information that they will "not . . . be providing." Language use is important here, as the chosen words seek not only to communicate to the user the agency's rationale for withholding information but present them as unchallengeable, expert-based, and authoritative. They speak to the user as a lay citizen rather than as a feral lawyer. The mention of the "taxpayers' right to know" is also significant here, as it seeks to close the exchange by framing it in the language of binary rights (the right to know versus the right not to know) rather than the more fluid *proficiency* to know that is at the core of feral lawyering. The coordinator's response also seeks to frame their withholding of records in terms of protecting "other democratic values," referring to a *responsibility to protect* the information of individuals and private companies. Finally, in the last sentence of their response, the coordinator encouraged us to contact them with "any other questions" about the agency's "expert" decision (rather than contact them to challenge or counter-argue it), again presented as something fixed and unchallengeable. This entire passage, which is typical when using ATI/FOI to research government agencies in Canada, exhibits many of the qualities of the official discourse surrounding ATI/FOI that feral lawyering is meant to challenge.

After receiving this response from the coordinator, we prepared a detailed analysis and counter-argument to this rationale and sent it to the local provincial IPC. Rather than a process of "dissatisfaction" and "complaint," feral lawyering involves disputing the decision of the blocking agency through lengthy, quasi-legal challenges and appeals framed in law and submitted to an IPC. Before filing an appeal with an IPC, feral lawyering ATI/FOI users prepare detailed letters, documenting all their communications with an ATI/FOI coordinator and crafting a persuasive counter-argument based in law establishing why they believe the coordinator is unjustified in withholding the information they are demanding access to. In our own appeal letters to the IPC, for example, we refer to precedent, propose alternative interpretations and applications of ATI/FOI law, highlight sections of ATI/FOI that strengthen our case, make "public interest" arguments about the information we are requesting, and sometimes even point to evidence of seeming ill-intention by the ATI/FOI coordinator in the context of formal and informal communications. We have also filed fee waiver requests with several agencies, an avenue of appeal that agencies do not always advertise or encourage but that can work well especially for students without sufficient financial resources to cover high costs. Finally, in some instances, we have gone as far as to threaten litigation, citing access to (admittedly sometimes exaggerated) research budgets, to gain access to information from agencies that simply will not budge otherwise.

In our letter to the IPC regarding the APD files, we explained how we had already filed this exact same request with other police agencies in the country and had received the information we requested. We also pointed to section 22(4)(a) of British Columbia's FOI law, which states that the disclosure of third-party information is not considered an unreasonable breach of privacy if "the third party has, in writing, consented to or requested the disclosure." The coordinator, who received a copy of this letter from the IPC, later responded to us again by email saying that they had contacted other agencies to confirm: "Since our last reply to your request we have consulted with several other police agencies to get their feedback regarding your type of request and confirm that they did agree to release the requested information to you, as such, we will follow suit." The coordinator, despite iterating at the start of another response letter that they had released all the information we had requested (an untrue statement), decided to "follow suit," giving in to the argument for precedent made in our letter to the IPC.

The process of request and appeal is unfortunately not always as straightforward as our above experience with the APD. Another example of feral lawyering comes from Randy K. Lippert (see Lippert, Walby, and Wilkinson 2016). Lippert and his colleagues submitted FOI requests to four police agencies in Ontario regarding similar policing practices to those we had requested from the APD. One of the agencies did not acknowledge receipt of the request or respond in any way within the required thirty-day period, despite having received a money order for the processing fee. After several months with no response, Lippert resubmitted his request in person, repaying the processing fee. When several months later there was still no response, Lippert submitted an appeal with the provincial IPC. In the appeal letter, Lippert detailed the actions he had taken to submit and resubmit the request and established precedence by showing how the other three agencies he submitted the same request to had already completed his requests. The IPC replied acknowledging his two requests to the police agency and indicated that they would be initiating a response from them. Soon after, the police service provided a fee estimate of $2,071 CDN, an amount twenty times higher than charged by the other three agencies.

Lippert contacted the IPC about this astonishingly high fee estimate and was encouraged to submit a fee waiver request to the agency. In the fee waiver letter, Lippert argued that the fee be abandoned or reduced because of the small amount of preparatory work required by the agency, the precedent set by the other three departments, and research budget limitations and because the research he was conducting was in the public interest. Under Ontario provincial FOI law, the agency is required to respond to this fee waiver request in ten days, but Lippert did not receive a response for two and half months, whereafter the agency denied his request on the grounds that every police service "is a different entity and is not required to keep the same database format" (Lippert, Walby, and Wilkinson 2016). In the letter, the department also explained that "your request dated May 17, 2012 and assigned our file number 12–2015 . . . duplicates 666 pages of this request. You may wish to amend your request and . . . and reduce your fees by $799.20" (2016). In other words, the agency had amalgamated the two duplicate requests under one file number resulting in a considerably higher fee estimate, a seemingly ill-intentioned tactic of stalling and blocking access (it may have been sheer incompetence, but this seems less likely given the broader context). By combining the two duplicate requests, and therefore planning to process the same disclosure twice, the department was able to justify a high processing cost *and* feign flexibility by offering to reduce the cost by only processing the request once. When Lippert appealed again with the IPC, the department used this rationale to justify their position and high cost, which the IPC, given its limited powers, was able to do little to challenge at the time. Two months later, Lippert received an email from the same IPC mediator explaining that the police department had agreed to release the information at a lower and more reasonable cost of $290 CDN. After paying this amount to the police agency, Lippert still did not receive any of the records from the agency. Unable to contact the IPC mediator, he eventually learned that his file had been transferred to a new IPC official. Lippert debriefed the new mediator, who agreed to initiate a "failure to disclose" appeal. A week later, Lippert and his colleagues received the information they requested. The lengthy and drawn-out fiasco took over a year to settle from the date of the initial request to final disclosure. In contrast to our example of requesting files from the APD, Lippert's experience was more complicated, drawn out, and even ridiculous at times. His experience perfectly demonstrates how far some agencies will go to prevent access to their records (even when they're as generally benign as these were). It also demonstrates just how persistent feral lawyering ATI/FOI users need to be when brokering access to records from such guarded agencies as the police.

We want to end with a note on ethics. Invoking precedent is one negotiation strategy that many feral lawyers use, but there are many other possibilities, some more seemingly risky from the standpoint of established scholarly ethics. How far a researcher practicing feral lawyering is willing to go in their argumentation tactics is an ethical matter. As we have argued elsewhere, ATI/FOI calls into question some ethical conventions in qualitative research (Walby and Luscombe 2017). Feral lawyers, who are generally viewed as submissive lay citizens by the power-wielding state, are "studying up" (Nader 1974) rather than "down" and, in our view, require a different procedural ethic than is applied in other research situations where the power relation is reversed (e.g., research interviews with prisoners or other victims of state violence). When studying the state using ATI/FOI requests, is there still an ethical duty for researchers-as-feral-lawyers to avoid deceiving coordinators in informal communications or to take caution when evidence of illegal or disreputable acts by state officials is obtained? When coordinators dubiously probe researchers about their research questions, intentions, and publication plans, are researchers still required to be totally transparent and forthcoming with them? The fact that coordinators sometimes inappropriately ask about users' intentions with the disclosed information, even though their decisions should not be made on such extralegal grounds, troubles established ethical practices of researcher-subject transparency applicable in other contexts and enforced by institutional review boards (also see Burr and Reynolds 2012; Prior 2010). While such questions remain unanswered and will vary by situational context, our goal here is simply to trouble mainstream ethical considerations in the context of ATI/FOI that, depending on the procedural and situational ethics of the researcher, will constrain or enable the use of different feral lawyering tactics.

Conclusion

In this chapter, we have developed a guiding conceptualization and research mentality through which to simultaneously study and practice ATI/FOI that is consistent with social studies of science and socio-legal studies. We have drawn attention to the need to foster more attention for research methods in socio-legal studies in Canada. Clarifying different methodological approaches to conducting socio-legal studies helps demarcate what socio-legal studies itself is and the direction it is headed (cf. Harris 1983). Specifically, we have developed the concept of "feral lawyering" in the context of ATI/FOI law as a way of cultivating a critical socio-legal analysis of law in action, moving away from reifying law as a privileged knowledge, and resituating academics, lawyers, activists, and other everyday people as capable users of law.

There is privilege involved in using law in this way, but the challenge is to do so in a manner that levels rather than reaffirms hierarchy. Indeed, using ATI/FOI in a feral manner is one of the only ways to investigate what the editors of this volume call the "slow violence" of the state (see the introduction). Such an insurgent approach cannot simply offer "a how-to manual revealing a linear cause-and-effect of the discipline (as generations of classical sociology thinkers and law 'and' society scholars suggested). Neither is law purely an aspect of social life" (McKnight 2015, 122). A social-legal approach needs to examine the making of law, the letter of the law, and law in action using new and existing conceptual and methodological tools rooted in the social sciences. The approach to feral lawyering used by us and many other ATI/FOI users in Canada and beyond attempts to level the playing field and dismantle the expert bureaucrat / lay citizen understanding of legal knowledge that marks official discourse on ATI/FOI and the legal field more generally. This approach to socio-legal research requires patience, grit, and the use of law to investigate practices of power and governance. There is also a subversive element to using ATI/FOI in this way, as these records can reveal embarrassing, wasteful, violent, and abhorrent government practices. This approach further acknowledges that law comes in many forms and is practiced by all kinds of players in the legal field (also see Tamanaha 2000; Merry 1988). Law is not simply what the state or legal experts say it is. As we have shown, ATI/FOI law is not reducible to case law or reviews of existing legislation. The goal of feral lawyering is to practice and study law in a non-obtuse, theoretically informed way to advance a socio-legal understanding of research methods and of ATI/FOI law in action.

Notes

1   It is not our contention that all government records should be publicly released. There are justifiable reasons for withholding records from the public. However, it is our assertion that many (possibly even most) of the records that governments deny access to do not fit this category of "justifiably withheld." Indeed, the specific documents we are interested in for our research are often mundane and bureaucratic. It is precisely these documents that can help show how law works in action.
2   There is also related literature in criminology (see Robert and Dufresne 2015).
3   Talk to any experienced user of ATI/FOI in the worlds of academia, journalism, or activism, and they will tell you that getting access to records requires more than just filing a request. ATI/FOI users have to go further by creatively bargaining, arguing, and bluffing. It is this difference in mentality and practice that we conceptualize as feral lawyering.

References

Banakar, R., and M. Travers, eds. 2005. "Introduction." In *Theory and Method in Socio-legal Research*, ix–xvi. London: Bloomsbury.

Brownlee, Jamie, and K. Walby, eds. 2015. *Access to Information and Social Justice: Critical Research Strategies for Journalists, Scholars and Activists*. Winnipeg, Manitoba: Arbeiter Ring.

Burr, J., and P. Reynolds. 2012. "The Wrong Paradigm? Social Research and the Predicates of Ethical Scrutiny." *Research Ethics* 6 (1): 128–33.

Callon, M. 1984. "Some Elements of the Sociology of Translation: Domestication of the Scallops and the Fishermen of St. Brieuc Bay." *Sociological Review* 32:196–233.

Canada. 2017. "How Access to Information and Personal Information Requests Work." Canada.ca. Last modified 12 August 2022. https://www.canada.ca/en/treasury-board-secretariat/services/access-information-privacy/access-information/how-access-information-personal-information-requests-work.html.

Cloatre, E. 2015. "Shifting Labels and the Fluidity of the 'Legal.'" In *Exploring the Legal in Socio-legal Studies*, edited by D. Cowan and D. Wincott, 91–115. London: Palgrave Macmillan.

Cordis, A., and P. Warren. 2014. "Sunshine as Disinfectant: The Effect of Freedom of Information Act Law on Public Corruption." *Journal of Public Economics* 115:18–36.

Cotterrell, R. 1998. "Why Must Legal Ideas Be Interpreted Sociologically?" *Journal of Law and Society* 25 (2): 171–92.

Cowan, D., and H. Carr. 2008. "Actor-Network Theory, Implementation, and the Private Landlord." *Journal of Law and Society* 35:149–66.

Creutzfeldt, N., A. Kubal, and F. Pirie. 2016. "Introduction: Exploring the Comparative in Socio-legal Studies." *International Journal of Law in Context* 12 (4): 377–89.

Duncan, Jamie, Alex Luscombe, and Kevin Walby. 2022. "Governing Through Transparency: Investigating the New Access to Information Regime in Canada." *Information Society*. https://doi.org/10.1080/01972243.2022.2134241.

Feenan, Dermot. 2009. "Foreword: Socio-legal Studies and the Humanities." *International Journal of Law in Context* 5 (3): 235–42.

Fitzpatrick, Peter. 1995. "Being Social in Socio-legal Studies." *Journal of Law and Society* 22 (1): 105–12.

Harris, D. R. 1983. "The Development of Socio-legal Studies in the United Kingdom." *Legal Studies* 3 (3): 315–33.

Hazell, R., and B. Worthy. 2010. "Assessing the Performance of Freedom of Information." *Government Information Quarterly* 27:352–59.

Hudson, Barbara. 2006. "Beyond White Man's Justice: Gender, Race and Justice in Late Modernity." *Theoretical Criminology* 10 (1): 29–47.

Hunt, A. 1981. "Dichotomy and Contradiction in the Sociology of Law." *British Journal of Law and Society* 8 (1): 47–77.

Jabbari, D. 1998. "Is There a Proper Subject Matter for 'Socio-legal Studies'?" *Oxford Journal of Legal Studies* 18 (4): 707–27.

Kagan, Robert A. 1995. "What Socio-legal Scholars Should Do When There Is Too Much Law to Study." *Journal of Law and Society* 22 (1): 140–48.

Katz, Joan M. 1969. "Games Bureaucrats Play: Hide and Seek Under the Freedom of Information Act." *Texas Law Review* 48:1261–84.

Kazmierski, V. 2009. "Something to Talk About: Is There a Charter Right to Access Government Information?" *Dalhousie Law Journal* 31:351–99.

———. 2011. "Accessing Democracy: The Critical Relationship Between Academics and the Access to Information Act." *Canadian Journal of Law & Society* 26 (3): 613–22.

———. 2013. "Lights, Judges, Access: How Active Judicial Review of Discretionary Decisions Protects Access to Government Information?" *Alberta Law Review* 51 (1): 49–76.

———. 2014. "How Much Law in Legal Studies? Approaches to Teaching 'Legal' Research and Doctrinal Analysis in a Legal Studies Program." *Canadian Journal of Law & Society* 29 (3): 297–310.

————. 2016. "Accessing with Dinosaurs: Protecting Access to Government Information in the Cretaceous Period of Canadian Democracy." *Constitutional Forum* 25 (3): 57–66.

Kline, M. 1994. "The Colour of Law: Ideological Representations of First Nations in Legal Discourse." *Social & Legal Studies* 3 (4): 451–76.

Larsen, M., and Kevin Walby, eds. 2012. *Brokering Access: Power, Politics, and Freedom of Information Process in Canada.* Vancouver: UBC Press.

Latour, B. 1987. *Science in Action.* Milton Keynes, UK: Open University Press.

Law, John. 2009. "Actor Network Theory and Material Semiotics." *New Blackwell Companion to Social Theory* 3:141–58.

Lefebvre, A. 2008. *The Image of Law: Deleuze, Bergson, Spinoza.* Stanford, CA: Stanford University Press.

Leonard, J., ed. 1995. *Legal Studies as Cultural Studies.* New York: SUNY Press.

Levi, Ron, and Mariana Valverde. 2008. "Studying Law by Association: Bruno Latour Goes to the Conseil d'Etat." *Law & Social Inquiry* 33 (3): 805–25.

Lippert, R., Kevin Walby, and B. Wilkinson. 2016. "Spins, Stalls and Shutdowns in Research on Security." *Qualitative Social Research* 17, no. 1. https://www.qualitative -research.net/index.php/fqs/article/download/2411/3920?inline=1.

Luscombe, A., and Kevin Walby. 2017. "Theorizing Freedom of Information: The Live Archive, Obfuscation, and Actor-Network Theory." *Government Information Quarterly* 34 (3): 379–87.

Luscombe, A., Kevin Walby, and R. K. Lippert. 2017. "Brokering Access Beyond the Border and in the Wild: Comparing Freedom of Information Law and Policy in Canada and the United States." *Law & Policy* 39 (3): 259–79.

Martel, J., B. Hogeveen, and A. Woolford. 2006. "The State of Critical Scholarship in Criminology and Socio-legal Studies in Canada." *Canadian Journal of Criminology and Criminal Justice* 48 (5): 633–46.

McKnight, J. 2015. "The Fourth Act in Socio-legal Scholarship: Playing with Law on the Sociological Stage." *Qualitative Sociology Review* 11 (1): 108–214.

Merry, Sally E. 1988. "Legal Pluralism." *Law & Society Review* 22 (5): 869–96.

Mol, A. 2010. "Actor-Network Theory: Sensitive Terms and Enduring Tensions." *Kölner Zeitschrift für Soziologie und Sozialpsychologie. Sonderheft* 50:253–69.

Nader, L. 1974. "Up the Anthropologist—Perspectives Gained from Studying Up." In *Reinventing Anthropology*, edited by D. Hymes, 284–311. New York: Vintage.

Nam, T. 2012. "Freedom of Information Legislation and Its Impact on Press Freedom: A Cross-National Study." *Government Information Quarterly* 29:521–31.

Prior, Lindsay. 2008. "Repositioning Documents in Social Research." *Sociology* 45 (5): 821–36.

———. 2010. "Qualitative Research Design and Ethical Governance: Some Problems of Fit." *Ethics Forum* 12:53–64.

Robert, D., and M. Dufresne. 2015. *Actor-Network Theory and Crime Studies.* Burlington, VT: Ashgate.

Roberts, A. 1999. "Retrenchment and Freedom of Information: Recent Experience Under Federal, Ontario, and British Columbia Law." *Canadian Public Administration* 42 (4): 422–51.

———. 2002. "Administrative Discretion and the Access to Information Act: An 'Internal Law' on Open Government?" *Canadian Public Administration* 45 (2): 175–94.

———. 2005. "Spin Control and Freedom of Information: Lessons for the United Kingdom from Canada." *Public Administration* 83 (1): 1–23.

Rooke, C., E. Cloatre, and R. Dingwall. 2012. "Actor-Network Theory and the Regulatory Governance of Nicotine in the United Kingdom: How Nicotine Gum Came to Be a Medicine, but Not a Drug?" *Journal of Law and Society* 39 (1): 39–57.

Shepherd, E., A. Stevenson, and A. Flinn. 2010. "Information Governance, Records Management, and Freedom of Information: A Study of Local Government Authorities in England." *Government Information Quarterly* 27:337–45.

Tamanaha, Brian Z. 2000. "A Non-essentialist Version of Legal Pluralism." *Journal of Law and Society* 27 (2): 296–321.

Thomas, Philip A. 1997. "Socio-legal Studies: The Case of Disappearing Fleas and Bastards." In *Socio-legal Studies*, 1–22. Aldershot, UK: Dartmouth.

Travers, Max. 2001. "Sociology of Law in Britain." *American Sociologist* 32 (2): 26–40.

Valverde, Mariana. 2016. "What Counts as Theory, Today? A Post-philosophical Framework for Socio-legal Empirical Research." *Brazilian Journal of Empirical Legal Studies* 3 (1): 172–81.

Walby, Kevin, and M. Larsen. 2012. "Access to Information and Freedom of Information Requests: Neglected Means of Data Production in the Social Sciences." *Qualitative Inquiry* 18 (1): 31–42.

Walby, Kevin, and A. Luscombe. 2017. "Criteria for Quality in Qualitative Research and Use of Freedom of Information Requests in the Social Sciences." *Qualitative Research* 17 (5): 537–53.

Yeager, Matthew. 2006. "The Freedom of Information Act as a Methodological Tool: Suing the Government for Data." *Canadian Journal of Criminology and Criminal Justice* 48 (4): 499–521.

7 Far from the Madding Crowds

Redefining the Field of Socio-legal Studies from Within

Nergis Canefe

Far from the madding crowd's ignoble strife / Their sober wishes never learn'd to stray; / Along the coolsequester'd vale of life / They kept the noiseless tenor of their way.

> —Thomas Gray, "Elegy Written in a Country Churchyard"

This chapter examines key questions regarding socio-legal studies and social change, with the central argument being that more needs to be done to *reorient the field toward questions of law's violence at a global scale and re-examine the politics of everyday life in our quest for radical social change.* To this end, it documents some of the problematic aspects of a select set of past endeavours and provides examples that successfully address law's relationship with history and sociality in a pointed way, including analyzing critical work emanating from the Global South and critical citizenship and migration studies. The chapter introduces questions of method that are endemic to the kind of inquiry that mark the field as distinct and concludes by identifying political philosopher Agnes Heller's work as a potential remedy for some of the ailments that have limited discussions on the nature of law and its contextual character. Walter Benjamin's work is also introduced, albeit briefly, and the focus is mainly on the questions Benjamin asks. Overall, laying out some of the main theoretical threads used by socio-legal studies scholars constitutes a point of entry for a dedicated debate on the changing meaning of interdisciplinarity, dissent, and discontent in the field. The central problematic of the chapter is not to define what exactly socio-legal studies is or has been. Rather, the chapter deals with a select group of canonized approaches to socio-legal studies that could potentially offer much more if they were to include an explicit framework concerning the politics of everyday life. As such, it invites us to reconsider the promise of the acute interest in everyday life articulated by Heller as a means to redefine the field from within.

Since the emergence of socio-legal studies as a distinct field and a transdisciplinary track of analysis back in the late 1960s, the maxims of being pluralistic, self-reflective, critical, and subversive became common markers of the scholarship associated with it. The combined study of law, legal institutions, legal processes, policy reform, politics, normative orders, the relationship between the state and the law, the production of criminality, jurisprudence, and much more was poised to surpass what the sociology of law, the anthropology of law, the psychology of law, legal history, criminology, and law and economics promised to deliver. One of the defining features of socio-legal studies, in contrast to traditional doctrinal law, has been its activist- or social-justice-oriented current, leading to the hand-in-hand march of activism, social and community engagement, and nuanced legal scholarship with a commitment to social change. This perspective informed the underlying premises of the Law and Society Associations on both sides of the Atlantic Ocean. Whether the "law and society discourse" indeed came to form a "second legal training" à la Galanter is to be debated, especially given the fact that many of the scholars populating contemporary law and society programs are not legally trained (Trubek and Galanter 1974; Merryman 1977). Debates on what constitutes law gradually penetrated the realms of social, political, and economic analysis. Early works like Philippe Nonet and Philip Selznick's *Law and Society in Transition* ([1978] 2017) explain the primary forms of law as a social, political, and normative phenomenon and generously speak of the fundamental difference between repressive law riddled with raw conflict and the accommodation of special interests and responsive law as the embodiment of the struggle to realize an ideal of polity. This recasting of jurisprudential issues from a social science perspective provided the initial framework for analyzing and assessing the worth of alternative modes of legal ordering. Such classic texts in law and society literature may not necessarily form parts of a canon in the strict sense of the word. Nonetheless, they are exemplary of law-and-society scholarship's sustained effort to prove the web of relations among history, sociology, philosophy, anthropology, and politics for the past half century. Indeed, as early as the 1980s, Marc Galanter's call of "down with the ringing grooves of change" was already attacking the past, present, and future of legal education for its lack of commitment to change and betterment. Forty years later, what is clear is that many of the untameable children of academia—including post-colonial studies scholars, those focused on feminist methodologies and theories, anti-racist critical methodologies advocates, proponents of anti-colonial and decolonial methodologies, and Marxist/post-Marxist political economy scholars—also turned their gaze onto law, entering the discussion on law in this newly established castle of myriad dreams called socio-legal studies (Darian-Smith and Fitzpatrick 1999; de Sousa Santos 2002; Riles 2004; Silbey 2005; Teubner 1997; Valverde 2009).

Despite these promising developments, in the following pages, I urge you to consider the possibility that the edifice of socio-legal studies incorporated some of the rigidities and silences that the field of inquiry set out to subvert in its dedication to social change and politically engaged legal scholarship. These issues largely pertain to what law is, how it functions, who uses it, and where it exists. This chapter provides an overview of some of the voices of discontent from within socio-legal studies in an attempt to decipher the sources of agony and anger that these critical voices articulate. It posits that we must pay more attention to the inner dynamics of the shaping and reshaping of socio-legal studies. There are lessons to be learned for the benefit of present and future generations who attempt to do advocacy work, activism, public intellectual engagement, compassionate community involvement, and scholarship all at once. This complex configuration corresponds to a realm much bigger than any particular designation could address within the field. Therefore, part of the future project for legal studies must be to turn the insights gained from our understanding of the subjects and objects of legal knowledge into further questions and inquiries about the self-imposed limits in select areas of socio-legal scholarship. Only then can we look deeper into conjunctures and commitments capable of challenging the academic disciplinary parochialisms that still haunt us.

Politics, the Law, and Scholarship: Contemporary Interventions

In the history of the field of socio-legal studies, the role of the law in politics was construed rather narrowly during its formative stages. In contradistinction, there has emerged a critical mass of work that looks at the role of politics in the making and practice of the law during the later decades (Vago 2015; Nonet 2017). A brief review of the relevant literature since the early 1990s demonstrates the presence of a sustained interest in legality that has been largely concentrated on the analysis of the role of politics in the making of new laws, the initiation of social change, and of course, law as a tool for social control and disciplining and hence a tool for disciplinary and institutionalized forms of violence (de Sousa Santos and Rodríguez-Garavito 2005; Loughlin 2000; Tamanaha 2004). Unfortunately, this view also implies a questionable acceptance of the distinction between public and private spheres as a reasonable guide for the study of law. In contradistinction, a more interactive view of the law characterizes legal mobilization and the invoking of legal norms as a form of political action by which the citizenry or political subjects at large use public authority on their own behalves (Rajagopal 2003; Levitsky 2015; McCann 2017). This form of public and political power, although contingent, is widely dispersed and thus open to various forms of mobilization on a global scale as well (Baker-Cristales 2008).

For rejuvenating the "older" socio-legal studies as defined by critical legal studies dating back to the 1970s, a full consideration of the factors that influence legal mobilization is important not only for understanding who uses the law and to which ends but also for predicting reactions to the implementation of public policy and legal regulations at both domestic and international levels (Cotterrell 2008). There is no doubt that politics strongly influences the form and extent of the implementation of laws and, in particular, the allocation of power and authority via the state. However, we must also consider the reverse and pay attention to how law interacts with, frames, responds to, and influences politics, society, and economics. To this end, in this section, I present a subset of critical interventions operationalized by socio-legal studies scholarship that engages with the politics-and-law relationship from multiple angles and via unsettling questions. This is also the lens through which I trace the reinvention of the field from within rather than simply responding to what existed before or outside. My preoccupation is with the distance between the academic studies of law in the progressive context of socio-legal studies and the politics of everyday life, social change, and transformation. The most current genre of socio-legal studies scholarship, which includes literatures on legal ethnography, legal consciousness, and law and the city with an acute interest in everyday life, is very keen on claiming to have closed that gap (Starr and Goodale 2002; Silbey 2005; Valverde 2012; Darian-Smith 2016; Hertogh 2018; Doll and Walby 2019). In my view, there is still more to be thought about.

In particular, in the larger context of law's dependency on both politics and society, the complex relationship between law and social movements is of great significance. Social movements use a wide variety of legal strategies in their programs—including litigation, lobbying, and administrative advocacy—to bring about social change. Law, particularly rights and rights claims, provides movements with political strategies and plays an important role in the cultural anatomy of a social movement. No doubt, law is a contested terrain for social movement struggles and movements that often rely on the rights discourse to frame their grievances, to generate and circulate collective identity claims, and to recruit and mobilize activists as well as to develop a system-level critique. Law and legal strategies can exert conservative or oppressive influences on social movements as well, sometimes channelling protests and more radical forms of action into the orbit of conventional political institutions. Overall, this complex interaction among social movements, politics, and the law constituted the key venue through which socio-legal studies scholarship redefined itself from within and with direct reference to everyday life.

A key example of this came from the Global South, where challenging government authoritarianism and enduring neocolonialism were important vectors of political struggles both within and beyond law schools. For instance, the impetus for a radical reform of the law school curriculum in the name of social relevance and critical awareness found one of its best expressions in the development of an interdisciplinary first-year foundation course on "Economic and Social Problems of East Africa" developed by the law faculty at Dar es Salaam, Ghana (Shivji 1986). In this regard, socio-legal studies had a direct link with the streets in the Global South more so than elsewhere: in geographies stretching from Brazil, Chile, Argentina, and Nicaragua to China, India, and Japan, from Mozambique, South Africa, and Zimbabwe to Sri Lanka, critical approaches to law were real platforms for social and political change throughout the last quarter of the past century. In other words, there are alternative histories in the Global South that link law and society movements and socio-legal studies scholarship with actual social movements and political struggles in real time (Dirlik 1994; Bayat 1997, 2000; Samaddar 2006; Mignolo 2010; Roy 2011). Whether that impetus has been sustained in the Global North and Western academia in general is a question yet to be answered.

There is a second conjuncture whereby we witness many interventions made to both established academic disciplines and everyday politics from the cohorts of socio-legal scholars. Issues of citizenship and immigration are critical for understanding ways that individuals, communities, and diasporas are created, sustained, excluded, exploited, and marginalized via the law and how they respond to their circumstances through politics. For socio-legal studies scholarship, this has been an area of growing interest and dedication, particularly in the Global North, where law defines, decides, divides, and excludes in very structured and formalized ways. Citizenship, broadly defined, includes legal status, membership rights, civic involvement, social participation, and political, economic, and cultural linkages to structures that delimit, transcend, and deconstruct the state. At the same time, it is essential to understand the discourses and practices that implicitly and explicitly define citizenship in particular contexts. Race, gender, national origin, religion, ethnicity, language, age, social class, and other markers of membership and exclusion determine the claiming or attribution of citizenship (Parmar 2015). Moreover, globalization, migration, and transnational processes constantly reshape both citizenship and, again, exclusion from it, positioning individuals and communities either within or outside of legal orders (Hyndman and Giles 2011; Hamlin 2012). In this context, legal management, governance, and control over immigration are clearly crucial concerns. Given the new realities emanating from the war on terrorism, the restructuring of immigration and refugee policies at a global level, and the resultant sharpening of inequalities, it is essential to examine how movements, rights, and statuses are being distributed or denied by legal orders (Malkki 1995; Lindley 2014).

Under the heading of migration, citizenship, and membership, there also emerged the category of "displaced/dispossessed peoples," which includes all those forced to migrate internally and internationally as a result of political, natural, or man-made issues (Glick Schiller and Salazar 2013; Casas-Cortes et al. 2015; Darling 2017). From homeless people, trafficked persons, and Indigenous peoples to asylum seekers, refugees, unaccompanied minors, and stateless people, millions are fleeing from Africa, South America, Southeast Asia, the Middle East, and Europe. Indeed, the heightened impact of recent migrant crises across the Mediterranean, Central America, Southeast Asia, Europe, and the Middle East demands new collaborative approaches to the millennia-old challenge of protecting those, especially children and women in the Global South, seeking refuge either regionally or across the North–South divide (Lems 2016). Forced displacement resulting from violent conflict, human rights abuses, climate change, natural disasters, economic disparity, or induced development leads to novel forms of marginalization and vulnerability because few legal instruments apply to safeguarding the rights of people on the move (Saunders 2014). Furthermore, the social, political, and legal issues of wealthy states favouring the immigration of select groups and brain-draining resource-poor countries of their highly educated citizens lead to the perpetuation of neocolonial oppression (Chimni 2009; Scheel and Ratfisch 2014). Unjust processes of migration are buried deep within the promising facade of globalization and new development models. These issues have been aptly discussed in the socio-legal studies canon.

Overall, since the early 1990s, the area of international law and politics indeed brought together a large group of scholars, teachers, researchers, and practitioners working on issues related to the politics of international legal thought, practice, method, and history. Institutions and organizations across the world, both in the Global North and South, have been employing a wide variety of theoretical and empirical approaches drawn from the disciplines of international law, anthropology, political science, history, political economy, sociology, international relations, and cultural studies in order to examine some of the most pressing problems related to the current global (dis)order and its normative underpinnings (Parfitt 2013; Grabham 2016; Nicholson 2016). The work of this group manifests a diverse range of political convictions. Their concerns range from a foundational critique of the practices of human rights and judicial activism to the development of Marxian, postcolonial, feminist, and queer legal theory and from the heterodox regulation of international finance and trade to the critical potential of international legal historiography (Parmar 2008; Eslava and Pahuja 2011, 2012; Gathii 2011; Parfitt 2014; Sreejith 2017). The increasing visibility of the disciplinary nature of international law in existing global, national, and local legal orders has led to contestations and reconfigurations of the separation between the domestic and the international realms (Rasulov 2010, 2016; Eslava 2015).

I see furthering of this project of analyzing law from local to global and back in critical theories pertaining to gender identities, critical race theories, feminism, and of course, post-colonial studies as they have been increasingly included in the socio-legal studies curricula. Cognizant of the brittle criticism that the original wave of feminist legal theory essentialized the feminine and excluded racialized and marginalized voices, since the 1990s, feminist socio-legal scholarship has been striving to become an energizing force again in a number of interrelated areas best characterized by the term *intersectionality*. In this larger context, another theme of critical importance is socio-legal studies' intent to broaden the conversation on sex work by bridging issues relating to sex with other labour contexts by examining their intersections (Jeffrey and Sullivan 2009; Hickle 2017). In addition to important theoretical work on intersectionality in general, conducting critical research on sex work with an emphasis on the regulation of sex(uality) in "mainstream" workplaces; facilitating comparisons among working conditions, labour standards, work-ers' rights in sex work, and "mainstream" labour; reflecting on how regulatory frameworks governing sex(uality) in the workplace both help and hinder workers in diverse contexts; and locating cross-national and geographically specific regulatory discourses governing sexuality, sexualization, and sexual harassment and exploitation in the workplace is one of the most important contributions made by contemporary socio-legal scholarship in this area (Raguparan 2017). All the same, the criminalization of the sex industry and the marginalization of people working therein remains a pressing issue, albeit made more visible (Law 2015).

The shared interest in gender and equality as related to race, class, sexual orientation, and disability cuts across many fields and hence encourages the cross-pollination of feminist critiques with debates on law, legality, normalcy, and order (Ahmed and Seshu 2014; Ahmed 2014, 2015; Baratosy and Wendt 2017). In a similar vein, queer theory's application to law focuses on disrupting established meanings while also questioning identity claims and disciplinary boundaries. Scholars and activists engaged in these fields are keen to shed light on the interconnectedness of patterns of domination engendered by legal technologies and narratives, in particular those initiated and sustained by biopolitics and the institutional governance of social life. Queering law, domestic or international, has become the means for examining and dis-rupting law's (re)production of the status quo through processes of othering in media, policy-making, legislation, adjudication, and litigation. Queering law also includes activism that addresses bodies, identities, and subjectivities in order to undermine the dominant conceptions of power and sovereignty. More generally, this theoretical approach seeks to undo law's boundaries and binaries that serve to uphold current structures of oppression that not only affect queer subjects but other gendered, racialized, classed, (dis)abled subjects. Furthermore, queer theory critically attends to legal technologies such as citizenship, immigration status, and similar determinations of capabilities through legal categories by exploring both the oppressive and emancipatory aspects of these practices of othering lying at the root of local, communal, and personal dimensions of politics. Whether this is socio-legal studies or queer theory focused on law is open to debate, though the former has its materials selected almost exclusively from the legal field.

Lastly, the body of work characterized by class analysis and the Marxist critique has been marked by genuine attempts to define what law is and what law does with visible emphases on politics and social change. In terms of their absorption by socio-legal studies scholarship, it is apt to suggest that Marxist socio-legal studies has been offering its own take on how to tackle the potent category of class (MacKinnon 1983; Pashukanis 2017). In a globalized late capitalist economy, there is a marked need for new approaches to the age-old challenge of protecting workers' rights and improving labour standards as well as addressing the global phenomenon of precarity and non-status people. Current forms of globalization affect both the nature of work and the character of the employment relationship itself in unprecedented ways. Improving competitiveness through restructuring workforces and production across national borders has indeed led to the emergence of a whole new class, that of the *precariat*, a term that began to define an entire field of study during the past two decades (Neilson and Rossiter 2008; Goldring and Landolt 2013; Tappe and Nguyen 2019). States in the North look for ways to preserve existing levels of employment and production while those in the South struggle simultaneously to promote growth and investment and to keep the labouring classes under control. Changes in production processes, locations of mass production, the effects of global market forces on redefining work, and worker's rights and conditions have no doubt led to variations on this theme in the North and South. In this context, exploring the role played by states, courts, and the legal establishment, as well as international and regional courts, unions, domestic non-governmental organizations, international non-governmental organizations, social and political movements, existing international institutions such as the International Labor Organization, social clauses in trade agreements, the World Bank and other international financial institutions, and globalized industries and transnational firms assumes paramount importance for scholarship on labour and law (Buchanan 2008). Similar lines of questioning mark scholarship on international and comparative analyses of laws governing global and national redefinitions of public health, covering areas concerning the management and erasure of health systems, social welfare policies, environmental health law and policy, warfare and public health, human rights law and policy, health disparities and inequities, subordination and law, and more (Purvis 1991; Trubek et al. 1993; Chimni 1999, 2004; Okafor 2008).

Methodological Openings

Many of the subfields of inquiry under the aegis of socio-legal studies have a distinct take on the "able-bodied individual," the "good citizen," and "the worthy member of society." They strive to incorporate feminist, critical race, social epidemiological, and critical disability theoretical perspectives on the distribution and socio-legal responses to illness, impairment, and injury. Similarly, using a critical and global lens is essential in areas concerning repro-genetics, genetic discrimination law and policy, medical ethics and law, medical testimony and the role of science in courts, and the regulation of genetic engineering, torts and malpractice law, health care discrimination, public health systems and services, and health care reform, as well as health outcomes specific to vulnerable or subordinated populations (Fidler 2002; Gostin, Wiley, and Frieden 2015). In this regard, socio-legal studies has enabled conversations that pinpoint the interactive and mutually constitutive relationships among law, public health, and medicine and between law and individual well-being, the latter understood as being both a socio-legal status and an embodied political experience (Powers and Faden 2006; Krieger 2015). Methodologies for conceptualizing the relationship between law and health are robust—incorporating public health, critical legal studies, and a canopy of related debates, disciplines, and fields. However, certain areas remain underdeveloped, such as the full-scale recognition of social stratification and the complex influence of economic and political systems on life chances and opportunities of individuals, groups, communities, and societies, a dangerous gap that is recognized by emerging scholarship (Fahrenwald et al. 2007; Lang and Heasman 2015).

On the critical issue of methodologies, ethnographic inquiries of law have also maintained a historic and steady position within the field. They were notably present particularly during the foundational years of law and society scholarship (Redding 2014). In more recent decades, renewed interest has arisen in an ethnography/law connection for the purposes of revisiting the character and shape of ethnographic methods of socio-legal scholarship and exploring the benefits and boundaries of ethnographic research practices in the production of knowledge (Starr and Goodale 2016). This has been particularly observable in areas such as criminology and the prison system as a separate heading due to the distinct nature of punitive measures used during incarceration (Werth 2012; Moore and Hirai 2014; Opsal 2015). Socio-legal scholarship in this area seeks to understand the social, political, economic, and cultural underpinnings of punishment in all its guises, not limited to prisons and executions or community-based corrective facilities, but also in immigrant detention facilities, mental institutions, welfare offices, schools, and neighborhoods. Examining punishment across time and space, penal policies established at the organizational, state, and national levels render punishment a socio-political practice that is experienced, constructed, and contested around the world, throughout history (Levine 1990; Israel 2004; Martel, Hogeveen, and Woolford 2006; Swiffen and Nichols 2017).

Another key methodological concern is that of doing comparative work. For instance, although societies in Asia and the Americas have their particularities regarding their positionality in the global history of capitalism and state formation as well as distinct challenges for engaged scholarship, many of the states in these regions share similar historical and political experiences such as their colonial backgrounds, post-colonial state-making, experiences of dictatorships, revolutions, democratic mobilizations, mass social movements, and civil wars. These geographically diverse societies, although different in their current legal and political cultures, also share constitutional values and paradigms. In this age of late capitalist globalization, as economic ties between these regions are gaining strength and momentum, issues such as the rule of law and rights struggles increasingly come to the fore as common themes. Examining legal developments, constitutional law and legal cultures from an interdisciplinary perspective allows for developing new insights concerning how political and historical paths cross. As already mentioned, a similar development of global analysis has also taken place in the field of labor rights. In hindsight, the socio-legal studies framework on rights formalized the scholarly dedication to supporting, promoting, and providing feedback for rights struggles. Focusing on the economic, political, social, and moral obligations of states, institutions, corporations, and other legal actors with regards to individuals, communities, and global society as a whole, this new generation of rights scholarship also attends to implications of global finance projects, corporate social responsibility, crowd funding, shareholder derivative actions, the restructuring of international financial markets, governance obligations of corporate boards, the morality of markets, and neoliberal policies of globalization (de Sousa Santos and Rodríguez-Garavito 2005; Gathii 2011; Cotterrell 2015; Harrington and Manji 2017). As such, socio-legal studies brought together an interdisciplinary group of scholars from around the world working on economic and social rights, including the rights to education, health, decent work, human dignity, social protection, an adequate standard of living, and the right to global commons and a clean environment. Scholars and practitioners in the field have made significant gains in both conceptualizing these rights and offering political and sometimes policy-relevant solutions to structural problems (Berman 2003; Gleeson 2009, 2010, 2016; Paret and Gleeson 2016). Needless to say, this area of work is closely related to the work on human rights and poverty, human development, capabilities, equality, and non-antidiscrimination law. This broader area began to address previously marginalized rights and the rights of disadvantaged groups, highlighting the possibility of existing human rights frameworks and concepts that could be more interruptive, inclusive, and systemic as well as methodologies for measuring the impact of the erasure and negation of economic and social rights on the well-being of individuals and communities.

Overall, these fields of comparative analysis have close relations with the more conventional debates on legal pluralism, although the critical literature on law, corporations, and globalization is quite weary of the pluralist perspective in its original format. Legal pluralism and non-state law debates traditionally had participation from a variety of disciplines, including anthropology, political science, economics, comparative law, legal history, and sociology (Galanter 1974; Sharafi 2007, 2008). With a focus on theoretical and practical problems resulting from the interaction of different types of law—such as religious law, customary law, state law, and international and transnational law as well as contestations of state law—legal pluralism initially provided an intellectual meeting ground for understanding "law in context." More recent examples of collaborative research on legal pluralism include studies of the comprehensive regulatory activities undertaken by government, civil society, and other legal actors in various fields of global capitalism; discourses on rights over land and natural resources that are both socially and politically contested; the increasing intertwining of human rights and development discourses on issues in legal pluralism; and the perplexing relationship among law, customs, and religion as competing sources of normative reasoning and social ordering in diverse societies. In these and other substantive areas, a key goal of what we may call the third generation of legal pluralism is to facilitate conversations among social scientists, lawyers, legal scholars, activists, and policy-makers (Shahar 2008; Nelson 2010; Tuori 2014).

On a related track of bridging activism and academia, the kind of scholarship that emerged under the roof of critical research on race and the law suggests an urgency in terms of expanding the socio-legal studies research agenda to include race and racial inequality in a much more pronounced and methodologically responsible fashion, reflecting the exciting work done in the legal academy over the past two decades under the critical race theory rubric (Cotterrell 1997, 2013; Delgado and Stefancic 2017). In this spirit, law and society scholars are increasingly drawing upon studies of race and ethnicity that incorporate cultural studies and/or critical theory (Freire 2000; Nelken 2004; Solórzano and Yosso 2002; Edelman, Smyth, and Rahim 2016; McElhattan, Nielsen, and Weinberg 2017).

As already mentioned briefly above, the interplay among the law, gender, and sexuality is an equally precarious one. On the one hand, the law and legal decision-making are rooted in a tradition of predictability, uniformity, consistency, and self-referentiality. On the other hand, gender and sexuality are identities that are increasingly understood as dynamic, non-discrete, and fluid. As gender- and sexuality-related issues are increasingly brought forward to be resolved in legislatures and the courtroom, the question of how to reconcile these seemingly competing paradigms has gained increasing relevance. While critically examining the law and its relationship to gender and sexual identities—that is, how the law constructs, constrains, and/or enables gender and sexual minorities at the municipal, state, and national level—socio-legal scholarship led the way for a comparative engagement with both domestic and international legal systems, identifying established and emergent patterns.

This line of work also touches upon the problem-laden, public-private divide in legal theory. There is a continuing debate over the role of legal institutions and processes in shaping the public-private dichotomy for public policy and institutions as well as people's private identities and lives (Mnookin 1981; Clunie and Psarras 2016). Demonstrating the critical impact of the law on how the public-private boundary is drawn is key in this regard.

Under this general heading of the politics of (international) law, two particular areas stand out almost as an outcry—namely, the jurisprudence of disasters and food management (Parks et al. 2015; Freeman 2014, 2015). Questions such as how the law contributes to the makings of catastrophic disasters related to weak land use regulation, public subsidies encouraging the population of dangerous places, construction in flood lands and plains, or whether law could facilitate or compel corrective measures in the realms of mitigation, preparation, response, and recovery are essential for determining the true nature of these disasters (Ballestero 2015; Ammons and Roy 2015; Chabay, Frick, and Helgeson 2015; Howe et al. 2016; Beuret and Brown 2016). These questions provide more than the thematic nexus as they encourage the application of perspectives and concerns such as those concerning civil rights and liberties as affected by disaster management, social and environmental justice, private rights and regulatory authority, the well-being of special-needs populations, equity and efficiency in resource allocation, the voluntary versus involuntary assumption of risk, and "soft law" versus "hard law" approaches to protecting the public good, public health, and safety. They also implicate topics such as law and scientific uncertainty, reciprocal obligation and moral community, and responses to climate change and risk (Burton 2002; Gauna 2008; Gottlieb 2009; Murray 2011; Pellow and Park 2002, 2011). In a similar vein, in the area of regulation of food, the legal scaffolding of modern food systems and the chain of activities that link food production, distribution, wholesale, retail, consumption, and disposal reveal a densely textured social and economic environment invoking law in multiple ways and across several jurisdictions and again hinging on issues of obligation, morality, commitment, and the public good as counterlogics to market mentality (Cross and Morales 2007; Morales 2010; Spalding et al. 2012).

The emerging field of biotechnology as an interdisciplinary discourse is also informed by these concerns. Socio-legal studies scholarship on issues related to bioethical and biotechnological disputes attempts to bridge the gap between biotechnology and its sister fields, bioethics and intellectual property, rather than casting them in disciplinary isolation. The result has been the critical examination of diverse issues underrepresented in conventional scholarship, including biopiracy, genetic determinism, human commoditization, genetic property, public health, and tort, property, and contract issues concerning the body. In addition, this body of work adds race, gender, socioeconomics, and public policy strategies to the analysis of biotechnology and bioethics, contemplating the nexus where law, politics, science, society, and medicine meet (Ayres 2005; Dolgin and Shepherd 2014; Rothman 2017). An extension of this work is found in the area of regulatory governance (Halliday and Shaffer 2015). The study of regulatory instruments, institutions, and actors, how law shapes and responds to economic activity, and how law informs privatization and globalization processes through regulatory and administrative institutions allows us to examine how traditional as well as emerging regulatory instruments operate in self-regulation, covenants, management systems, market-based regulation, and societal responses to market expansions. Here, particular attention has been paid to the increasing demands of accountability and legitimacy in both domestic and international settings.

On a final note, the processes through which international organizations and transnational networks create law and legal norms and concomitantly shape national and international social, political and economic arenas have led to increasing concern across the field. International organizations, transgovernmental networks, and the regular involvement of non-state actors at the global level, including corporations and non-governmental organizations, affect and govern public and private interactions more extensively and intensively than ever before. Examination of the role of actors and mechanisms in the creation of transnational law, norms, and legal orders and their impact on domestic law and practice through processes of transformation and resistance also constitute the grounds upon which law school and socio-legal studies curricula began to overlap. As new technologies stand poised to initiate a global paradigm shift concerning the workings of legal institutions, new tools for regulatory governance and law enforcement generate novel forms of knowledge that confront traditional notions of due process and reshape norms around harm, damage, risk, and accountability. For instance, *inter alia*, the use of technologies that attempt to control social and political actors, provide or prohibit access to legal institutions and the polity, change societal understandings and expectations of what law is and how it is experienced, and present novel ethical and normative questions around privacy, ownership, access, and compliance that have now become part and parcel of syllabi on public and administrative law as taught from a socio-legal studies perspective.

In this context, the meaning of the law for both the colonized and the colonizers is also changing. The presumption of colonial continuity is a double-edged sword. For instance, in examining the extent and nature of colonial influence on legal institutions and legal culture, are we not unduly privileging the colonial encounter? As the new forms of scholarship in the field attest to, developing a fuller understanding of the interaction between law and colonial and post-colonial processes requires that we update our very notion of what law is and what it does. The study of law and indigeneity in both domestic and global contexts is a case in point. The much-needed interaction and comparative inquiry between scholars began to allow for the discussion of the similarities and differences among colonial/post-colonial/ neoimperial conditions with respect to native peoples, with the hope of expanding the discussion beyond the discourses of resistance and human rights and to foreground other ways that Indigenous peoples engage with and redefine the law (Inman 2014; Birrell 2016). By doing so, socio-legal scholars aim at promoting inquiries of the complex legal landscape that involves multiple layers and meanings of what constitutes law for Indigenous peoples. By stressing the multiple sites of knowledge production that inform issues of indigeneity and that contextualize the engagement of native peoples with formal and informal legal institutions, understanding legality in Indigenous societies also leads to acknowledgement of the law's ever-present connections to national identity and state power (Hunt 2014; Johnson 2016).

Through these aforementioned interventions and many more that are not included in this brief synopsis, new generations of scholars engaged in socio-legal studies actively seek to facilitate broad interdisciplinary conversations, collaborations, and action, challenging preconceived notions of "the legal" and "theory" while examining their own roles and complicities in structures of both oppression and emancipation (Beare, Des Rosiers, and Deshman 2014; Arthurs 2017). Despite this promise of redefining the field from within, as each of these movements responds to challenges that emerged from within the field rather than being responsive to impositions from outside, there remain dangers concerning how one thinks about and deals with law in context. For this, in the next section, I will venture an invitation to further engage with the political, philosophical, and historical critiques of everyday life and its relationship to both power/hegemony and subversive/authentic acts, the law constituting a paramount example.

The Call of Everyday Life and the Law

The topics browsed through in the previous sections have one thing in common: they attempt to bring socio-legal studies scholarship out of the university onto the street and into the flow of everyday life. Everyday life is not an altogether new addition to the critical framework of Marxist and post-Marxist thought. Since it was introduced by the French theorist Henri Lefèbvre (*Critique de la vie quotidienne I*, 1947; *The Critique of Everyday Life*, 1991), the critique of everyday life gradually took the form of a steady response to the continuing endurance of late capitalism and the absorption of formerly radical elements of society within capitalism's logic of containment. In this context, I will try to illuminate how some of the key developments in the field of socio-legal studies in effect emulated this strategy in their redefinition of the work to be done under the aegis of the study of law.

Before proceeding with this observation, however, I will first reintroduce the basic premises of a key intervention in this area: Agnes Heller's work on everyday life. Heller's writings illuminate the integrative tendencies of the all-encompassing systems of both capitalism and real socialism during the Cold War years (Canefe 1998). Though Heller's contributions to social theory range across numerous disciplines, from sociology to literary theory and political philosophy, her use of the phrase "prism of alienation" specifically refers to the act of chronicling totalitarianism and grounded resistance to it. While Heller's "The Marxist Theory of Revolution and the Revolution of Everyday Life" touches on numerous issues that confronted the radical political movements of the late 1960s, its most enduring aspect is the author's focus on the phenomenology of personhood in the context of systemic alienation. Yearning for a radical restructuring of everyday life, the human subject of Heller's critique is a particularistic person in that her subjectivity persists in abstraction from the totality of everyday life (Heller 2015). Heller further argues that the *fetish character* of everyday life is concomitant with the person's incapacity to relate to herself in her uniqueness and thus feels alienation from her subjectivity. The result is a social agent geared exclusively toward self-preservation who seeks only what serves to propagate herself and her perceived needs. In contrast to this "particular" person, Heller offers us the possibility of a genuine individual who is characterized by the distance she is able to assume between herself and her particular needs, motives, and desires. By appropriating higher-level values within the constellation of her everyday life, the individual is then able to decipher, resist, and remake the demands placed upon her by the socio-political system that embraces her existence (2015). She thus strives to consciously choose what she does, a strategy that in turn leads to the defetishization of everyday life.

Crucially for Heller, individual self-consciousness and morality cannot emerge in isolation from the community. The individual is able to transcend her particularistic identification with conventions via her participation in the conscious construction of human relationships constituted around shared interests and norms. In other words, the political and economic transformation of society alone, Heller concludes, is insufficient to bring about the end of the existing society and its oppressive makeup. It must be accompanied by the revolution of everyday life, which in her view is inseparable from the *praxis* of authentic community formation. Suffice to say, social movements scholars, particularly those studying the decentralized and radical anarchistic elements of these movements, have long indicated the emergence of prefigurative politics to transcend law's violent foundations. In this regard, Heller is accompanied by a long tradition of anarchist thought. Assessing new possibilities for the construction of radical alternatives within and against global capitalism, many elements of the "new" social movements have taken a turn away from a universalizing conception of social change that is characteristic of the hegemonic logic they developed within. Instead, these activist currents are driven by an "anarchist logic of affinity," which is defined as the possibility of moving away from a politics of demand and response and into the territory of asking unanswerable questions if one remains within the system (Graber 2002).

In summary, according to Heller's take on everyday life, the community is always present. The particularistic individual can live in a world of mediated relationships conceived as quasi-transcendent and at least partially cut off from the integrated totalities into which she was born. In contradistinction, the new *individual* has the capacity to defetishize the world. In this sense, Heller's critique of everyday life transcends the concrete political agendas touted by many of the movements that were in force during the latter half of the twentieth century, at the time of her writing this particular treatise. Though the possibilities facing contemporary political movements differ significantly from those that Heller confronted, her insight into the structures of conformity retains its power and relevance well into the twenty-first century. Law is no exception in this regard. The professionalization, commodification, commercialization, and ideological uses of the law are supported by the general milieu of egoism, utility, and self-interest, the pillars defining Heller's particular individual. Her reconstruction of the links between self-interest and social conformity gives a clear indication of the consequences engendered by the continued hegemony of our alienated system of values, including the law.

Heller's critique of everyday life is both wide-ranging in scope and subtle in nuance. "The Marxist Theory of Revolution and the Revolution of Everyday Life" (Heller 1970) should indeed be regarded as an illuminating introduction for a substantive critique of the law. As I have discussed in the previous section, the overall critique offered by the socio-legal studies perspective focuses on the problems associated with the analytic separation of law and society, law and politics, law and history, and so on, attempting to bring the critical study of the law into each of these contexts. And yet, often resorting to an instrumentalist methodology, law, legality, and judicial systems have also been treated without a systematic consideration of the socio-economic underpinnings of the very definition of justice that is dominant in a given context. Furthermore, there remains a prevalent presence of the correctionalist impulse in studies on law leading to the prima facie interpretation of legal systems via hypostatization of the law, continuing to separate law from its actual socio-political context, a.k.a. Heller's everyday life.

No doubt, socio-legal studies' overall perspective on law embodies a heterogeneous, interdisciplinary approach. While sharing a keen interest in law as a socially constructed and politically sustained phenomenon, both shaping and being shaped by society, the field is keen on shedding light on law's violence. However, I would argue that its drawing on different epistemological and methodological foundations has led to risk-laden divisions and bifurcations in the field as well as obstruction of the overall view of law in the history of making and remaking capitalism and its permeation in everyday life. We must never lose sight of the fact that the relationship between law and violence remains paradoxically structured: law is supposedly the opposite of violence, since legal forms of decision-making are intent on disrupting the spell of violence while generating more violence. At the same time, law itself is a kind of structural violence, since it imposes a judgment that determines the fate of its subjects and follows them like a curse. Socio-legal studies' offerings of social and political inquiry provide a useful conceptual link between doctrinal methods and non-legal methodologies of analyzing, understanding, and contextualizing the law. Although most socio-legal studies work involves case-based, in-depth analyses of specific problems, the field is also highly sensitive and responsive to normative questions and power relationships rather than the focus being on finding immediate pragmatic solutions. Still, I would argue that for socio-legal scholarship to fulfill its full promise, it needs to stand closer to larger critiques of everyday life and violence as embodied in the work of thinkers such as Agnes Heller, among others (Sarat and Kearns 2009). In this regard, Heller's take on everyday life could be read as a step forward toward bringing socio-legal studies scholarship into the centre of the sociality, historicity, and politics it declares to be a part of.

Conclusion

In his introductory essay "Ghosts of Law and Humanities," Marett Leiboff (2012) teases out the ghosts of the law and humanities past to decipher the pattern of the relationship between these two fields. He cautiously asks whether it is the case that law has forgotten about its past and has created an imagined present for itself in order to manufacture a relationship with the humanities. If law attempted to do so while dissociating the "human" from humanities, the end result would no doubt be violent. The intersections and interdisciplinarity that constitute and shape the humanities in their broadest conceptions—of the human, of the civic, the politics, and the community—might end up missing from a law-and-humanities-combined future too keen on the legal side of things.

But there is another question that really remains baffling, despite all the riches offered by the rich traditions of socio-legal studies: Why do people believe that violence is acceptable if it is legal? Normative beliefs about the acceptability of violence to achieve social control and social change indicate that deliverance of procedural justice is strongly correlated with law's legitimacy and that positive judgments about law's legitimacy are associated with social justice (Jackson et al. 2013). However, legitimacy has an additional, hitherto unrecognized, empirical property—it is constitutive of the belief that the law monopolizes the rightful use of force in society. Certainty and uncertainty undoubtedly intersect in the case of challenges and injustices created or protected by the law. For instance, settler's entitlement to Indigenous lands has been constructed in past colonial and current national laws, land policies, and ideologies as a certainty (Mackey 2014). Though one persistent characteristic of settler colonialism is settler certainty and entitlement, decolonization—especially in the area of jurisprudence—means embracing this certainty as uncertainty. Many of the examples discussed in the above pages concerning interdisciplinary interventions of socio-legal studies canon reveal something similar in nature: the creation of uncertainties where law and legality once stood as epitomes of certainty.

As a case in point, immigration judges of states with a British settler-colonial background (Canada, the United States, and Australia) regularly make consequential decisions that fundamentally affect the basic life chances of thousands of non-citizens and their family members every year. Yet until recently, we knew very little about how immigration judges make these decisions, including decisions about whether to release or detain non-citizens pending the completion of their immigration cases. Working on long-term immigrant detainees, socio-legal scholars began to analyze judicial decision-making in immigration bond hearings, and their findings reveal many an undercurrent gone unnoticed until then (Rehaag 2009; Ryo 2016). These reveal that there are wide variations in the average bond grant rates and bond amount decisions among judges. If so, where is the certainty of law? It appears that the detainees' prior criminal history is the only significant legally relevant factor in both the grant/deny and bond amount decisions among other possible relevant factors. In other words, immigration courts might claim to be exercising crime control through administrative proceedings, which begs further questions about the cross-sectionality of administrative law, race, gender, class, and status. Law must be put in context again and again to make sense of this normalized set of aberrant decisions.

And yet, studying law in "social context" is never enough. The concept of embeddedness defined as such is imprecise and inadequate (Cotterrell 2013b). Socio-legal scholarship must also be apt in addressing the moral-political concerns that its methodologies reflect (McCann 2014). In this sense, now is a propitious time to renew the dialogue between socio-legal studies scholarship and other fields of analysis and work attending to politics, culture, society, economics, and history. Relational work has an enormous impact on the outcomes of rethinking the relationship between law and all other spheres of human sociality (Block 2013). Devotion to relationality must be reinvigorated. Overall, the socio-legal study of the law is an investigation into both a set of ideals in terms of treating law and legality as normative questions and a set of practices in terms of the rule of law being considered as *praxis*. Studying the law involves understanding the contingent nature of its ideals as well as investigating the actual work that lawyers, judges, state officials, aid workers, activists, advocacy groups, and others do in specific legal contexts. These overlapping layers of the study of the law provides socio-legal studies its distinct framework with tools for understanding how we experience institutional power and respond to or refute it. Indeed, reviewing research on the politics of law, law and social movements, law and inequality, and law and social change allows us to examine the conditions under which legal institutions could potentially promote inequality-reducing structural social change in late capitalism (Stryker 2007). Law induces social change through a combination of adaptation to legal structures, cultural-meaning making and institutional diffusion, and political mobilization and counter-mobilization. For instance, substantive and effects-oriented administrative, adjudicative, and organizational interpretations of welfare legislation maximize inequality reduction, whereas procedural interpretations do the opposite. These interpretations are most likely to be achieved through a combination of collective mobilization for strategic litigation in conjunction with sustained political mobilization from below and direct involvement in implementation and active monitoring of the law. This is not to negate law's propensity to violence but to underline its potential uses to create forms of anti-systemic violence.

This chapter examined some of the more recent frames of analysis that socio-legal studies scholars use to understand the law in context. As discussed above, across the field, critical exploration of issues ranging from defining/redefining justice, ethics, law, truth-telling, and responsibility has been a common trend since the 1980s. These developments are significant in light of the violent foundational histories of the states and societies known today. Colonial and post-colonial quests for supremacy, racial purity, and accumulation of property have been facilitated by oppressive exercises of institutional power and its most pristine expression: the law. The trauma that has arisen from past oppressive exercises of legality being used as a shield for unjust practices and the manner in which legal positivism and formalist methodology attempt to maintain privilege at the expense of the multiple others of the polity clearly demonstrate the inherent tensions pertaining to law and its societal legitimacy. Socio-legal studies operates in the midst of ongoing injustices being committed against oppressed and marginalized groups. In this context, investigating the role that the law plays in facilitating and formalizing systemic violence against groups who are targeted as undesirable and the manner in which the past continues to permeate the present is of paramount importance. However, in order to do so, socio-legal studies must approach legal consciousness not just as a theoretical concept or topic of research but as an inherent aspect of legal hegemony, particularly in relation to how the law sustains its institutional power despite persistent gaps between the letter of the law and the law in action. In order to understand why people acquiesce to a legal system that, despite its promises of equal treatment, systematically reproduces inequality, we must take a closer look at the kind of critique advanced by Agnes Heller regarding the kind of politics of everyday life capitalism dictates and its alternative formulations. In this sense, recent studies in the field have both broadened and narrowed the enterprise's overall reach. Rather than explaining how the different experiences of law become synthesized into systemic behavior, the literature often tracks what particular individuals, groups, or communities do in reaction to the law. As long as the relationship among legal consciousness, ideology, and hegemony remains unexplained, socio-legal studies runs the risk of falling short of developing into a wholesome area of sustained substantive critical interventions.

References

Ahmed, Aziza. 2014. "Think Again: Prostitution." *Foreign Policy* 204:74.
———. 2015. "Trafficked? AIDS, Criminal Law and the Politics of Measurement." *University of Miami Law Review* 70:96.
Ahmed, Aziza, and Meena Seshu. 2014. "We Have the Right Not to Be 'Rescued' . . ." *Global Human Trafficking: Critical Issues and Contexts* 2:169.
Ammons, Elizabeth, and Modhumita Roy. 2015. *Sharing the Earth: An International Environmental Justice Reader*. Athens: University of Georgia Press.
Arthurs, Harry. 2017. "The Commonwealth of Lawyers?" *International Journal of the Legal Profession* 24 (1): 13–17.
Ayres, Susan. 2005. "The Powers of Stories: Gloucester Tales." *Tex. Wesleyan L. Rev.* 12:1.
Baker-Cristales, Beth. 2008. "Magical Pursuits: Legitimacy and Representation in a Transnational Political Field." *American Anthropologist* 110 (3): 349–59.
Ballestero, Andrea. 2015. "The Ethics of a Formula: Calculating a Financial–Humanitarian Price for Water." *American Ethnologist* 42 (2): 262–78.

Baratosy, Roxana, and Sarah Wendt. 2017. "'Outdated Laws, Outspoken Whores': Exploring Sex Work in a Criminalised Setting." *Women's Studies International Forum* 62:34–42.

Bayat, Asef. 1997. "Un-civil Society: The Politics of the 'Informal People.'" *Third World Quarterly* 18 (1): 53–72.

———. 2000. "From 'Dangerous Classes' to 'Quiet Rebels': Politics of the Urban Subaltern in the Global South." *International Sociology* 15 (3): 533–57.

Beare, Margaret E., Nathalie Des Rosiers, and Abigail C. Deshman, eds. 2014. *Putting the State on Trial: The Policing of Protest During the G20 Summit.* Vancouver: UBC Press.

Benjamin, Walter. 1978. "Critique of Violence." In *Reflections: Essays, Aphorisms, Autobiographical Writings*, edited by Peter Demtez, 277–300. New York: Schocken.

Berman, Jennifer. 2003. "The Needle and the Damage Done: How Hoffman Plastics Promotes Sweatshops and Illegal Immigration and What to Do About It." *Kan. JL & Pub. Pol'y* 13:585.

Beuret, Nicholas, and Gareth Brown. 2016. "The Walking Dead: The Anthropocene as a Ruined Earth." *Science as Culture* 26 (3): 1–25.

Birrell, Kathleen. 2016. *Indigeneity: Before and Beyond the Law.* London: Routledge.

Block, Fred. 2013. "Relational Work and the Law: Recapturing the Legal Realist Critique of Market Fundamentalism." *Journal of Law and Society* 40 (1): 27–48.

Buchanan, Ruth. 2008. "Writing Resistance into International Law." *International Community Law Review* 10 (4): 445–54.

Burton, Lloyd. 2002. *Worship and Wilderness: Culture, Religion, and Law in Public Lands Management.* Madison: University of Wisconsin Press.

Canefe, Nergis. 1998. "Sovereign Utopias: Civilisational Boundaries of Greek and Turkish Nationhood, 1821–1923." PhD thesis, York University.

Casas-Cortes, Maribel, Sebastian Cobarrubias, Nicholas De Genova, Glenda Garelli, Giorgio Grappi, Charles Heller, Sabine Hess, et al. 2015. "New Keywords: Migration and Borders." *Cultural Studies* 29 (1): 55–87.

Chabay, Ilan, Martin Frick, and Jennifer Helgeson, eds. 2015. *Land Restoration: Reclaiming Landscapes for a Sustainable Future.* Cambridge, MA: Academic Press.

Chimni, Bhupinder S. 1999. "Marxism and International Law: A Contemporary Analysis." *Economic and Political Weekly* 34 (6): 337–49.

———. 2004. "An Outline of a Marxist Course on Public International Law." *Leiden Journal of International Law* 17 (1): 1–30.

———. 2009. "The Birth of a 'Discipline': From Refugee to Forced Migration Studies." *Journal of Refugee Studies* 22 (1): 11–29.

Clunie, Gregor, and Haris Psarras. 2016. *The Public in Law: Representations of the Political in Legal Discourse.* London: Routledge.

Cotterrell, Roger. 1997. *Law's Community: Legal Theory in Sociological Perspective.* Oxford: Oxford University Press.

———. 2008. "Transnational Communities and the Concept of Law." *Ratio Juris* 21 (1): 1–18.

———. 2013a. *Law, Culture and Society: Legal Ideas in the Mirror of Social Theory.* New York: Ashgate.

———. 2013b. "Rethinking 'Embeddedness': Law, Economy, Community." *Journal of Law and Society* 40 (1): 49–67.

———. 2015. "From Living Law to Global Legal Pluralism: Rethinking Traditions from a Century of Western Socio-legal Studies." *Kobe University Law Review* 49:229.

Cross, John, and Alfonso Morales, eds. 2007. *Street Entrepreneurs: People, Place, & Politics in Local and Global Perspective.* London: Routledge.

Darian-Smith, Eve. 2016. "The Crisis in Legal Education: Embracing Ethnographic Approaches to Law." *Transnational Legal Theory* 7 (2): 199–227.

Darian-Smith, Eve, and Peter Fitzpatrick, eds. 1999. *Laws of the Postcolonial.* Ann Arbor: University of Michigan Press.

Darling, Jonathan. 2017. "Forced Migration and the City: Irregularity, Informality, and the Politics of Presence." *Progress in Human Geography* 41 (2): 178–98.

Delgado, Richard, and Jean Stefancic. 2017. *Critical Race Theory: An Introduction.* New York: NYU Press.

de Sousa Santos, Boaventura. 2002. *Toward a New Legal Common Sense: Law, Globalization, and Emancipation.* Cambridge: Cambridge University Press.

de Sousa Santos, Boaventura, and César A. Rodríguez-Garavito, eds. 2005. *Law and Globalization from Below: Towards a Cosmopolitan Legality.* Cambridge: Cambridge University Press.

Dirlik, Arif. 1994. "The Postcolonial Aura: Third World Criticism in the Age of Global Capitalism." *Critical Inquiry* 20 (2): 328–56.

Dolgin, Janet, and Lois L. Shepherd. 2014. *Bioethics and the Law.* Wolters Kluwer Law & Business.

Doll, Agnieszka, and Kevin Walby. 2019. "Institutional Ethnography as a Method of Inquiry for Criminal Justice and Socio-legal Studies." *International Journal for Crime, Justice and Social Democracy* 8 (1): 147.

Edelman, Lauren B., Aaron C. Smyth, and Asad Rahim. 2016. "Legal Discrimination: Empirical Sociolegal and Critical Race Perspectives on Antidiscrimination Law." *Annual Review of Law and Social Science* 12:395–415.

Eslava, Luis. 2015. *Local Space, Global Life.* Cambridge: Cambridge University Press.

Eslava, Luis, and Sundhya Pahuja. 2011. "Between Resistance and Reform: TWAIL and the Universality of International Law." *Trade L. & Dev.* 3:103.

———. 2012. "Beyond the (Post) Colonial: TWAIL and the Everyday Life of International Law." *Verfassung und Recht in Übersee/Law and Politics in Africa, Asia and Latin America* 45 (2): 195–221.

Evans-Cowley, Jennifer S., and Angel Arroyo-Rodríguez. 2016. "Integrating Food Waste Diversion into Food Systems Planning: A Case Study of the Mississippi Gulf Coast." *Journal of Agriculture, Food Systems, and Community Development* 3 (3): 167–85.

Fahrenwald, Nancy L., Janette Y. Taylor, Shawn M. Kneipp, and Mary K. Canales. 2007. "Academic Freedom and Academic Duty to Teach Social Justice: A Perspective and Pedagogy for Public Health Nursing Faculty." *Public Health Nursing* 24 (2): 190–97.

Fidler, David P. 2002. "A Globalized Theory of Public Health Law." *Journal of Law, Medicine & Ethics* 30 (2): 150–61.

Freeman, Andrea. 2014. "'First Food' Justice: Racial Disparities in Infant Feeding as Food Oppression." *Fordham L. Rev.* 83:3053.

———. 2015. "Transparency for Food Consumers: Nutrition Labeling and Food Oppression." *American Journal of Law & Medicine* 41 (2–3): 315–30.

Freire, Paulo. 2000. *Pedagogy of the Oppressed*. Bloomsbury.

Galanter, Marc. 1974. "Why the 'Haves' Come Out Ahead: Speculations on the Limits of Legal Change." *Law & Society Review* 9 (1): 95–160.

Gathii, James Thuo. 2011. "TWAIL: A Brief History of Its Origins, Its Decentralized Network, and a Tentative Bibliography." *Trade L. & Dev.* 3:26.

Gauna, Eileen. 2008. "El Dia De Los Muertos: The Death and Rebirth of the Environmental Movement." *Envtl. L.* 38:457.

Gleeson, Shannon. 2009. "From Rights to Claims: The Role of Civil Society in Making Rights Real for Vulnerable Workers." *Law & Society Review* 43 (3): 669–700.

———. 2010. "Labor Rights for All? The Role of Undocumented Immigrant Status for Worker Claims Making." *Law & Social Inquiry* 35 (3): 561–602.

———. 2016. *Precarious Claims: The Promise and Failure of Workplace Protections in the United States*. Berkeley: University of California Press.

Glick Schiller, Nina, and Noel B. Salazar. 2013. "Regimes of Mobility across the Globe." *Journal of Ethnic and Migration Studies* 39 (2): 183–200.

Goldring, Luin, and Patricia Landolt, eds. 2013. *Producing and Negotiating Non-citizenship: Precarious Legal Status in Canada*. Toronto: University of Toronto Press.

Gostin, Lawrence O., Lindsay F. Wiley, and Thomas R. Frieden. 2015. *Public Health Law: Power, Duty, Restraint*. Berkeley: University of California Press.

Gottlieb, Robert. 2009. "Where We Live, Work, Play . . . and Eat: Expanding the Environmental Justice Agenda." *Environmental Justice* 2 (1): 7–8.

Graber, David. 2002. "A Movement of Movements? The New Anarchists." *New Left Review* 13:61.

Grabham, Emily. 2016. *Brewing Legal Times: Things, Form, and the Enactment of Law*. Toronto: University of Toronto Press.

Grappi, Giorgio, Charles Heller, Sabine Hess, et al. 2015. "New Keywords: Migration and Borders." *Cultural Studies* 29 (1): 55–87.

Halliday, Terence C., and Gregory Shaffer, eds. 2015. *Transnational Legal Orders*. Cambridge: Cambridge University Press.

Hamlin, Rebecca. 2009. *Let Me Be a Refugee: Asylum Seekers and the Transformation of Law in the United States, Canada, and Australia*. Berkeley: University of California Press.

Hamlin, Rebecca. 2012. "International Law and Administrative Insulation: A Comparison of Refugee Status Determination Regimes in the United States, Canada, and Australia." *Law & Social Inquiry* 37 (4): 933–68.

Harrington, John, and Ambreena Manji. 2017. "The Limits of Socio-legal Radicalism: Social and Legal Studies and Third World Scholarship." *Social & Legal Studies* 26 (6): 700–715.

Heller, Agnes. 1970. "The Marxist Theory of Revolution and the Revolution of Everyday Life." *Telos*, no. 6, 212–23.

———. 2015. *Everyday life*. Vol. 3. London: Routledge.

Hertogh, Marc. 2018. *Nobody's Law: Legal Consciousness and Legal Alienation in Everyday Life*. London: Palgrave Pivot.

Hickle, Kristine E. 2017. "Resiliency and Women Exiting Sex Trade Industry Work." *Journal of Social Work* 17 (3): 302–23.

Howe, Cymene, Jessica Lockrem, Hannah Appel, Edward Hackett, Dominic Boyer, Randal Hall, Matthew Schneider-Mayerson, et al. 2016. "Paradoxical Infrastructures: Ruins, Retrofit, and Risk." *Science, Technology, & Human Values* 41 (3): 547–65.

Hunt, Sarah. 2014. "Ontologies of Indigeneity: The Politics of Embodying a Concept." *Cultural Geographies* 21 (1): 27–32.

Hyndman, Jennifer, and Wenona Giles. 2011. "Waiting for What? The Feminization of Asylum in Protracted Situations." *Gender, Place & Culture* 18 (3): 361–79.

Inman, Derek. 2014. "Indigenous Peoples as Users of Human Rights: Pushing the Boundaries of Indigeneity and Influencing International Law." *Hum. Rts. & Int'l Legal Discourse* 8:258.

Israel, Mark. 2004. "Strictly Confidential? Integrity and the Disclosure of Criminological and Socio-legal Research." *British Journal of Criminology* 44 (5): 715–40.

Jackson, Jonathan, Aziz Z. Huq, Ben Bradford, and Tom R. Tyler. 2013. "Monopolizing Force? Police Legitimacy and Public Attitudes toward the Acceptability of Violence." *Psychology, Public Policy, and Law* 19 (4): 479.

Jeffrey, Leslie, and Barbara Sullivan. 2009. "Canadian Sex Work Policy for the 21st Century: Enhancing Rights and Safety, Lessons from Australia." *Canadian Political Science Review* 3 (1): 57–76.

Johnson, Miranda C. L. 2016. *The Land Is Our History: Indigeneity, Law, and the Settler State*. New York: Oxford University Press.

Krieger, Nancy. 2015. "Public Health, Embodied History, and Social Justice: Looking Forward." *International Journal of Health Services* 45 (4): 587–600.

Lang, Tim, and Michael Heasman. 2015. *Food Wars: The Global Battle for Mouths, Minds and Markets*. London: Routledge.

Law, Tuulia. 2015. "Licensed or Licentious? Examining Regulatory Discussions of Stripping in Ontario." *Canadian Journal of Law & Society* 30 (1): 31–50.

Leiboff, Marett. 2012. "Ghosts of Law and Humanities (Past, Present, Future)." *Australian Feminist Law Journal* 36 (1): 3–17.

Lems, Annika. 2016. "Placing Displacement: Place-Making in a World of Movement." *Ethnos* 81 (2): 315–37.

Levine, Felice J. 1990. "Goose Bumps and 'the Search for Signs of Intelligent Life' in Sociolegal Studies: After Twenty-Five Years." *Law & Society Review* 24 (1): 7–33.

Levitsky, Sandra R. 2015. "Law and Social Movements: Old Debates and New Directions." *The Handbook of Law and Society*, edited by Austin Sarat and Patrick Ewick, 382–98. Oxford: Wiley-Blackwell.

Lindley, Anna, ed. 2014. *Crisis and Migration: Critical Perspectives*. London: Routledge.

Loughlin, Martin. 2000. *Sword and Scales: An Examination of the Relationship Between Law and Politics*. Portland, OR: Hart.

Mackey, Eva. 2014. "Unsettling Expectations: (Un) Certainty, Settler States of Feeling, Law, and Decolonization." *Canadian Journal of Law & Society* 29 (2): 235–52.

MacKinnon, Catharine A. 1983. "Feminism, Marxism, Method, and the State: Toward Feminist Jurisprudence." *Signs: Journal of Women in Culture and Society* 8 (4): 635–58.

Malkki, Liisa H. 1995. "Refugees and Exile: From 'Refugee Studies' to the National Order of Things." *Annual Review of Anthropology* 24:495–523.

Martel, Joane, Bryan Hogeveen, and Andrew Woolford. 2006. "The State of Critical Scholarship in Criminology and Socio-legal Studies in Canada." *Canadian Journal of Criminology and Criminal Justice* 48 (5): 633–46.

McCann, Michael. 2014. "The Unbearable Lightness of Rights: On Sociolegal Inquiry in the Global Era." *Law & Society Review* 48 (2): 245–73.

McCann, Michael, ed. 2017. *Law and Social Movements*. London: Routledge.

McElhattan, David, Laura Beth Nielsen, and Jill D. Weinberg. 2017. "Race and Determinations of Discrimination: Vigilance, Cynicism, Skepticism, and Attitudes About Legal Mobilization in Employment Civil Rights." *Law & Society Review* 51 (3): 669–703.

Merryman, John Henry. 1977. "Comparative Law and Social Change: On the Origins, Style, Decline & Revival of the Law and Development Movement." *American Journal of Comparative Law* 25:457–91.

Mignolo, Walter. 2010. "Cosmopolitanism and the De-colonial Option." *Studies in Philosophy and Education* 29 (2): 111–27.

Mnookin, Robert H. 1981. "Public/Private Dichotomy: Political Disagreement and Academic Repudiation." *U. Pa. L. Rev.* 130:1429.

Moore, Dawn, and Hideyuki Hirai. 2014. "Outcasts, Performers and True Believers: Responsibilized Subjects of Criminal Justice." *Theoretical Criminology* 18 (1): 5–19.

Morales, Alfonso. 2010. "Planning and the Self-Organization of Marketplaces." *Journal of Planning Education and Research* 30 (2): 182–97.

Murray, Kali. 2011. "Changing Conceptions of Water in the Law." *Marquette Law Review* 95 (1): 1.

Neilson, Brett, and Net Rossiter. 2008. "Precarity as a Political Concept, or, Fordism as Exception." *Theory, Culture & Society* 25:51–72.

Nelken, David. 2004. "Using the Concept of Legal Culture." *Austl. J. Leg. Phil.* 29:1.

Nelson, Matthew J. 2010. "Persistent Legal Pluralism and the Challenge of Universal Human Rights." *Journal of Human Rights Practice* 2 (3): 401–7.

Nicholson, Matthew. 2016. "Walter Benjamin and the Re-Imageination of International Law." *Law and Critique* 27 (1): 103–29.

Nonet, Philippe, and Philip Selznick. (1978) 2017. *Law and Society in Transition: Toward Responsive Law*. New York: Routledge.

Okafor, Obiora Chinedu. 2008. "Critical Third World Approaches to International Law (TWAIL): Theory, Methodology, or Both?" *International Community Law Review* 10 (4): 371–78.

Opsal, Tara. 2015. "'It's Their World, So You've Just Got to Get Through': Women's Experiences of Parole Governance." *Feminist Criminology* 10 (2): 188–207.

Paret, Marcel, and Shannon Gleeson. 2016. "Precarity and Agency through a Migration Lens." *Citizenship Studies* 20 (3–4): 277–94.

Parfitt, Rose. 2013. *The Unequal Equality of Sovereigns: A Brief History of "Peripheral Personality."* New York: New York University School of Law.

Parfitt, Rose. 2014. "The Spectre of Sources." *European Journal of International Law* 25 (1): 297–306.

Park, Lisa Sun-Hee, and David N. Pellow. 2011. *The Slums of Aspen: Immigrants Vs. the Environment in America's Eden*. New York: NYU Press.

Parks, Gregory S., Shayne E. Jones, Rashawn Ray, and Matthew W. Hughey. 2015. "White Boys Drink, Black Girls Yell: A Racialized and Gendered Analysis of Violent Hazing and the Law." *J. Gender Race & Just.* 18:93.

Parmar, Pooja. 2008. "TWAIL: An Epistemological Inquiry." *Int'l Comm. L. Rev.* 10:363.

———. 2015. "Nation and Family: Personal Law, Cultural Pluralism, and Gendered Citizenship." *Law & Society Review* 49(3): 807–9.

Pashukanis, Evgeny. 2017. *The General Theory of Law and Marxism*. New York: Routledge.

Pellow, David N., and Lisa Sun-Hee Park. 2002. *The Silicon Valley of Dreams: Environmental Injustice, Immigrant Workers, and the High-Tech Global Economy*. New York: NYU Press.

Powers, Madison, and Ruth R. Faden. 2006. *Social Justice: The Moral Foundations of Public Health and Health Policy*. Oxford: Oxford University Press.

Purvis, Nigel. 1991. "Critical Legal Studies in Public International Law." *Harv. Int'l. LJ* 32:81.

Raguparan, Menaka. 2017. "'If I'm Gonna Hack Capitalism': Racialized and Indigenous Canadian Sex Workers' Experiences Within the Neo-liberal Market Economy." *Women's Studies International Forum* 60:69–76.

Rajagopal, Balakrishnan. 2003. *International Law from Below: Development, Social Movements and Third World Resistance*. Cambridge: Cambridge University Press.

Rasulov, Akbar. 2010. "Writing About Empire: Remarks on the Logic of a Discourse." *Leiden Journal of International Law* 23 (2): 449–71.

———. 2016. "From Apology to Utopia and the Inner Life of International Law." *Leiden Journal of International Law* 29 (3): 641–66.

Redding, Jeffrey A. 2014. "The Case of Ayesha, Muslim 'Courts,' and the Rule of Law: Some Ethnographic Lessons for Legal Theory." *Modern Asian Studies* 48 (4): 940–85.

Rehaag, Sean. 2009. "Bisexuals Need Not Apply: A Comparative Appraisal of Refugee Law and Policy in Canada, the United States, and Australia." *International Journal of Human Rights* 13 (2–3): 415–36.

Riles, Annelise. 2004. "Property as Legal Knowledge: Means and Ends." *Journal of the Royal Anthropological Institute* 10 (4): 775–95.

Rothman, David J. 2017. *Strangers at the Bedside: A History of How Law and Bioethics Transformed Medical Decision Making*. New York: Routledge.

Roy, Ananya. 2011. "Slumdog Cities: Rethinking Subaltern Urbanism." *International Journal of Urban and Regional Research* 35 (2): 223–38.

Ryo, Emily. 2016. "Detained: A Study of Immigration Bond Hearings." *Law & Society Review* 50 (1): 117–53.

Samaddar, Ranabir. 2006. "Law and Terror in the Age of Colonial Constitution Making." *Diogenes* 53 (4): 18–33.

Sarat, Austin, and Thomas R. Kearns, eds. 2009. *Law in Everyday Life*. University of Michigan Press.

Saunders, Natasha. 2014. "Paradigm Shift or Business as Usual? An Historical Reappraisal of the 'Shift' to Securitisation of Refugee Protection." *Refugee Survey Quarterly* 33 (3): 69–92.

Scheel, Stephan, and Philipp Ratfisch. 2014. "Refugee Protection Meets Migration Management: UNHCR as a Global Police of Populations." *Journal of Ethnic and Migration Studies* 40 (6): 924–41.

Shahar, Ido. 2008. "State, Society and the Relations between Them: Implications for the Study of Legal Pluralism." *Theoretical Inquiries in Law* 9 (2): 417–41.

Sharafi, Mitra. 2007. "A New History of Colonial Lawyering: Likhovski and Legal Identities in the British Empire." *Law & Social Inquiry* 32 (4): 1059–94.

———. 2008. "Justice in Many Rooms since Galanter: De-Romanticizing Legal Pluralism through the Cultural Defense." *Law and Contemporary Problems* 71 (2): 139–46.

Shivji, Issa G., ed. 1986. *Limits of Legal Radicalism: Reflections on Teaching Law at the University of Dar es Salaam*. Dar es Salaam, Tanzania: University of Dar es Salaam.

Silbey, Susan S. 2005. "After Legal Consciousness." *Annu. Rev. Law Soc. Sci.* 1:323–68.

Solórzano, Daniel G., and Tara J. Yosso. 2002. "Critical Race Methodology: Counter-storytelling as an Analytical Framework for Education Research." *Qualitative Inquiry* 8 (1): 23–44.

Spalding, B., N. Czarnecki, W. Hallman, and N. Fitzgerald. 2012. "Can Farmers Markets Improve Access and Consumption of Fruits and Vegetables in Vulnerable Populations?" *Journal of the Academy of Nutrition and Dietetics* 112 (9): A72.

Sreejith, S. G. 2017. "An Auto-Critique of TWAIL's Historical Fallacy: Sketching an Alternative Manifesto." *Third World Quarterly* 38 (7): 1511–30.

Starr, June, and Mark Goodale. 2002. "Introduction: Legal Ethnography: New Dialogues, Enduring Methods." In *Practicing Ethnography in Law*, 1–10. New York: Palgrave Macmillan.

———, eds. 2016. *Practicing Ethnography in Law: New Dialogues, Enduring Methods*. New York: Palgrave Macmillan.

Stryker, Robin. 2007. "Half Empty, Half Full, or Neither: Law, Inequality, and Social Change in Capitalist Democracies." *Annual Review of Law and Social Science* 3:69–97.

Swiffen, Amy, and Joshua Nichols, eds. 2017. *Legal Violence and the Limits of the Law: Cruel and Unusual*. London: Routledge.

Tamanaha, Brian Z. 2004. *On the Rule of Law: History, Politics, Theory*. Cambridge: Cambridge University Press.

Tappe, Oliver, and Minh T. N. Nguyen. 2019. "Southeast Asian Trajectories of Labour Mobility: Precarity, Translocality, and Resilience." *TRaNS: Trans-Regional and-National Studies of Southeast Asia* 7 (1): 1–18.

Teubner, Gunther. 1997. "The King's Many Bodies: The Self-Deconstruction of Law's Hierarchy." *Law & Society Review* 31:763–87.

Trubek, David M., and Marc Galanter. 1974. "Scholars in Self-Estrangement: Some Reflections on the Crisis in Law and Development Studies in the United States." *Wisconsin Law Review*, 1062–1102.

Trubek, David M., Yves Dezalay, Ruth Buchanan, and John R. Davis. 1993. "Global Restructuring and the Law: Studies of the Internationalization of Legal Fields and the Creation of Transitional Arenas." *Case W. Res. L. Rev.* 44:407.

Tuori, Kaius. 2014. *Lawyers and Savages: Ancient History and Legal Realism in the Making of Legal Anthropology*. London: Routledge.

Vago, Steven. 2015. *Law and Society*. New York: Routledge.

Valverde, Mariana. 2009. *Law's Dream of a Common Knowledge*. Princeton, NJ: Princeton University Press.

———. 2012. *Everyday Law on the Street: City Governance in an Age of Diversity*. Chicago: University of Chicago Press.

Werth, Robert. 2012. "I Do What I'm Told, Sort of: Reformed Subjects, Unruly Citizens, and Parole." *Theoretical Criminology* 16 (3): 329–46.

Yon, Daniel A. 2001. Review of *Laws of the Postcolonial*, edited by Eve Darian-Smith and Peter Fitzpatrick. *Social & Legal Studies* 10 (2): 280.

Afterword

Toward the Law of Anti-laws: Notes on Prefigurative Politics and Radical Imaginations

Mariful Alam and Irina Ceric

The root of the prevailing lack of imagination cannot be grasped unless one is able to imagine what is lacking, that is, what is missing, hidden, forbidden, and yet possible, in modern life.

—*Situationist International*

As we write this afterword, there are calls to disarm and abolish the police across the United States and Canada following the murder of George Floyd, yet another Black man killed by a white police officer in the United States. The call has also brought into the mainstream conversations regarding alternatives to incarceration and prisons as a solution to interpersonal violence and structural racism, a timely discussion that chapter 4 in this volume on the #MeToo movement engages with. Only a few months ago, these kinds of conversations were almost unimaginable in mainstream media and public policy debates. This rapid progression has given thinkers such as Dr. Angela Davis—a pioneer in the prison abolition movement—hope for a transformative future. When "many of us began to talk about abolishing these [policing and carceral] institutions back in the 1970s," Davis states in a recent interview with Boston University's WBUR radio station, "We were treated as if we were absolutely out of our minds. . . . This is the opportunity for us to begin to reimagine the meaning of [public safety]" (Mosley and Hagan 2020). It seems that now, more than ever, the contribution of socio-legal scholars to the discussion of state violence is needed. The conversation on police violence will, among other things, centre questions around possibilities of moving outside and beyond law's power and toward transformative—not retributive—justice. In what follows, we believe a dialogue between critical legal scholarship and radical social movement organizing can be fruitful for thinking through these possibilities.

In this volume's introduction, the editors map how legal regimes animate oppressive power relations. We build on these observations to make a bold claim: *It will never be possible* to separate the force of law from violence, whether that violence is metaphysical, social, or political. As Jacques Derrida famously explained, the relationship among law, violence, and justice is, and will always remain, paradoxical (1992). This tense and often contradictory relationship is clearly demonstrated in several of the chapters in this volume. Chapter 1 and chapter 2, for example, remind us that decolonization and racial justice for Indigenous peoples cannot be achieved without radically reimagining how we can deconstruct and transform settler-colonial legal regimes that are inherently designed to erode and eliminate Indigenous peoples and their sovereignty (see also Walia 2014). Similarly, chapters 3 and 4 illustrate how legal discourses, knowledge, and strategies are essential in the (re)production of racial and gendered violence and subjugation.

The chapters in this volume suggest to us that a "just world," where subjects are free from oppressive power relations, will consequently require the imagination of communities where the state and its law cease to exist. This claim may seem "utopian," "naive," and "impossible" to either imagine or put into practice, but the recent events that have unfolded in relation to police violence and the compelling argument put forward in the last chapter (chapter 7)—that socio-legal scholarship must continue to find ways to benefit the marginalized and oppressed—serve as reminders that activists and academics must not give up on transformative imaginations or dreams of radical alternatives. Unfortunately, as the editors noted in the introduction, much of the discussion of social transformation and resistance in socio-legal studies centres around the question of whether and how law can be used to achieve practical change. What alternatives to law could look like—that is, how communities could organize their everyday lives and how they could address social and interpersonal conflicts outside of an apparatus of violence—is an underexplored and underdeveloped question in the field. It is here where we think socio-legal scholarship could look to elements within new social movements and the practice of prefigurative politics to generate a dialogue on radical possibilities.

Social movement scholars have extensively documented that, unlike older radical movements that were often organized hierarchically through vanguard political party structures, newer social movements are not striving to take control of the state and its legal apparatus (Holloway 2010). Instead, they are attempting to develop new forms of self-organization that can run parallel to existing forms of governance (Day 2005; Gautney 2012; Graeber 2002, 2009; Juris 2008; Maeckelbergh 2009, 2011). What uniquely distinguishes these new movements is the emphasis on employing non-violent forms of social inter-action in their organizations. These practices manifest the very forms of social relationships, albeit in a miniature form, that activists hope to achieve in the longer term. Social movement scholars have conceptualized this as a form of *prefigurative politics*, which seeks to collapse the distinction between means and ends (Franks 2003, 145; see also Dixon 2014; Gautney 2012). The idea is as follows: by organizing direct actions and developing alternative community initiatives based on the principles of mutual aid, solidarity, and transformative justice, not only are activists practically challenging institutions and symbols of oppression, but they are also simultaneously opening space to experiment with and (re)imagine "radical models of democracy" (Juris 2008, 126).

For example, activists have long organized their own radical legal support structures to defend movements, resist criminalization, and support arrested or detained comrades. Beginning in the 1970s and then re-emerging during the alterglobalization movement, law collectives and other activist legal projects have provided legal support to thousands of activists and protesters by facilitating access to lawyers, fielding legal observers, staffing legal hotlines, and organizing court and jail support. Radical legal support organizers have provided countless workshops and trainings, from basic "Know Your Rights" sessions for protesters to impromptu solidarity trainings in police wagons and more advanced train-the-trainer workshops on organizing legal support for the movement. Such popular legal education efforts—like the legal guides, manuals, comic books, videos, websites, and other popular legal education resources developed by activist legal support providers—are resolutely political, aimed at defending and building movements for radical social change. The provision of direct support and legal assistance alongside legal information and resources is approached as a movement-building tactic, grounded in the need to counter state repression at every stage of organizing (Ceric 2020). These dual roles—popular legal education and direct support—are also evidence of a commitment to prefigurative movement praxis. In their largely involuntary engagements with law, radical legal support organizers strive toward what one activist legal support project described as "forms of individual and collective empowerment that are alien to the legal process, where we are usually objects rather than agents" (CRASS 2010).

As responses to repression and criminalization, the capacity-building and movement defence praxes of activist legal support organizers demonstrate the counter-hegemonic and prefigurative potential of radical legal work. Especially when carried out by non-lawyers, this work points toward a mode of movement lawyering *from below*, a mutual aid project that does not take the legitimacy of the legal system as a given and recognizes that repression can breed resistance as well as demobilization (Ceric 2020). The work of radical legal support organizers in shaping post-arrest experiences into mobilizing ones and the broader pedagogical interventions it builds on are evidence of a distinct orientation toward law and the state, one that engages with the law as it is without fully conceding its legitimacy or acknowledging it as the boundary of emancipatory possibilities (2020). This example points to a form of prefiguration that aims to advance analyses of the criminalization of dissent that go beyond frames of liberal constitutionalism to theorize and actually construct alternate notions of justice, accountability, and redress, both within our own movements, communities, and/or organizations and in terms of challenging the state on its own terrain. The work of radical legal support organizers is one example of prefiguration, which socio-legal scholars could draw on to begin a dialogue between critical legal scholarship and social movement organizing in order to sketch imaginations and alternative possibilities to law and state violence.

Another example comes from migrant justice activists, such as the No One is Illegal networks operating across North America and Europe that have successfully implemented initiatives to turn their local municipalities into sanctuary cities. A sanctuary city is a space where the municipal government, its local police forces, and all in-city public services pledge to neither deny undocumented immigrants access to social services nor report their immigration status to the federal government to ensure their safety and protection. Although seemingly paradoxical, sanctuary cities are an example of how alterglobalization activists organize their revolution both within *and also* outside of the confinements of law and state power. More importantly, sanctuary cities reflect the vision of open borders not merely as a policy goal but also as a move toward abolishing the violence of borders and law *all together* (see Squire and Bagelman 2014).

Similarly, anti-carceral and Black, Indigenous, and people of colour (BIPOC) feminist organizations such as INCITE! and Philly Stands Up in the United States are offering practical visions on how to organize against interpersonal and sexual violence within their communities without relying on the police or criminal justice system. INCITE!, for example, offers tools and intervention strategies based on transformative justice and community accountability, a process in which "a group of friends, a family, a church, a workplace, an apartment complex, a neighborhood" can work together to address a community "member's abusive behavior" by "creating a process for them to account for their actions and transform their behavior" (INCITE! n.d.). INCITE! also seeks to develop ways to provide safety and support "to community members who are violently targeted that respects their self-determination" (ibid.; see also INCITE! 2016; Law 2014).

Like INCITE!, Philly Stands Up is another collective of feminist activists working in Philadelphia "to confront sexual assault" in various communities by using "a transformative justice framework" (Philly Stands Up n.d.). The collective directly intervenes and works with both perpetrators and survivors to resolve conflicts and harms using community-based strategies without relying on the criminal justice system. As the collective's mandate states, in dealing with perpetrators, the group seeks to "recognize and change [their] behavior, rather than ostracizing and allowing future assaults elsewhere." Furthermore, they support "their healing process, and challenge them on their behavior in order to prevent future assaults" (Philly Stands Up n.d.). As Esteban Lance Kelly (2011–12) writes, the group's belief is that the violence of prison systems cannot solve issues that require transforming socio-economic conditions. On the contrary, prisons reinforce cycles of sexual violence, as it systemically targets low-income and working-class communities of colour, particularly Black and Brown communities, and destabilizes families in the process (Kelly 2011–12, 50; see also Law 2014). By practicing a community-oriented approach, the group creates a "culture of care" that opens space for individuals to develop skills and knowledge that offers not only an image of what a world without the violence of the state and prisons could look like but also a practical approach in challenging sexual violence and social harm (ibid., 51).

In chapter 4 of this volume, the authors highlight how carceral and criminal justice solutions to interpersonal conflicts and sexual violence has merely led to a prison-industrial complex that has disproportionately targeted poor Black, Indigenous, and other people of colour. The initiatives and models used by groups such as INCITE! and Philly Stands Up offer other opportunities for socio-legal scholars to engage in dialogues reimagining what justice *could* look like and how we can think through ways to address and respond to interpersonal community conflicts without having to perpetuate or rely on state violence (see also Gaarder 2009).

The examples noted above are only a few out of many examples in which activists are creatively and democratically organizing. All this is not to suggest that the visions and models discussed above should be understood as essentializing blueprints and schematics. They are not without their own sets of contradictions and limitations. Radical legal support can often wind up recreating the very top-down professionalized and service-oriented models it set out to challenge, and a lack of intergenerational movement infrastructure means that this sort of organizing is often crisis-driven and reactive. The long-term maintenance of sanctuary cities requires constant vigilance against both state and non-state incursion as forms of securitization evolve and often privatize. Despite the rapid diffusion of abolitionist critiques, communities attempting to address sexual violence without resorting to force must grapple with complex procedural and practical questions (such as, What do you when someone refuses to participate in an accountability process?) that often prove divisive and exhausting in practice. All these examples are subject to critiques of scale: (How) Can hyper local and/or culturally marginal projects challenge the hegemony of state law and market forces? Can insurgent legalities take root outside of activist (sub)cultures? Finally, and fundamentally, none of these examples speak to the possibilities posed by decolonization and the potential reordering of settler-colonial legal regimes prefigured by assertions and enactments of Indigenous sovereignty and jurisdiction.

Despite the limitations, the various examples discussed above reveal that human possibilities and resilience are not fixed. Not only do these examples of collective actions and acts of solidarity, even if small in scale, offer visions of a future in which our communities can organize themselves and address social harms in ways that are humane and just, without relying on the repression of the state and its laws, but they also reveal practical examples of resistance and emancipation. The intersection of socio-legal studies and grassroots organizing initiatives would strengthen efforts to abolish systems of domination and repressive power and enable us to think through ways in which we can live in a better world.

References

Alam, Mariful. 2013. "From Deconstruction to the Possibilities of Radical Alternatives: Anarchy within the Matrix of Domination." Master's thesis, Carleton University.

Ceric, Irina. 2020. "Lawyering from Below: Activist Legal Support in Contemporary Canada and the US." PhD diss., Osgoode Hall Law School of York University.

CRASS (Community RNC Arrestee Support Structure). 2010. *Untitled, or What to Do When Everyone Gets Arrested*. https://www.sproutdistro.com/catalog/zines/legal/untitled-arrestee-support.

Day, Richard J. F. 2005. *Gramsci Is Dead: Anarchist Currents in the Newest Social Movements*. London: Pluto.

Derrida, Jacques. 1992. "Force of Law: The 'Mystical Foundation of Authority.'" In *Deconstruction and the Possibility of Justice*, edited by Drucilla Cornell, Michel Rosenfeld, and David Gray Carlson, 3–67. London: Routledge.

Dixon, Chris. 2014. *Another Politics: Talking Across Today's Transformative Movements*. Berkeley: University of California Press.

Franks, Benjamin. 2003. "The Direct Action Ethic." *Anarchist Studies* 11 (1): 13–41.

Gaarder, Emily. 2009. "Addressing Violence Against Women: Alternatives to State-Based Law and Punishment." In *Contemporary Anarchist Studies: An Introductory Anthology of Anarchy in the Academy*, edited by Randal Amster, Abraham DeLeon, Luis A. Fernandez, Anthony J. Nocella, and Deric Shannon, 46–56. New York: Routledge.

Gautney, Heather. 2012. *Protest and Organization in the Alternative Globalization Era: NGOs, Social Movements, and Political Parties*. New York: Palgrave Macmillan.

Graeber, David. 2002. "The New Anarchists." *New Left Review* 62 (13): 61–73.

———. 2009. *Direct Action: An Ethnography*. Oakland, CA: AK.

Holloway, John. 2010. *Change the World Without Taking Power: The Meaning of Revolution Today*. London: Pluto.

INCITE! n.d. "About." Accessed June 2020. https://incite-national.org/history.

INCITE! Women of Color Against Violence, ed. 2016. *Color of Violence: The INCITE! Anthology*. Durham, NC: Duke University Press.

Juris, Jeffrey S. 2008. *Networking Futures: The Movements Against Corporate Globalization*. Durham, NC: Duke University Press.

Kelly, Esteban Lance. 2011–12. "Philly Stands Up: Inside the Politics and Poetics of Transformative Justice and Community Accountability in Sexual Assault Situations." *Social Justice* 37 (4): 44–57.

Law, Victoria. 2014. "Against Carceral Feminism." *Jacobin Magazine*, 17 October 2014. https://www.jacobinmag.com/2014/10/against-carceral-feminism.

Maeckelbergh, Marianne. 2009. *The Will of the Many: How the Alterglobalisation Movement Is Changing the Face of Democracy*. London: Pluto.

———. 2011. "Doing Is Believing: Prefiguration as Strategic Practice in the Alterglobalization Movement." *Social Movement Studies: Journal of Social, Cultural and Political Protest* 10 (1): 1–20.

Mosley, Tonya, and Allison Hagan. 2020. "'An Extraordinary Moment': Angela Davis Says Protests Recognize Long Overdue Anti-racist Work." WBUR, Boston University. 19 June 2020. https://www.wbur.org/hereandnow/2020/06/19/angela-davis-protests-anti-racism.

Philly Stands Up. n.d. "About." Accessed June 2020. https://phillystandsup.wordpress.com/about.

Squire, Vicky, and Jennifer Bagelman. 2014. "Taking Not Waiting: Space, Temporality and Politics in the City of Sanctuary Movement." In *Citizenship, Migrant Activism and the Politics of Movement*, edited by Peter Nyers and Kim Rygiel, 146–64. London: Routledge.

Walia, Harsha. 2014. "Decolonizing Together: Moving beyond a Politics of Solidarity toward a Practice of Decolonization." In *The Winter We Danced: Voices from the Past, the Future, and the Idle No Movement*, 44–45. Oakland, CA: AK.

Contributors

Mariful Alam is a Toronto-based musician, union organizer, and doctoral student at York University. His research interests focus on critical theories of law and state violence, political policing and surveillance, and social movement mobilization.

Timothy Bryan is an assistant professor in the Department of Sociology at the University of Toronto. His primary research interests include the policing of hate crime, race and racism, and criminal justice reform in Canada. His work has appeared in the *Journal of Hate Studies*, the *Oñati Socio-legal Series*, and the *Canadian Journal of Law & Society*. He has also conducted policy research for the Ontario Association of Chiefs of Police and Nova Scotia's Department of Justice.

Nergis Canefe (PhD, SJD) is a professor of political science, public policy, and law at York University. Her areas of expertise are international public law and ethics, mass human suffering—including war crimes, crimes against humanity, and genocide—the global politics of dispossession, transitional justice, memory and trauma, and critical citizenship studies. Her latest book is *Crimes Against Humanity: The Limits of Universal Jurisdiction in the Global South* (University of Wales Press, 2021).

Irina Ceric is an assistant professor at the University of Windsor Faculty of Law and holds a PhD from Osgoode Hall Law School. She is a former criminal defence and clinical lawyer, as well as a long-time activist legal support organizer. Ceric's research interests lie at the intersection of law and social movements, with a particular focus on the regulation and criminalization of dissent by movements for social and environmental justice and Indigenous sovereignty.

Stacy Douglas is an associate professor in the Department of Law and Legal Studies at Carleton University in Ottawa, Canada. She has published work on constitutionalism and legal theory in *Law and Critique, Law, Culture, and the Humanities*, the *Australian Feminist Law Journal*, and *Feminist Legal Studies*. Her book, *Curating Community: Museums, Constitutionalism, and the Taming of the Political* (University of Michigan Press, 2017), argues against the centrality of sovereignty in our political and juridical imaginations. Her current work explores narratives of law's violence in popular culture as well as activist campaigns for individuals facing extraordinary charges.

Patrick Dwyer is a PhD candidate in the socio-legal studies program at York University. His dissertation research examines how knowledge about prisoners' deaths in federal penitentiaries is produced. His research interests include socio-legal theory, the sociology of punishment, the governance of mental health, risk management, crime prediction technologies and governing practices, and state accountability.

Yavar Hameed is a human rights lawyer and a sessional lecturer in Carleton University's Department of Law and Legal Studies. Since September 11, 2001, he has represented clients in national security investigations by CSIS, the seizure of assets by the RCMP in anti-terrorism cases, the listing of a terrorist entity under the Criminal Code, immigration security certificate cases, and racial profiling complaints relating to national security policing.

Emily Lockhart is a socio-legal scholar whose research lies in the areas of critical youth studies, feminist legal studies, and critical sexuality studies. She is interested in the legal and moral regulation of sexuality, young peoples' technology-mediated sexualities, youth legal consciousness, and legal mobilization.

Alex Luscombe is a PhD candidate at the Centre for Criminology & Socio-legal Studies at the University of Toronto. His research interests include policing studies, social inequality, freedom of information law, and computational social science. He is coeditor of *Freedom of Information and Social Science Research Design* (Routledge, 2019) and *Changing of the Guards: Private Influences, Privatization, and Criminal Justice in Canada* (University of British Columbia Press, 2022).

Jeffrey Monaghan is an associate professor of criminology and sociology at Carleton University in Ottawa. His research examines practices of security governance, policing, and surveillance. He is the author of *Security Aid: Canada and the Development Regime of Security* (2017) and the coauthor, with Andrew Crosby, of *Policing Indigenous Movements: Dissent and the Security State* (2018) as well as the coeditor, with Lucas Melgaço, of *Protests in the Information Age: Social Movements, Digital Practices and Surveillance* (2018) and, with Kelly Fritsch and Emily van der Meulen, of *Disability Injustice: Confronting Criminalization in Canada* (2022).

Carmela Murdocca is the York Research Chair in Reparative and Racial Justice and a professor in the Department of Sociology at York University. She is appointed to graduate programs in sociology, socio-legal studies, and social and political thought. She has been a Fulbright Scholar and Visiting Fellow at the Center for the Study of Law and Culture at Columbia University's law school. Her research examines the intersections of racialization, criminalization, and the social and legal politics of restorative justice, redress, and reparations.

Katrin Roots is an assistant professor in the department of criminology at Wilfrid Laurier University. Her work examines the carceral focus of Canada's anti-trafficking efforts. She is the author of *The Domestication of Human Trafficking: Law, Policing and Prosecution in Canada* (University of Toronto Press, 2023) and the author or coauthor of numerous peer-reviewed articles and book chapters on trafficking law, enforcement, and policing technologies.

Heather Tasker is a PhD candidate in the socio-legal studies program at York University. Her research explores gendered conceptions of harm and justice in conflict-affected and post-conflict contexts. Her dissertation focuses on community responses to sexual exploitation and abuse committed by MONUSCO peacekeepers in the Democratic Republic of the Congo. Through her work with the Conjugal Slavery in War (CSiW) partnership, she has conducted collaborative research on the rights and needs of children born of war, experiences of harm and access to justice for survivors of forced marriage in conflict, and the development of international criminal law around sexual and gender-based violence.

Shaira Vadasaria is a lecturer in race and decolonial studies in the School of Social and Political Science at the University of Edinburgh. Her research and teaching draw on interdisciplinary and methodologically driven thought that is attentive to race, law, and social regulation under imperial rule and settler-colonial nation building, with close attention to Israel and Palestine. She currently serves as codirector of RACE.ED, a university-wide research and teaching hub concerned with the study of race, racialization, and decoloniality, which she cofounded. Some of her publications can be found in *Social Identities: Journal for the Study of Race, Nation and Culture, Critical Studies on Security,* and *Oñati Socio-legal Series,* as well as in edited volumes including *Gaza on Screen* (Duke University Press, 2023).

Kevin Walby is an associate professor in the criminal justice program at the University of Winnipeg. He is the coauthor of *Police Funding, Dark Money, and the Greedy Institution* (Routledge, 2022) as well as the coeditor of *Disarm, Defund, Dismantle: Police Abolition in Canada* (Between the Lines, 2022) and *Changing of the Guards: Private Influences, Privatization, and Criminal Justice in Canada* (University of British Columbia Press, 2022). He is the director of the Centre for Access to Information and Justice and the coeditor of the *Journal of Prisoners on Prisons.*